Exam Ref 70-688 Supporting Windows 8.1

Joli Ballew

PUBLISHED BY
Microsoft Press
A Division of Microsoft Corporation
One Microsoft Way
Redmond, Washington 98052-6399

Library of Congress Control Number: 2014940675
ISBN: 978-0-7356-8473-7

Printed and bound in the United States of America.

First Printing

Microsoft Press books are available through booksellers and distributors worldwide. If you need support related to this book, email Microsoft Press Book Support at mspinput@microsoft.com. Please tell us what you think of this book at http://www.microsoft.com/learning/booksurvey.

Acquisitions Editor: Anne Hamilton
Developmental Editor: Karen Szall
Editorial Production: Box Twelve Communications
Technical Reviewer: Randall Galloway and Brian Svidergol
Cover: Twist Creative • Seattle

Contents at a glance

Contents

What do you think of this book? We want to hear from you!

Microsoft is interested in hearing your feedback so we can continually improve our
books and learning resources for you. To participate in a brief online survey, please visit:

www.microsoft.com/learning/booksurvey/

Chapter 2   Support resource access   93

What do you think of this book? We want to hear from you!

Microsoft is interested in hearing your feedback so we can continually improve our
books and learning resources for you. To participate in a brief online survey, please visit:

www.microsoft.com/learning/booksurvey/

Introduction

This book is written for IT professionals who want to earn the Microsoft Certified Solutions Associate Windows 8.1 certification. This certification includes two exams:

- **70-687** Configuring Windows 8.1
- **70-688** Supporting Windows 8.1

Exam 70-688, the focus of this book, serves as the second exam in the path to the Windows 8.1 MCSA certification. This book is written specifically for IT professionals who want to demonstrate that they have the primary set of Windows 8.1 skills, relevant across multiple solution areas in a business environment, to support Windows 8.1 across any size or type of enterprise. Starting in January 2014, this exam covers topics that include new features and capabilities introduced in Windows 8.1.

The two exams—Exam 70-687 and Exam 70-688—allow you to earn the Windows 8.1 MCSA certification without any prior certification. Together, these include 10 domains of broader skills and 35 more specific objectives, each having many subobjectives. The 70-688 exam tests three domains and 12 objectives that comprise the core knowledge needed to support a Windows 8.1 infrastructure. Each of the 12 objectives includes several subobjectives.

In order to create a book that is a manageable study tool, I've focused on covering the new features and capabilities of Windows 8.1, while not ignoring likely test subjects that were introduced in earlier versions of Windows 8.1. I cover every objective and subobjective here too, offering links to information you'll want to read that I didn't have room to add to this book.

While this book covers every exam objective, it does not cover every exam question. Only the Microsoft exam team has access to the exam questions themselves and Microsoft regularly adds new questions to the exam, making it impossible to cover specific questions. You should consider this book a supplement to your relevant real-world experience and other study materials. If you encounter a topic in this book that you do not feel completely comfortable with, use the links you'll find in the book to find more information—and then take the time to research and study the topic. Valuable information is available on MSDN, TechNet, and in blogs and forums.

Microsoft certifications

Microsoft certifications distinguish you by proving your command of a broad set of skills and experience with current Microsoft products and technologies. The exams and corresponding certifications are developed to validate your mastery of critical competencies as you design and develop, or implement and support, solutions with Microsoft products and technologies both on-premises and in the cloud. Certification brings a variety of benefits to the individual and to employers and organizations.

> **MORE INFO** **ALL MICROSOFT CERTIFICATIONS**
>
> For information about Microsoft certifications, including a full list of available certifications, go to *http://www.microsoft.com/learning/en/us/certification/cert-default.aspx*.

Acknowledgments

I have written nearly 60 books and I always say that it takes a good, strong, competent team to get it done. I just write the words. Behind the scenes are acquisition editors, project managers, technical editors, copy editors, layout designers, and many others I am sure that I don't even know about. I also have a supportive family, pets to keep me company while I write, and a group of friends that let me talk about tech stuff, even when I know they aren't really interested.

By name these people include Acquisitions Editor Karen Szall, Technical Editors Randall Galloway and Brian Svidergol, Copy Editor Susan Dunn, and Indexer Angie Martin. My Project Manager is Jeff Riley. My family includes Cosmo, Jennifer and Andrew, two lovely granddaughters, my 93-year-old father, and a handful of pets.

I'd like to thank everyone at Studio B, too, including my agent, Stacey Czarnowski, and the person who takes care of my money, Katrina Bevin. I also continue to acknowledge my (retired) agent, Neil Salkind, who managed my work for over a decade.

Errata, updates, & book support

We've made every effort to ensure the accuracy of this book and its companion content. You can access updates to this book—in the form of a list of submitted errata and their related corrections—at:

> *http://aka.ms/ER688R2*

If you discover an error that is not already listed, please submit it to us at the same page.

If you need additional support, email Microsoft Press Book Support at mspinput@microsoft.com.

Please note that product support for Microsoft software and hardware is not offered through the previous addresses. For help with Microsoft software or hardware, go to *http://support.microsoft.com*.

We want to hear from you

At Microsoft Press, your satisfaction is our top priority and your feedback is our most valuable asset. Please tell us what you think of this book at:

http://aka.ms/tellpress

The survey is short, and we read every one of your comments and ideas. Thanks in advance for your input!

Stay in touch

Let's keep the conversation going! We're on Twitter: *http://twitter.com/MicrosoftPress*.

Preparing for the exam

Microsoft certification exams are a great way to build your resume and let the world know about your level of expertise. Certification exams validate your on-the-job experience and product knowledge. While there is no substitution for on-the-job experience, preparation through study and hands-on practice can help you prepare for the exam. We recommend that you round out your exam preparation plan by using a combination of available study materials and courses. For example, you might use the Training Guide and another study guide for your "at home" preparation and take a Microsoft Official Curriculum course for the classroom experience. Choose the combination that you think works best for you.

CHAPTER 1

Support operating system and application installation

You must pass two exams to earn the Microsoft Certified Solutions Associate (MCSA) certification. The first, Configuring Windows 8.1 (70-687), deals mainly with how to install and configure the operating system. The second, Supporting Windows 8.1 (70-688), deals mainly with how to support those installations and configurations for the long term. Because the common factor between these two exams is Windows 8.1, you'll see some overlap. For instance, you learn how to install Windows To Go while preparing for Exam 70-687, and you learn how to support Windows To Go while preparing for Exam 70-688. That's a fine line; make sure that as you work through this book you understand that installations and configurations might already have been performed, and that those who write the exam questions might simply assume that you know how to do it. That said, you will still see how to perform some installation and configuration tasks in this chapter, especially those you might not be familiar with.

> **IMPORTANT**
> ## Have you read page xiii?
> It contains valuable information regarding the skills you need to pass the exam.

In this chapter you'll learn how to support various operating system installations that are, for the most part, already in place, ranging from the most basic Windows 8.1 installations to native virtual hard disks to specialty Windows installations unique to a single enterprise. You'll learn how to support desktop apps in many ways, too, including how to run those apps in virtual, cloud, or remote environments when running them on each workstation isn't ideal. Finally, you'll learn how network administrators can make their own apps available to users in a process called sideloading.

Objectives in this chapter:

- Objective 1.1: Support operating system installation
- Objective 1.2: Support desktop apps
- Objective 1.3: Support Windows Store and cloud apps

Objective 1.1: Support operating system installation

You can install an operating system in many ways beyond the familiar upgrade-with-a-DVD or boot-to-a-DVD method. You can install Windows 8.1 as Windows To Go, native virtual hard disk (VHD), and as part of a multiboot system, for example.

You also can customize an installation. As an enterprise network administrator, you can configure a reference computer exactly as you want it, install drivers, software, specialty screen savers, and so on, and then create an image of that computer to use for workstation installations. You can also perform installations via a network by enabling the computers to locate the installation files on a network server. Installations can be lite-touch and zero-touch, too, and include unique answer files to reduce the amount of human contact required during the installation process. In this objective you'll learn how to support many of these types of installations.

> **This objective covers how to:**
> - Support Windows To Go
> - Manage boot settings, including native virtual hard disk (VHD) and multiboot
> - Manage desktop images
> - Customize a Windows installation by using Windows Preinstallation Environment (Windows PE)

Supporting Windows To Go

To create a Windows To Go workspace, you must have access to a Windows 8-based Enterprise edition computer. Windows 8.1 Enterprise has a Windows To Go Creator Wizard just for that purpose. You create and save the workspace to a certified Windows To Go USB flash drive. After it's created, you give authorized users the configured flash drive, which they can use to run Windows from a computer other than their own, assuming that the computer can be configured to start to a USB drive and run a compatible operating system.

> **MORE INFO** **CREATING A WINDOWS TO GO DRIVE**
>
> A step-by-step wiki available at TechNet explains how to create a Windows To Go USB drive: *http://social.technet.microsoft.com/wiki/contents/articles/6991.windows-to-go-step-by-step.aspx*. How to install Windows To Go is an objective on Exam 70-687, Configuring Windows 8.1.

A few things are unique about Windows To Go:
- You can create a Windows To Go workspace only from a Windows 8-based Enterprise edition computer, and you need the Windows 8-based Enterprise installation files

to do so. Installation files can be in the form of an International Organization for Standardization (ISO) file, installation media such as a DVD, or a Windows Image file (.wim).

- The Windows To Go drive can hold the same image used on your enterprise workstations.

- The USB drive must be at least 32 gigabytes (GB) or larger and must be Windows To Go certified.

- You can't use Trusted Platform Model (TPM) with Windows To Go drives. TPM protects a specific computer from unauthorized access, and Windows To Go is used on more than one. When BitLocker is used, though, you can configure a startup password.

- Hibernate and sleep aren't enabled by default, although they can be through Group Policy.

- Windows Recovery Environment (Windows RE) isn't available, nor is resetting or refreshing. You should reimage problematic drives.

- For Windows To Go images that run Windows 8.1 Enterprise edition, Windows Store apps can roam between multiple PCs on a Windows To Go drive.

Hosting Windows To Go

The host computer is the computer used to start to the Windows To Go USB drive. The host computer must:

- Have hardware that has been certified for use with either Windows 7 or Windows 8 operating systems

- Not be a Windows RT or Mac computer

- Be thought of as a temporary host, because Windows To Go is only a short-term solution when the user can't be at his or her workstation

- Meet additional requirements listed in Table 1-1 and Table 1-2

Note also that the host computer's internal hard disks aren't accessible. This is to ensure that data isn't accidentally or maliciously accessed by the temporary user. Likewise, Windows To Go won't be listed in File Explorer.

TABLE 1-1 Computer requirements when hosting Windows To Go

Item	Requirement
Startup and firmware	The computer must be able to start to a USB drive and firmware must be USB enabled.
Processor architecture	The architecture must support the image on the Windows To Go drive (see Table 1-2).
USB port	The host must have an available USB port that can't be part of a USB hub and must be 2.0 or later.
Processor, RAM, graphics	The host must meet minimum standards for Windows 8, including a 1-GHz processor or higher, 2 GB of RAM or higher, and a DirectX 9 graphics device with WDDM 1.2 or greater driver.

TABLE 1-2 Architecture requirements for hosting Windows To Go

Firmware/Processor	Compatible architecture
Legacy 32-bit BIOS	32-bit
Legacy 64-bit BIOS	32-bit and 64-bit
UEFI 32-bit BIOS	32-bit
UEFI 64-bit BIOS	64-bit

Starting to Windows To Go

If a host meets the requirements for starting to a Windows To Go USB drive, you should change the startup options on the host to ensure that it will do exactly that when a USB Windows To Go drive is inserted.

To change the Windows To Go startup options on a host running Windows 8.1, follow these steps:

1. Log on as an administrator.

2. Right-click the Start button and Control Panel.

3. Click Hardware And Sound.

4. Under Devices And Printers, click Change Windows To Go Startup Options.

5. Click Yes (see Figure 1-1).

6. Click Save Changes.

When you're ready, turn off the host computer, insert the Windows To Go USB drive into an applicable USB port, and restart the computer. During this first restart, the host scans for the Windows To Go drive and installs any required drivers. The information is cached so that next time the process won't be repeated. When the Windows To Go workspace opens, you use it as you would any Windows 8.1 installation, but understand the limitations detailed earlier (such as Hibernate being disabled and internal drives unavailable).

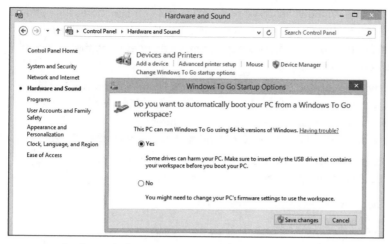

FIGURE 1-1 Configure the host computer to start to a Windows To Go workspace.

Configuring Group Policy for Windows To Go

Administrators configure and apply Group Policy to control what workers, guests, user groups, and even computer groups can do or access, either locally or on a domain. For example, you might use Group Policy to keep users from accessing the Windows Store or from copying data to removable drives. You might also require that all computers on a company network use a specific desktop background. Group Policy helps you maintain a secure (and sometimes identical) work environment for everyone. This makes managing large networks easier.

On domains, you configure Group Policy by using the Group Policy Management Console (gpmc.msc) or the Group Policy Editor (gpedit.msc). On a workgroup, you use the Local Group Policy Editor on each computer.

> **MORE INFO** **USING GROUP POLICY OBJECTS (GPOS)**
>
> At the highest level, network administrators create and configure Group Policy Objects (GPOs) to define settings that determine how users and computers will function. GPOs exist for Windows To Go as well. GPOs are then associated with Active Directory containers such as physical or virtual sites, entire domains, or other (perhaps smaller) organizational units.

Three Windows To Go settings are available:

- **Allow Hibernate (S4) When Starting From A Windows To Go Workspace** When this setting is enabled, the PC can go into hibernation mode when started from a Windows To Go workspace. If this setting is disabled or not configured, the PC can't.
- **Windows To Go Default Startup Options** When this setting is enabled, the host computer can start to a Windows To Go workspace when one is discovered during startup, and users can't change this setting in Control Panel. If this setting is disabled,

the host can't start to a Windows To Go workspace unless a user configures the option manually in the BIOS or other boot order configuration. If it's not configured, users who are members of the Administrators group can make changes using the Windows To Go Startup Options Control Panel item.

■ **Disallow Standby Sleep States (S1-S3) When Starting From A Windows To Go Workspace**   If this setting is enabled, when started from the Windows To Go workspace, Windows can't use standby states to let the computer sleep. If this setting is disabled or not configured, Windows can use standby states to make the PC sleep.

To locate and explore the available Windows To Go Local Group Policy settings, and to enable Windows To Go Default Startup Options, follow these steps:

1. Press Windows logo key+R to open a Run dialog box.

2. Type **gpedit.msc** and press Enter.

3. Navigate to Computer Configuration, Administrative Templates, Windows Components, Portable Operating System.

4. Double-click and explore each of the three available settings, and then return to the second one, Windows To Go Default Startup Options.

5. Click Enabled (see Figure 1-2).

6. Click OK.

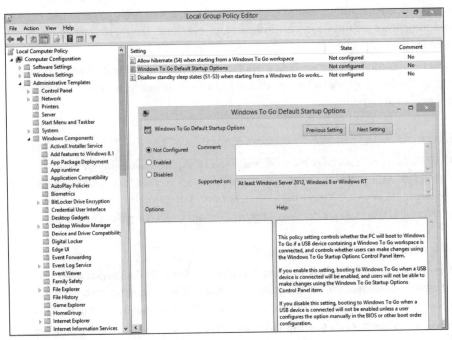

FIGURE 1-2 Locate and configure Windows To Go Local Group Polices.

Managing boot settings

Startup settings determine how a computer starts by default. When multiple operating systems are available, a list of startup entries generally appears from which users can choose what they want. BCDedit and BCDboot are command-line utilities used to configure and control the process. Startup configuration parameters are stored in the Boot Configuration Data (BCD) Store, which you manage with the BCD Editor (Bcdedit.exe).

Although these command-line tools might be new to you, you might already be familiar with a related end-user option available from the System tool in Control Panel. Click Advanced System Settings to see the dialog box shown in Figure 1-3 on the left, and click Settings under Startup and Recovery to see the Startup And Recovery dialog box shown on the right. The Startup And Recovery dialog box in Figure 1-3 also shows that Windows 8.1 is the default operating system. If multiple operating systems exist on the machine, the list of startup options remains on the screen (and available for selection) for 30 seconds before the default operating system automatically starts. When you need to make simple changes (such as changing the default operating system), you can make those changes in the Startup And Recovery dialog box.

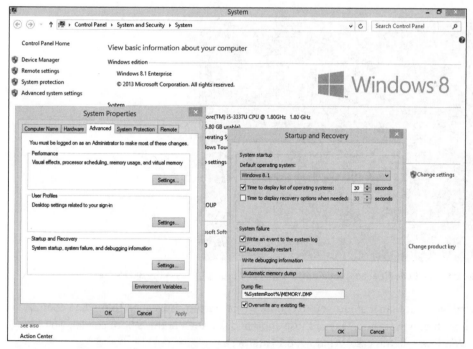

FIGURE 1-3 Change basic startup settings from the Startup And Recovery dialog box.

You can also change how Windows starts by using the System Configuration utility (Msconfig.exe) and the BCD Windows Management Instrumentation (WMI) provider. The System Configuration utility is more advanced than the Startup And Recovery dialog box and offers more tools with capabilities that include */debug*, */safeboot*, */bootlog*, */noguiboot*, */basevideo*, and */numproc*. The latter is a management interface that you can use to script utilities that modify BCD.

EXAM TIP

The BCD Store holds the startup configuration parameters. It replaces the older ntldr/Boot.ini file, so if you see this latter term on the exam, it's likely there to throw you off—that is, unless the question involves a multiboot system with something earlier than Windows Vista installed. Bootcfg is also an outdated term, now replaced with BCDedit. The BCD Store is located in one of two places on Windows Vista, Windows 7, and Windows 8-based machines. On legacy BIOS machines, it's in \Boot\BCD. On Extensible Firmware Interface machines, it's on the EFI system partition.

Using BCDedit

Bcdedit.exe is a command-line utility that replaced Bootcfg.exe in Windows Vista. Figure 1-4 shows this command and the resulting information regarding the BCD Store on a computer running only Windows 8.1 Enterprise. Notice the Administrator command prompt. The results show two entries: Windows Boot Manager and Windows Boot Loader.

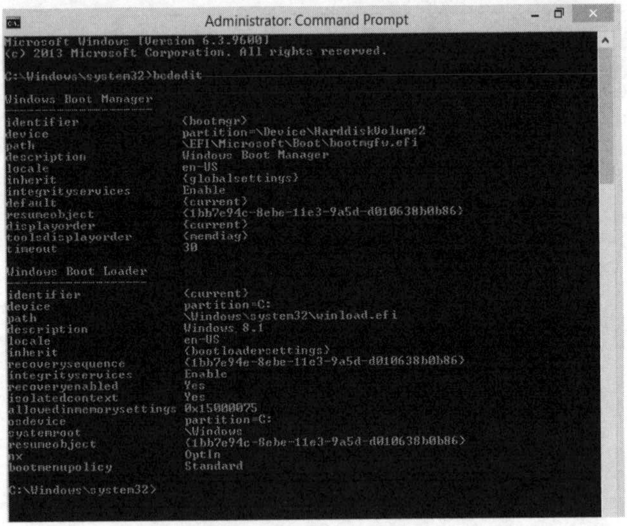

FIGURE 1-4 Type **bcdedit** at an Administrator command prompt to view the BCD Store.

Windows Boot Manager lets you to choose which startup application to run and controls that process during startup. One of those applications is the Windows Boot Loader, which loads Windows—in this case, Windows 8.1 Enterprise.

You can do much more with the *bcdedit* command than simply showing the BCD Store information. You can do the following, for example:

- Add entries to an existing BCD Store, and modify or delete existing entries
- Export entries to a BCD Store or import from one

- Apply a global change (to all the entries)
- Change the default time-out value

You'll likely be tested on the various parameters you can use with the *bcdedit* command. Here are some with which you should be familiar (you can find a more complete list at *http://technet.microsoft.com/en-us/library/cc709667(v=WS.10).aspx*):

- **/create store**   Use this to create a new empty startup configuration store
- **/export** or **/import**   Use */export* to export store information or */import* to restore using what you've saved from the */export* parameter
- **/copy**   Use this to copy entries in the store
- **/delete**   Use this to delete entries in the store
- **/boot sequence**   Use this to configure a one-time startup sequence for the boot manager
- **/default**   This sets the default startup entry
- **/displayorder**   This sets the startup order in a multiboot system
- **/timeout**   This sets the boot manager timeout value

Using BCDboot

Installing Windows 8.1 or any other operating system on a hard disk automatically creates partitions. The system partition contains the files required to start the operating system (as well as the Boot folder) that tells the computer where the operating system is stored. The boot partition contains the Windows operating system files. The active partition, a system partition, is the one used to start Windows. You can have multiple startup partitions—and you will if you have a multiboot system. BCDboot helps you manage these partitions.

Bcdboot.exe (as well as Bcdedit.exe) is located in the Windows\System32 folder of a Windows 8.1 computer. You can copy startup files from the Windows directory with this command:

```
x:\Windows\System32\bcdboot x:\Windows
```

You can use the *bcdboot* command to do the following, for example:

- Configure a computer to boot to a virtual hard disk (VHD) file
- Repair the system partition by replacing damaged files with undamaged copies
- Set up or repair the startup menu on a multiboot PC

You can view the parameters listed here by typing **bcdboot /Windows** at an Administrator command prompt, as shown in Figure 1-5.

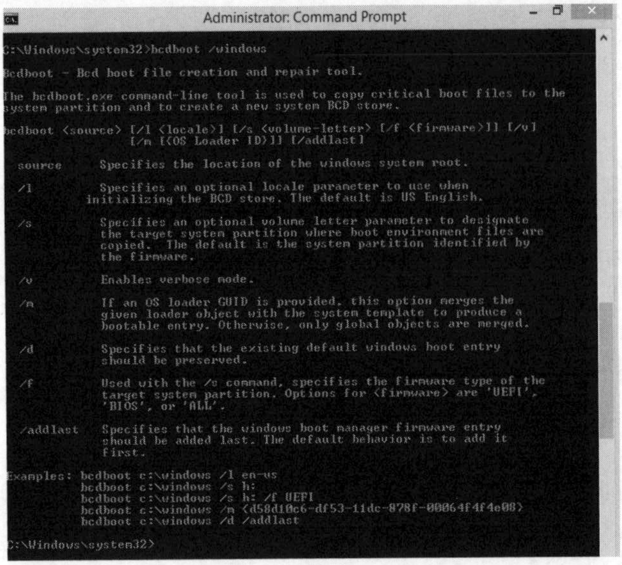

FIGURE 1-5 Type **bcdboot /windows** to view available parameters for the command.

You should be familiar with these *bcdboot* parameters:

- */l* specifies an optional language for the BCD Store. The default is U.S. English.
- */s* specifies a volume letter for the system partition. This shouldn't be used in typical deployment scenarios but can be used to specify a system partition for a drive on a USB flash drive or a secondary hard drive. The default is the partition designated in the firmware.
- */v* specifies verbose mode, which provides details regarding what the computer is doing and what drivers and software it's loading during startup.
- */m* specifies that you want to merge the values from an existing startup entry into a new startup entry. This option merges only global objects by default. You can specify an operating system loader GUID to merge a specific loader object.
- */d* specifies that you want to preserve the existing startup entry.
- */f*, when used with */s*, specifies the firmware type. Options are *UEFI*, *BIOS*, and *ALL*.

You can view the current partitions for any Windows 8.1 computer in Disk Management, as shown in Figure 1-6.

> **MORE INFO BCDBOOT**
>
> TechNet offers a lot of information about BCDboot. You can start at *http://technet. microsoft.com/en-us/library/hh824874.aspx.*

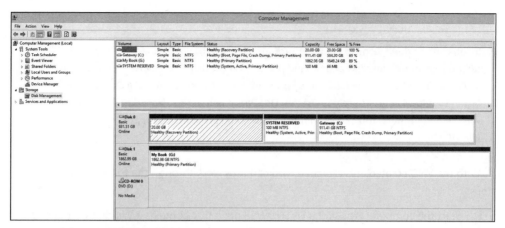

FIGURE 1-6 View partitions in Disk Management.

Adding a native VHD to the startup menu

A virtual hard disk (VHD) is a single file that functions as a unique, separate drive with its own operating system. If you studied for Exam 70-687, Configuring Windows 8.1, you learned how to create a VHD inside an existing operating system by using the Disk Management console, and then how to install Windows on it by using tools in the Windows Assessment and Deployment Toolkit (ADK). You learned how to attach the VHD and then run it "on top of" your Windows 8.1 default installation in its own separate window and space. In this instance, the VHD had a parent operating system.

VHDs can also run on their own, without the need for a parent operating system. These are called native VHDs. You can create a native VHD and use it to start by using the computer's actual hardware. This is easier to do if the computer already has an operating system on it, but it's not required that it does. In fact, you can run this kind of VHD on a computer with no existing virtual machine or hypervisor.

EXAM TIP

Read "Understand Virtual Hard Disks with Native Boot" at *http://technet.microsoft.com/ en-us/library/hh825689.aspx*. You'll be glad you did.

Adding a native VHD to a computer with an operating system

If the computer has an operating system, you can create and attach a VHD by using the Disk Management console. From the Action menu select Create VHD to get started. Then use the Action menu again to attach the newly created VHD. (Creating a VHD was covered in *Exam Ref 70-687: Configuring Windows 8.1.*)

With the VHD created and attached, you can now work through the following general steps:

1. Start the computer by using a DVD or USB drive that contains a Windows 8.1 Enterprise image (or whatever you want to install). This can be a simple installation DVD or something you've created via other methods.

2. Opt to start to the DVD or USB drive, and start the installation process.

3. When you get to the Windows Setup page that asks where you want to install Windows, choose the partition that houses the VHD you created. If you don't see it, you might have to restart at step 1 and press Shift+F10 to attach the VHD.

4. Work through the rest of the installation process as prompted.

5. When installation is complete, on restart, you'll see two entries, one for the existing operating system and one for the new VHD. The new VHD should be on top.

Adding a native VHD to a computer without an operating system

If a computer doesn't have an operating system, you need some way to communicate with it and make the desired configurations—in this case, adding a native VHD to the startup menu. You do this by creating and using a Windows Preinstallation Environment (Window PE) 8.1 disk and a Windows Image (.wim) file.

To get started, you need to install the Windows ADK on another Windows 7 or Windows 8-based technician computer. Use the Windows ADK to create the Windows PE disk. You use this disk and various tools to apply the .wim you want to install. You use the Deployment Image Service and Management (DISM) tool to apply an existing Windows 8 image, perhaps one you created for your enterprise (or to modify the image). This image can include drivers, for example.

Assuming that the computer doesn't have an operating system on it and has at least 30 GB of free disk space, you first must use the DiskPart tool to create, attach, partition, and format a new virtual hard disk. At a command prompt, type the following, noting that you can generally use different parameters than what you see here for size, type, drive letter, and so on as desired:

```
Diskpart
create vdisk file=C:\windows.vhdx maximum=25600 type=fixed
select vdisk file=C:\windows.vhdx
attach vdisk
create partition primary
assign letter=v
format quick label=vhdx
exit
```

To apply the desired Windows image and to use the DiskPart tool to detach the virtual disk after applying it, type

```
Dism /apply-image /imagefile:install.wim /index:1 /ApplyDir:V:\
diskpart
select vdisk file=C:\windows.vhdx
detach vdisk
exit
```

To copy the VHDX file to a network share or USB hard drive, if applicable, type

```
net use n: \\server\share\
md N:\VHDXs
copy C:\windows.vhdx n:\VHDs\
```

Start the destination computer with the Windows PE disk, and then format the hard disk and create a system and primary partition. Type

```
Diskpart
select disk 0
clean
create partition primary size=350
select partition 1
format fs=ntfs label="System" quick

active
create partition primary
format fs=ntfs label="Windows" quick
assign letter=c
exit
```

Copy the VHDX file and attach it on the destination computer by typing the following:

```
copy N:\VHDs\Windows.vhdx C
diskpart
select vdisk file=C:\windows.vhdx
attach vdisk
```

Note the letter given to the VHD in the volume list. To exit the DiskPart tool, type

```
list volume
select volume <volume_number_of_attached_VHD>
assign letter=v
exit
```

Copy the boot-environment files from the \Windows directory in the VHD to the system partition. The BCDboot tool creates the BCD configuration required to start from the VHD. Type

```
cd v:\windows\system32
bcdboot v:\windows
```

Use the DiskPart tool to detach the virtual disk and then restart the destination computer. Type

```
Diskpart
select vdisk file=C:\windows.vhdx
detach vdisk
exit
```

On restart, the Boot Manager starts via the .vhdx file.

EXAM TIP

Spend some time studying the terms associated with hard disks: GPT, MBR, UEFI, BIOS, and so on.

Working with multiboot systems

A multiboot system has two or more operating systems installed on it. In a multiboot configuration, each operating system uses its own unique partition, and the operating systems are completely independent of one another. Most network administrators use (or formerly used) multiboot systems to test new operating systems and to determine compatibility with existing software and hardware. Most end users choose this type of setup when they need to run a legacy application that isn't compatible with Windows 8.1 and can't be forced into compatibility with Program Compatibility Mode. (Most users don't understand, have never heard of, or can't configure a VHD to resolve these kinds of problems.)

Creating a multiboot system is easier than you might think, assuming that your computer has a large enough hard drive to create a new partition for a second operating system. Only a few steps are involved: Shrink an existing partition so that you can use the new, unused space to create a second partition; create the new partition; and then install the operating system on it. You use Disk Management to shrink a partition:

1. Press the Windows logo key+R to open a Run dialog box.

2. In the Run dialog box, type **diskmgmt.msc**.

3. Select a partition, likely C, to shrink. Right-click this partition and select Shrink Volume (see Figure 1-7).

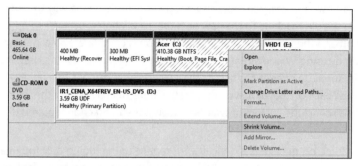

FIGURE 1-7 Shrink a volume to make room for a new partition.

4. Enter the amount of space to shrink in megabytes. You might opt for 40000. Click Shrink.

5. Right-click the new unallocated space and select New Simple Volume.

6. In the New Simple Volume Wizard, click Next, and then specify the volume size in megabytes. You can select the default size and click Next.

7. On the Assign Drive Letter Or Path page, leave Assign The Following Drive Letter selected and choose a letter. Click Next.

8. On the Format Partition page, leave the defaults selected, but type a name for the new partition in the Volume Label box. Click Next.

9. Click Finish.

You should see the new partition in the Disk Management window. You can now insert a bootable DVD that contains the operating system you want to install. Restart the computer, start to the DVD, and during the installation process select Custom to select the new partition. Windows installs the second operating system onto that partition. After the installation is complete, you should see the new operating system as an option at startup. Remember, you can change the defaults from the Startup And Recovery dialog box detailed earlier in this chapter.

Managing desktop images

Network administrators can opt to use a standard Windows Image (.wim) file to perform installations on their enterprise workstations. The standard image is the out-of-the-box installation file you receive when you purchase a Windows 8.1 DVD. When taking this route, you must then, using some method, also install the desired Office applications, device drivers, and so on, and configure each computer so that it meets company standards. Because this is quite time-consuming, enterprise administrators often opt to create a custom Windows image that contains all these things and more, so that fewer after-the-installation tasks need to be completed.

Beyond building your own images, you must also design and implement a way to move existing user data from the old machine to the new or, if the installation is performed on a single PC, to move it off and then back on when the installation is complete. You can do this in several ways, including by using Windows Easy Transfer for small migrations or the User State Migration Tool (USMT) for large ones. If neither fits the scenario, you can opt to manually move data off the PC and then back on. Beyond even that, installations of images (and the folders that hold them) might also include custom answer files to limit the interaction required during the installation process.

Knowing what you'll see on the exam is difficult with regard to managing desktop images, because the area of study is extensive. You might need to know how to create or deploy a custom image, or only how to modify an existing image. You might be required to know how to include options to migrate user data during image deployment, or you might not. The goal of the next few pages is to introduce you to many of the facets of desktop imaging, but because everything can't be covered, links are provided where you can learn more.

EXAM TIP

With regard to USMT, which you'll learn about in this section, make sure that you are familiar with some of the terms associated with it, including but not limited to MigDocs, MigApp, /nocompress, /hardlink, and others that you'll find at *http://technet.microsoft. com/en-us/library/hh825256.aspx*.

Understanding desktop images

An image is an installation file. An image can be customized so that it is unique to the company and meets the company's specific needs. In larger enterprises, administrators likely create multiple desktop images. One image might be for the Sales team's laptop computers, another for the desktop computers in the Human Resources department, and another for the tablets used by high-ranking administrators. These images can be used for more than just installations, though. When a computer needs to be reimaged—perhaps when a user leaves the company or a computer becomes unstable—you can use the desired image to reinstall the computer quickly. By using data stored on network servers, you can quickly transfer user data also. Desktop images can also be serviced rather than rebuilt if an image itself becomes corrupt.

Images can contain device drivers, applications, specific settings for the desktop background, and so on. A *thin* image has little or no customization, and most of the device drivers, applications, and updates are installed by using another method on each client computer. A *thick* image includes applications, device drivers, and updates (for example) and requires much more planning, network bandwidth, and other resources than thin images. A *hybrid* image is lightly customized. It might be used as a base image for an entire organization's desktop computers. Thin images are recommended in most instances because they can reduce installation time, maintenance time, storage requirements, and costs, for example. The Microsoft Deployment Toolkit (MDT) makes using thin images with the Lite-Touch, High-Volume Deployment strategy pretty straightforward for experienced network administrators. For more information, visit *http://technet.microsoft.com/en-us/windows/dn282138*.

Creating a desktop image

To create an image, you need the MDT, the Windows ADK, and a file server to hold the installation files (as a share). When you're ready to deploy that image, you need media that you can use to start the computers during deployment or a server configured with the Windows Deployment Services (WDS) role, and network cards on the PCs to upgrade that can start to the installation image. If you have all this in place, you should create an image and deploy it as Lite-Touch, High-Volume Deployment if your enterprise has between 200 and 500 computers, or use a Zero-Touch, High-Volume Deployment if your enterprise has 500 or more machines.

EXAM TIP

Although you won't be asked how to configure a WDS server, you might be asked how you would start a machine so that it could connect to it. Often the answer includes customizing a Windows PE image and booting the machine with it. The image can point the machine to the desired WDS server and deployment image, for example.

Many steps are involved in creating a custom installation, and a high-level outline is provided here:

1. On a technician computer, install the Windows ADK. (Note that you also can use Microsoft Hyper-V to build an image.)

2. Create a share on the network to hold the installation files and other files related to the deployment of Windows 8.1, such as the answer file. (An answer file can be created to answer some of the questions posed during the installation, such as the language or time zone, or even what partition to install the image to.)

3. Create a reference computer that can serve as a template for the desktop image you want to create, complete with all the software you want to install, language packs, settings, required device drivers, custom wallpapers, and anything else you want to include.

4. Prepare the reference computer for imaging by removing certain values unique to the reference computer. Use the following commands:

    ▪ *Sysprep /generalize* to remove unique IDs. You might add other command-line options, such as */oobe*, to give the installation an "out-of-the-box" experience.

    ▪ *Copype.cmd* to create a Windows PE startup disk, with the proper command-line options such as *c:\winpe* (to note the location of the required Windows PE files).

- *Oscdimg.exe* to package the Windows PE files into a sector-based image file, along with proper command-line options.

5. Capture an image of the reference computer that results in an image file. By using this file, you can install as many desktops as you want and apply your image to all of them to create uniformity. Use these commands in place of the deprecated command *ImageX* along with *net use*, appropriately adapted for your enterprise:

- *Dism /Capture-Image /ImageFile:c:\myimage.wim /CaptureDir:C:\ /Name:"Myimagecapture"*

- *Dism /Capture-Image /ImageFile:s:\mysystempartition.wim /CaptureDir:S:\ /Name:"Mysystempartition"*

- *Net use* with command-line options including something like *z: \\server\share* to denote the location of the network share where the files are stored

6. Create an answer file to automate the installation partially or an unattended answer file to completely automate the answers asked during installation. Use tools including Windows System Image Manager (SIM, available in Windows ADK) to select the image and create and apply the answer file.

7. Start the target computers with either a Windows PE disk or a boot image that the computer can download from the server.

8. Apply the reference computer image to create your duplicate workstations. This can include copying and applying the desired image.

EXAM TIP

You will probably see questions that ask when you would use a specific tool such as SysPrep, a Windows PE disk, DISM, and so on. Make sure that you understand what each tool is used for, why, when, and how.

Modifying or repairing a desktop image

If you create an image and then need to modify it, you can use the DISM command-line tool, available from the Windows ADK. You learned a little about this tool earlier in the chapter when you saw how to add a native VHD to a computer without an operating system. There, you used it to mount the installation file.

You should know some more facts about DISM:

- You can use it to install, uninstall, configure, and update Windows features, packages, drivers, and international settings in an existing .wim file.

- You can use the DISM servicing commands to make changes to a VHD.

- DISM commands are generally used on offline images, but servicing a running operating system is possible.

- You can use DISM to repair an image.

Use the commands in Table 1-3 to repair an image.

TABLE 1-3 Commands for repairing an image

Action	Command
To check for corruption	*Dism /Online /Cleanup-Image /ScanHealth*
To check whether corruption has been detected	*Dism /Online /Cleanup-Image /CheckHealth*
To repair an offline image by using a mounted image as a repair source	*Dism /Image:C:\offline /Cleanup-Image /RestoreHealth /Source:c:\test\mount\windows*
To repair an image by using your own sources without involving Windows Update	*Dism /Online /Cleanup-Image /RestoreHealth /Source:c:\test\mount\windows /LimitAccess*

To modify an image, you need to know quite a bit more about DISM. You can find command sets that enable you to do the following:

- Add or remove drivers.
- Enable or disable Windows features.
- Add or remove language packs.
- Sideload apps.
- Customize the Start screen.

This isn't a complete list, of course. Each modification requires that you type a set of commands. For example, to add or remove a language pack, assuming that your image is already mounted (this is the easiest to achieve), you would follow this sequence:

1. On the Start screen, type **Deployment**, and then right-click Deployment and Imaging Tools Environment.

2. Click Run As Administrator.

3. Type the following commands, in order:

   ```
   Dism /Get-MountedImageInfo
   ```

   ```
   Dism /Image:C:\test\offline /ScratchDir:C:\Scratch /Add-Package /PackagePath:C:\
   packages\package1.cab /PackagePath:C:\packages\package2.cab ...
   ```

   ```
   Dism /Commit-Image /MountDir:C:\test\offline
   ```

4. To configure international settings, type these commands, in order:

   ```
   Dism /Mount-Image /ImageFile:C:\test\images\install.wim /Index:1 /MountDir:C:\
   test\offline
   ```

   ```
   Dism /Image:C:\test\offline /Set-SKUIntlDefaults:en-us
   ```

   ```
   Dism /Unmount-Image /MountDir:C:\test\offline /Commit
   ```

The Windows image is now ready to be deployed.

EXAM TIP

The MDT includes DISM PowerShell cmdlets, DISM API, Windows SIM, and OSCDIMG. It
also includes the Volume Activation Management Tool (VAMT), Windows Performance
Toolkit (WPT), Windows Assessment Toolkit, and Windows Assessment Services. Make sure
that you are familiar with these tools. An overview is available at *http://msdn.microsoft.*
com/en-us/library/windows/hardware/hh825486.aspx.

Using Windows Easy Transfer and the User State Migration Tool

You can use the Windows Easy Transfer (WET) Wizard to migrate user data (such as profile
information) off a computer to complete a clean installation on it. After the installation is
complete, you can migrate the data back. You also can use WET to move data from one
computer to another. You would use this method to migrate data only for a small number of
computers; you wouldn't want to use it in an enterprise.

EXAM TIP

You can't use WET to transfer files from a 64-bit operating system to a 32-bit operating
system (USMT doesn't work either). In this case, you should back up files manually.

You can use the scriptable command-line User State Migration Tool (USMT) to migrate
user data from a previous edition of Windows to Windows 8.1. By using USMT, you can copy
the user data you select, exclude any data that doesn't need to be migrated, and then transfer
the selected data back to the computer after it's installed clean with Windows 8.1. You can
also transfer the data to a brand new or newly installed Windows 8.1 computer.

USMT provides much of the same functionality as Windows Easy Transfer. However,
although USMT has the same basic capabilities as WET, USMT is a command-line tool and
WET is graphical. This isn't a disadvantage in a large organization, because administrators can
use USMT to incorporate USMT tasks into scripts, which are better suited for domains, enterprises, and automated deployments. (Scripts, task sequences, answer files, and so on are what
help automate a deployment.) Two tools included with USMT are ScanState and LoadState,
both command-line tools. When you use USMT, you'll also use Windows PE, which you learn
about next.

EXAM TIP

Windows PE and USMT are available in the Windows ADK; you might be required to know this to select the proper solution, given a scenario. You also might see an exam question regarding ScanState and LoadState and their related parameters. To learn about the parameters available for these two commands, refer to the USMT Technical Reference sheet offered at *http://technet.microsoft.com/en-us/library/hh825256.aspx*.

MORE INFO   USING MDT

No matter how many images you create and store, you can use MDT to manage and maintain them. MDT 2013 supports the Windows ADK for Windows 8.1, supports the deployment of Windows 8.1, and supports zero-touch installations if you also use System Center 2012 R2 Configuration Manager.

Customizing a Windows installation by using Windows Preinstallation Environment (Windows PE)

When you create a custom installation, you also create a Windows PE disk. It's unique to your image. You can use the Windows PE disk to start the installation process on a client computer. Before focusing more on this, though, you should look at what Windows PE actually is.

Exploring Windows PE

The startup process has changed over the years. When Windows ME was retired, so was MS-DOS. Windows 8, Windows 7, and Windows Vista no longer rely on MS-DOS for any part of the installation and startup process. To replace MS-DOS, Windows uses Windows PE, a minimal operating system that you can use to prepare a computer for a Windows installation. Windows PE can start a computer that has no operating system or has other problems. When deploying Windows 8.1, you can use Windows PE to partition and format hard drives, copy disk images to a computer, and initiate Windows Setup from a network share. You can create a Windows PE disk by using the tools in the Windows ADK. With regard to USMT, you use a customized Windows PE startup disk to start the source computer (the computer that holds the files to migrate) and use the tools available on the disk to collect the data you want to migrate.

EXAM TIP

Windows PE can help you deploy custom Windows 8.1 images to computers. It can also help you create disk partitions and format hard drives, but most notably it helps initiate an installation from a network share. Also, something called the Windows Recovery Environment (Windows RE) is built from Windows PE, which makes sense. Both assist in installations (and recovery).

Windows PE offers the following improvements and advantages over MS-DOS. As you read through this list, think about how important each item is to automated and custom operating system deployments:

- Native 32-bit or 64-bit support (MS-DOS is a 16-bit operating system)
- Native 32-bit and 64-bit driver support, or the ability to use the same drivers as a full Windows 8 installation
- Internal networking support
- Internal NTFS support
- Scripting language support for a subset of Win32 application programming interface (API), Windows Management Instrumentation (WMI), Windows Data Access Components (Windows DAC), HTML Applications (HTAs), and Windows Script Host (You can create scripts that are much more robust than the MS-DOS batch files.)
- Myriad startup options, including CDs, DVDs, USB devices such as flash drives, a temporary folder on a hard disk, RAM disk, network share, and Windows Deployment Services (WDS) server
- Support for offline sessions and offline servicing of images
- Inclusion of Hyper-V drivers (except display drivers), which enables Windows PE to run in a hypervisor (support includes mass storage, mouse integration, and network adapters)

Windows PE has various restrictions, not limited to the following:

- It restarts after 72 hours, so it can't be used as an operating system for the long term.
- It supports TCP/IP and NetBIOS over TCP/IP, but doesn't support other methods, such as the Internetwork Packet Exchange/Sequenced Packet Exchange (IPX/SPX) network protocol.
- It doesn't support applications that are packaged via Windows Installer (.msi) files.
- It doesn't support cross-platform scenarios, like installing a 64-bit Windows image on a 32-bit computer (among others).

> **MORE INFO** **WINDOWS PE**
>
> Visit *http://technet.microsoft.com* and type **What is Windows PE?** in the Search box to locate related technical information.

Copying the Windows PE files and creating a standard Windows PE DVD disk

You need to copy the Windows PE files to your computer before you can work with them or create a custom Windows PE disk. You can copy and create 32-bit or 64-bit sets, or both, using the *Copype* command as detailed in the following steps. You can also create an ISO file if you want to create a standard, bootable Windows PE DVD. You must complete steps 1–3 before you can continue with the next section.

To create a standard, bootable Windows PE DVD disk, follow these steps:

1. Install the Windows ADK from *www.microsoft.com/en-us/download/details.aspx?id=39982*. Also be sure to install the necessary deployment tools: Deployment and Imaging Tools Environment and Windows PE.

2. At the Start screen, type **Deploy** and then right-click Deployment And Imaging Tools Environment. Click Run As Administrator.

3. Type **copype amd64 C:\WinPE_amd64** (or replace with 32 as applicable). Press Enter.

4. Insert a writeable DVD into the appropriate drive.

5. Type **MakeWinPEMedia /ISO C:\winpe_amd64 c:\winpe_amd64\winpe.iso**. Press Enter.

6. Verify that Success appears (see Figure 1-8).

FIGURE 1-8 Create a Windows PE ISO file.

7. If desired, in File Explorer, navigate to C:\winpe_amd64, right-click winpe.iso, and select Burn To Disc.

8. Follow the prompts to create a DVD. Alternatively, you can wait and customize Windows PE by working through the next section.

Mounting and modifying Windows PE

You can customize Windows PE to meet your own needs. A more common customization is to add device drivers, but you can also add languages, add an app, replace the background image, add answer file settings, add a startup script, and more. Before you continue here, however, make sure that you've installed the required Windows ADK tools and worked through steps 1–3 in the preceding section to install the Windows ADK and copy the appropriate Windows PE files to your hard drive.

As an example of what you can do, you can follow these steps to mount and modify a Windows PE image specifically to change the desktop background:

1. At the Start screen, type **Deploy** and then right-click Deployment And Imaging Tools Environment. Click Run As Administrator.

2. Mount the PE Image. Type **Dism /Mount-Image /ImageFile:"C:\WinPE_amd64\media\sources\boot.wim" /index:1 /MountDir:"C:\WinPE_amd64\mount"** (see Figure 1-9).

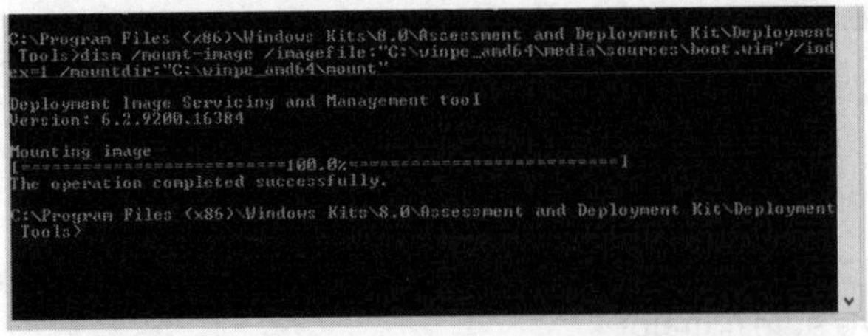

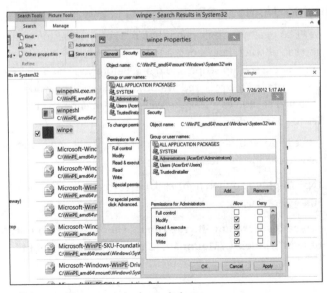

FIGURE 1-9 Use DISM to mount Windows PE.

Before you can customize Windows PE by replacing the background image, you must first change the security permissions of the background image file so that you can modify it. The default image file is at \windows\system32\winpe.jpg. Follow these steps to make the required modifications:

1. In File Explorer, navigate to C:\WinPE_amd64\mount\windows\system32.

2. Right-click the winpe.jpg file and select Properties, Security tab, Advanced.

3. Next to Owner, select Change.

4. In the Enter The Object Name To Select box, type **Administrators** and press Enter.

5. Click Apply and then OK. Click OK again.

6. Right-click the winpe.jpg file and select Properties, Security tab, Advanced.

7. Click Administrators and then Edit.

8. Click Administrators, and select the Full Control Allow check box to give Administrators full access (see Figure 1-10).

FIGURE 1-10 Change required permissions.

9. Click OK twice.

10. Replace the winpe.jpg file with your own image file.

To learn how to perform other customizations, you can refer to the steps at *http://technet. microsoft.com/en-us/library/hh824972.aspx*. You'll find the commands you need to modify other areas of Windows PE. For example, to add device drivers to the Windows PE image, use these commands at the DISM Administrator prompt:

- To add a device driver: *Dism /Add-Driver /Image:"C:\WinPE_amd64\mount" /Driver:"C:\SampleDriver\driver.inf"*

- To verify that driver packages have been added: *Dism /Get-Drivers /Image:"C:\WinPE_ amd64\mount"*

To add an app, use these commands:

- To create an app directory: *md "C:\WinPE_amd64\mount\windows\<MyApp>"*

- To copy the app files: *Xcopy C:\<MyApp> "C:\WinPE_amd64\mount\ windows\<MyApp>"*

- To test the app by booting Windows PE and running the application from the X directory: *X:\Windows\System32> X:\Windows\<MyApp>*

Thought experiment

Testing a Windows Image before deployment

In this thought experiment, apply what you've learned about this objective. You can find answers to these questions in the "Answers" section at the end of this chapter.

You created a Windows Image (.wim) file that you want to deploy across your organization. You want to test it thoroughly before performing the deployment—specifically, you want to test it against the same hardware your desktops use. You want do this with a VHD. You've chosen to use a computer that now has no operating system on it.

1. What term is used to describe a VHD that you install on a computer with no parent operating system?

2. What application should you use to create the required Windows PE disk?

3. Your image is ready to go. What application or tool can you use to apply that image?

4. How much free hard disk space does this computer need to have to support this VHD?

Objective summary

- You can use Windows To Go to work from any computer that enables you to start to a USB drive and meets Windows To Go host requirements.
- You can use Group Policy to control how Windows To Go and the host interact.
- Startup settings determine how a computer starts by default, and many tools are available to help you manage the startup process, including but not limited to BCDedit and BCDboot.
- You can add a native VHD to the startup menu and start to it, even if no parent operating system exists.
- Multiboot systems house two or more operating systems, each on its own partition.
- Enterprise administrators often create specialized, personalized installation images for deployment in their organizations.
- You can modify and repair desktop images rather than rebuild them.
- Windows PE is a preinstallation environment that you can use to install a new operating system, for example, or repair one. It replaces the older MS-DOS and offers many more features.
- You can create customized Windows PE images and add your own drivers, apps, Start screen configurations, and more.

Objective review

Answer the following questions to test your knowledge of the information in this objective. You can find the answers to these questions and explanations of why each answer choice is correct or incorrect in the "Answers" section at the end of this chapter.

1. Which of the following are true regarding Windows To Go? (Choose all that apply.)

    A. You can create a Windows To Go workspace only from a Windows 8-based Enterprise edition computer, and you need the Windows 8-based Enterprise installation files to do so.

    B. The USB drive must be at least 32 GB or larger and must be Windows To Go certified.

    C. You can't use a Trusted Platform Model (TPM) with Windows To Go drives.

    D. When a Windows To Go drive starts having problems, you can refresh or restore it by using recovery options in PC Settings.

    E. You can use Windows To Go when a Windows RT computer is the host.

2. You want to host Windows To Go on your personal computer but don't want to allow the computer to hibernate. How should you configure Local Group Policy?

   A. Disable Allow Hibernate (S4) when starting from a Windows To Go workspace or leave the default, Not Configured.

   B. Enable Allow Hibernate (S4) when starting from a Windows To Go workspace.

   C. Disable Disallow Standby Sleep States (S1-S3) when starting from a Windows To Go workspace.

   D. Enable Disallow Standby Sleep States (S1-S3) when starting from a Windows To Go workspace.

3. Where are the startup configuration parameters stored?

   A. Boot.ini

   B. BCD Editor (BCDedit)

   C. BCDboot

   D. BCD Store

4. You need to create a new, empty startup configuration store and configure what starts by default. You plan to use BCDedit. What two command parameters do you use?

   A. /import

   B. /create store

   C. /boot sequence

   D. /default

   E. /displayorder

   F. /new

5. You have a Windows 8.1 computer with a 500-GB hard drive, all available from the C drive. You're using only a small portion of that hard drive now. You want to create a multiboot system that runs both the existing Windows 8.1 operating system and Windows 7. What do you do first?

   A. Start to the Windows 7 DVD

   B. Create a new simple volume.

   C. Open Disk Management and shrink the C partition.

   D. Format the drive.

6. What type of custom image includes many applications, device drivers, and updates and requires a lot of planning, network bandwidth, and other resources?

   A. Thin

   B. Thick

   C. Hybrid

   D. All custom images include these things.

7. Which of the following do you need to create your own custom image?

   A. MDT

   B. Windows ADK

   C. A network share

   D. A reference computer

   E. All of the above

   F. B, C, and D

8. To create an image and then modify it, you need the DISM command-line tool, which is available from which of the following?

   A. MDT

   B. Windows ADK

   C. SIM

   D. ACT

9. Which of the following commands might you use to copy the Windows PE files from Windows ADK to your hard drive?

   A. *copype amd64 C:\WinPE_amd64*

   B. *copype amd32 C:\WinPE_amd32*

   C. *MakeWinPEMedia /ISO C:\winpe_amd64 c:\winpe_amd64\winpe.iso*

   D. *Dism /Get-MountedImageInfo*

10. Which of the following does MDT include?

    A. DISM PowerShell cmdlets

    B. DISM API

    C. Windows System Image Manager (Windows SIM)

    D. OSCDIMG

    E. The Volume Activation Management Tool (VAMT)

    F. All of the above

    G. Only A, B, C, and D

Objective 1.2: Support desktop apps

Although Windows 8.1 comes with a set of default apps on the Start screen, these aren't widely used in large enterprises by end users who need to perform work. Instead, administrators often opt to install traditional desktop apps. This isn't to say that apps aren't used at all; they are. In fact, administrators can (and do) create their own apps and make them available using a process known as sideloading, detailed later in Objective 1.3. However, this objective focuses on supporting only desktop apps.

Quite a few issues can arise while supporting desktop apps. The desktop app might not be compatible, period. Because you need to know this sooner rather than later, you use the Application Compatibility Toolkit (ACT) to determine how widespread the problem is and learn how to fix it before proceeding with an organization-wide installation of Windows 8.1 or the application after the fact. Other issues include the need to run two or more versions of an app side by side, and in these cases and similar scenarios you might opt for technologies such as Hyper-V, RemoteApp, and AppV. You might also opt to run a problematic or noncompliant app virtually or remotely. Other options available for additional desktop app scenarios and functionality include User Experience Virtualization (UE-V) and Windows Intune, which also are discussed in this section.

This objective covers how to:

- Support desktop app compatibility by using ACT, including shims and compatibility databases
- Support desktop application coexistence by using Hyper-V, RemoteApp, and App-V
- Support installation and configuration of User Experience Virtualization (UE-V)
- Deploy desktop apps by using Windows Intune

Supporting desktop app compatibility by using ACT

ACT is included with the Windows ADK and can be used to detect which enterprise applications, devices, and computers will likely be incompatible (or cause problems) with Windows 8.1 after installation. ACT can also help you find solutions to those problems.

ACT is used in stages:

1. You have to install all of the required software and set up or have previously set up an ACT database.

2. You need to inventory computers and applications in your enterprise. This lets ACT know what to test.

3. You need to gather compatibility information based on what's found by testing for compatibility on the desired platform and comparing that to known issues.

4. You need to test applications and obtain compatibility results.

5. You need to analyze the data.

6. You finally can implement solutions and test again.

Before you dive into the inventory process (the first step to using ACT), look at what ACT includes.

> **NOTE** **PREPARING FOR THE ACT**
>
> If you haven't yet installed Windows ADK on your computer, do that before continuing. Alternatively, you can download and install just ACT for Windows 8.1. To use ACT, you also need an active and compatible SQL Server database.

Understanding ACT tools and how to get started

You should be familiar with several ACT tools before working with the program:

- The Windows Assessment Console is a graphical user interface that enables you to group assessments, create and run jobs, and view and manage the results of those jobs.

- Assessments are a combination of files that induce specific states on a computer for the purpose of measuring activities during testing. These assessments provide a starting point for necessary remediation.

- The Assessment Platform comprises the items necessary to develop assessments, extend assessments, and reliably run jobs and display results.

As noted previously, you have to set up or have previously set up an ACT database before you can use ACT. The requirements for doing so include having in place a SQL Server database that stores your enterprise inventory, as well as .NET Framework 4. If you have all of that, you can begin to work through the wizard available from the Microsoft Application Compatibility Manager, which guides you through the setup process. The wizard also helps you create an ACT log share, where the collected log files can be stored, and set up an ACT Log Processing Service user account, which has read and write access. To get started, at the Start screen type **application compat**, and click Application Compatibility Manager. (You need to run this with elevated privileges.)

Creating an inventory collector package

You create an inventory collector package to collect information about the computers in your enterprise. The data collected includes hardware information such as memory capacity and processor speed, as well as information about the make and model of those PCs. Of course, it also inventories the installed software so that you can later determine whether that software is compatible with the Windows edition you want to install. (If you have hundreds of computers, you can likely inventory them all; however, if you have thousands, you can opt to inventory representative groups of computers. You can do this only if you have groups of computers on similar platforms and with similar installations.)

To create an inventory collector package, follow these steps:

1. Open the Microsoft Application Compatibility Manager.

2. Click File, and then click New.

3. Click Inventory Collection Package.

4. Input the required information (name, output location, and label) and click Create.

5. Browse to the location to save the required Windows Installer (.msi) file for the package. You might opt for a network share that can be reached by client computers.

6. Type a name for the file and click Save.

7. Click Finish.

Deploying the inventory collector package

Now you must deploy the package you created. If your network isn't too large and your users are computer-savvy, you might opt to send an email with a link to the deployment folder and let the users install the package themselves. You could also burn the .msi file to a DVD or other removable media and pass that around. Users need administrator privileges either way. Alternatively, you can opt for a Group Policy software installation. This requires more infrastructure, but you would probably already have the required items in place in a large organization. For Group Policy to work, the computers you want to inventory need to be part of the Active Directory forest; you'll need to create a Group Policy Object (GPO) for publishing; you'll need to assign the GPO to the appropriate organizational units (OUs); and you'll need to create and publish the software installation.

More complicated ways require scripting or using additional hardware. You can, for instance, assign a logon script. You can also deploy the package by using System Center Configuration Manager.

Creating a runtime-analysis package

The testing compatibility process involves a few steps, all of which must be completed before creating the runtime-analysis package:

1. Decide which applications to test. You can use information gathered from the previous steps to make those decisions.

2. Use the Microsoft Compatibility Exchange to get the latest compatibility ratings.

3. Organize the applications you want to test.

With that complete, you are ready to create your runtime-analysis package:

1. In ACM, click Collect.

2. Click File, and then click New.

3. Click Runtime Analysis Package.

4. Provide the required information (name, output location, and label) and click Create.

5. Browse to the location to save the required Windows Installer (.msi) file for the package.

6. Type a file name for the .msi file, and then click Save.

7. Click Finish.

MORE INFO **USING THE MICROSOFT COMPATIBILITY EXCHANGE**

During the inventory and testing process, you need to use the Microsoft Compatibility Exchange to compare what you found on your own network with what others also encountered. The exchange collects and stores compatibility data from many places including Microsoft, software vendors, and ACT users (who opt to be part of the ACT community and document and share their own experiences and results). You can sync the data you've collected with data in the exchange from the ACM to share what you've learned with others too:

1. Navigate to the Analyze screen.

2. Click Send And Receive.

3. Click Review The Data Before Sending.

4. (Optional) Click Review All Data.

5. Type a name for the .txt file and click Save.

6. Review the file, as desired.

7. When you are ready to send the data, click Send.

Review what's offered as results arrive and use the information to help your decision-making processes. After your first sync, subsequent syncs include only the changes made since the last synchronization. The process won't resend all the information. Again, updates might be available, or you might be notified that no updates exist.

Deploying a runtime-analysis package

You can now deploy the package. You can use Group Policy, Configuration Manager, a logon script, removable media, a network share, and so on to do so. If you opt to let users work with the package, they'll need to run Microsoft Compatibility Monitor. However you opt to deploy, Compatibility Monitor needs to be run.

To run a deployed runtime-analysis package, follow these steps:

1. On the target computer, open Microsoft Compatibility Monitor. Note that if you run the .msi file Microsoft Compatibility Monitor installs automatically.

2. Click Start Monitoring.

3. Use each application that you want to test for a few minutes.

4. After you test the required applications, click Stop Monitoring. Data is sent automatically to the ACT database.

Reviewing report data

You view application compatibility reports from the ACM. Several types of reports are available, with names such as Computers, Devices, and Internet Explorer Add-ons. What you're interested in here is the Applications report. To open this report, follow these steps:

1. Open ACM.

2. In the Quick Reports pane, click Analyze.

3. In the same pane, under the operating system heading, click Applications.

Here are a few things you'll see in this report:

- Application names
- Application vendors
- Application versions
- The count of active issues for the application
- Whether the information for the application is included in the synchronization process with the Microsoft Compatibility Exchange
- Compatibility ratings unique to your organization
- Compatibility ratings provided by the vendor
- The number of computers that have the application installed

Fixing problems

When application compatibility problems are uncovered, you have to decide how you will deal with them. It might be time to move from a little-known office application suite to something more mainstream, such as Microsoft Office. It might be time to simply retire an application. Or, you might decide (and likely will in most cases) to fix the problem and continue to use the application. Fixing the problem can involve modifying the code or applying shims.

A common way to fix a compatibility issue is to alter the code. Microsoft recommends this over changing Registry settings or trying other risky or short-term workarounds. Changing the code requires resources (like money and time) on the front end, but the result might be worth it in the end, at least for a while. If you change the source code for Windows, however, you do create a long-term challenge for yourself and future administrators on many levels, including a risk of causing unexpected problems with other applications you run, with Windows Updates, and so on. A better option to consider is to create shims.

UNDERSTANDING SHIMS

If you opt to use the Shim Infrastructure, you can apply the fix (shim) to a specific application and application version only. Shims you create remain independent of the core Windows functions. (If you're unsure of what the word "shim" means, consider this real-life example: When you fold up a piece of paper and place it under a single table leg that is uneven and causing the table to wobble, you're creating a shim.)

Technically, but on a high level, Shim Infrastructure involves application programming interface (API) hooking; the shim redirects API calls from Windows to some other code, which is the shim itself. Windows manages and secures shims just as it would the original application code. Thus, you can't use shims to work around security mechanisms already in place by the operating system, including User Account Control (UAC) prompts. You also can't use a shim to fix kernel-mode code, specifically to fix issues with device drivers. Shims can fix compatibility issues, though, and are often applied as the desired solutions to compatibility problems.

KNOWING WHEN TO USE SHIMS

Deciding to use shims is a process, like anything else. You must first decide whether the problem merits a shim and is worth the time it takes to create it. Here are a few reasons you might opt for a shim:

- The vendor who created the application is out of business and no updates are available. The source code isn't available either, so shims are the only option.

- Your company created the application. If you don't have the time available to rewrite the code, a shim is the next best alternative.

- The vendor is still in business but has yet to create an update or fix, or a company-created application can be modified in the future, but no immediate update is available. In these cases, a shim can work temporarily, until an update or fix becomes available in the future.

CREATING SHIMS

Teaching you how to create a shim for an application is beyond the scope of this book; besides, the number of applications that might need shims is seemingly endless. So, rather than try to address this specifically, this section offers an overview and then points you to a few TechNet articles that can offer overviews and provide solution options.

One tool you might opt to use to resolve application compatibility issues is Compatibility Administrator, available from ACT (see Figure 1-11).

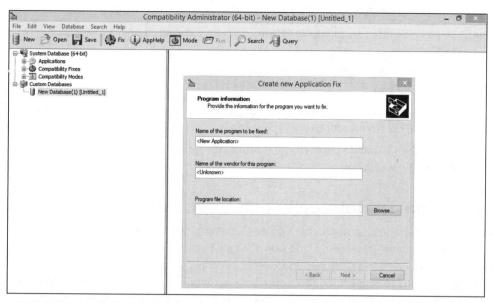

FIGURE 1-11 Compatibility Administrator enables you to create and apply application compatibility fixes.

This tool provides

- Compatibility fixes, compatibility modes, and AppHelp messages that you use to resolve specific compatibility issues
- Tools that enable you to create your own customized compatibility fixes, compatibility modes, AppHelp messages, and compatibility databases
- A tool that you can use to query and search for installed compatibility fixes on your organization's computers

To use this tool, you first create a new compatibility database (.sdb), select your problematic application, and then select and apply the desired fix. You then test that fix and, when you're ready, deploy it throughout your organization. To learn how to use this tool, refer to the Compatibility Administrator Users' Guide at *http://technet.microsoft.com/en-us/library/hh825182.aspx*.

EXAM TIP

If you discover that problems are the result of UAC issues, you can use the Standard User Analyzer (SUA) Wizard to guide you through the process of locating and fixing compatibility issues. Alternatively, you can use the SUA tool (without a wizard) with which you can perform an in-depth analysis first, and then then fix issues on your own. You use the SUA tool to test applications, monitor API calls, and detect issues related to UAC in Windows.

The following TechNet articles provide more detail:

- Compatibility Fixes for Windows 8, Windows 7, and Vista at *http://technet.microsoft. com/library/dn383989.aspx*

- Managing Shims in an Enterprise at *http://technet.microsoft.com/en-us/windows/ jj863250.aspx*

- Application Compatibility at *http://technet.microsoft.com/en-us/windows/application- compatibility.aspx*

- Create Shim Database-Management Strategies at *http://technet.microsoft.com/en-us/ library/dd835543(v=ws.10).aspx*

- Custom Shim Database Deployment at *http://technet.microsoft.com/en-us/library/ dd837647(v=ws.10).aspx*

Supporting desktop application coexistence

You can further test and run applications on new operating systems by using technologies such as Client Hyper-V, RemoteApp, and App-V. Client Hyper-V lets you run applications on virtual machines (VMs) in a dedicated space you can easily manage. RemoteApp lets you access applications remotely through Remote Desktop Services, and the apps themselves are housed and managed on network servers. App-V lets you virtualize applications so that you can use the applications side by side on the same system. All three options let you test applications in various scenarios before deployment. You can then make decisions based on what solution and environment works best in your enterprise.

Understanding and supporting Client Hyper-V

With Windows 8.1 Pro and Windows 8.1 Enterprise, you can create virtual machines that are housed inside a single operating system on a single computer. These virtual machines can run their own operating systems, and you can separate and secure them with virtual switches. A hypervisor keeps these "child" operating systems separate from the parent operating system. This enables network administrators to combine multiple machines into one, which saves money, power consumption, resources, space, and so on. In Windows 8.1, this technology is called Client Hyper-V and is a free element. With regard to supporting applications, you will install applications that you want to test in these environments to check compatibility, perhaps after shims or other fixes are applied.

To use Client Hyper-V, you'll need the following:

- Windows 8.1 Pro or Windows 8.1 Enterprise, 64-bit

- Second Level Address Translation (SLAT) processor

- 4 GB of RAM

- BIOS-level hardware virtualization support

If you have a compatible computer, you can create and configure a virtual machine. However, you must first enable Client Hyper-V from Control Panel, under Programs And Features.

Click Turn Windows Features On Or Off, locate Hyper-V, and select all related entries (see Figure 1-12). When it's enabled, click OK and restart the computer. After restarting, you'll have access to two new tiles when you log on as an administrator: Hyper-V Manager and Hyper-V Virtual Machine Connection.

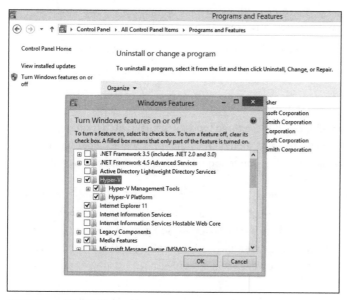

FIGURE 1-12 Enable Hyper-V.

NOTE

You might have to enter the BIOS to enable virtualization support.

EXAM TIP

You can enable Hyper-V in Windows PowerShell with the *Enable-WindowsOptionalFeature –FeatureName Microsoft-Hyper-V –All command.*

IMPORTANT **WHEN HYPER-V PLATFORM IS UNAVAILABLE**

If you don't see any entries for Hyper-V in the Windows Features dialog box, the computer is either Windows 8.1 (not Pro or Enterprise) or is 32-bit. If you see everything but Hyper-V Platform is unavailable for selection, everything else is okay, but the computer's processor isn't SLAT.

How to create, configure, and then install virtual machines by using the Hyper-V Manager is covered in the book, *Exam Ref 70-687: Configuring Windows 8.1*. This book also covers the types of virtual switches available and how to create them. You can create three types of virtual switches (from the Action pane, click Virtual Switch Manager):

- External, to let the VM connect to a network interface controller (NIC) on the computer to communicate with the external network, perhaps for the purpose of connecting to the Internet. If you want, it can also be configured to connect to the host computer. The physical NIC can connect to only one network in this scenario.
- Internal, to let the VM communicate with other VMs and to the host computer.
- Private, to let the VM communicate with other VMs but not the host computer.

EXAM TIP

More than likely you'll see something about the three types of virtual switches on the exam: External, Internal, and Private. You also should know that pretty much anything you want to do in the Hyper-V Manager requires you to log on with an administrator account.

Because creating and installing VMs were objectives for Exam 70-687, you wouldn't think you would need to know how to do these things for Exam 70-688. But as you learned earlier in this chapter, the exams will likely have quite a bit of overlap. So learning how to perform these tasks is in your best interest, specifically creating a VM, installing a VM, running a VM, and creating a virtual switch. This section, however, focuses only on supporting application compatibility with Client Hyper-V.

You can install applications on a virtual machine the same way you would install one in any other circumstance. You open Hyper-V Manager, right-click the desired VM and select Connect, in the VM window click Action and then Start, and then perform the desired application installation. During the testing process you can use the Hyper-V snapshot feature to take a snapshot of the original state of the VM so that you can return to a known state after application testing. (Snapshots are now called *checkpoints*.) You manually create a checkpoint to save the state of a virtual machine. This saves all the hard disk's contents, including application data files, settings, and configurations. When you're sure you don't need the checkpoint anymore, you can delete it (because these files can be quite large). Also, checkpoints are portable.

To create a checkpoint, follow these steps:

1. In Hyper-V Manager, click the new VM you just created and configured.
2. As needed, click Action and then Start, or click Action and then Connect.
3. Right-click the VM and select Checkpoint.
4. In the Checkpoints pane, right-click the new checkpoint and select Rename.
5. Name the checkpoint appropriately (Day1AfterInstall, for instance).

To test a checkpoint, follow these steps:

1. Inside the virtual machine, make a change, such as the desktop background.

2. In Hyper-V Manager in the Virtual Machines pane, right-click the VM and select Revert.

3. Click Revert again to verify.

4. Return to the running VM and note that the change has been undone.

EXAM TIP

A *differencing disk* is a virtual hard disk you create to quarantine changes you've made to a virtual hard disk or the guest operating system. You store these changes in a separate file. The differencing disk is associated with an existing virtual hard disk and can be any kind of virtual disk. You choose the disk when you create the differencing disk. This virtual hard disk is called the parent disk and the differencing disk is the child disk.

Understanding and supporting RemoteApp

Remote Desktop Services (RDS) lets you virtualize a computing session. You can opt to virtualize the entire desktop or, in this chapter, only individual applications. You use Remote-App tools and technologies to virtualize applications. When you do, applications look and feel as though they're running on the computer a user is sitting in front of, but in reality the app is being hosted elsewhere. As you might guess, this could be used to resolve compatibility problems with specific apps, as well as provide another means to test the apps before deployment. You can use RemoteApp with local apps, and they can be added to the Start screen.

RemoteApp programs are stored on an RD Session Host server; virtual desktops are hosted on an RD Virtualization Host server. These virtual environments can be accessed remotely from a configured client machine. The Windows server running the RDS role must have the following services configured and available:

- RD Session Host enables a server to host the desired applications (and perhaps full desktops). Users connect to this server to run the programs. Users also save files and access other network resources available on the server, as applicable.

- RD Virtualization Host, with Hyper-V, hosts the virtual machines and makes them available to users as virtual desktops. These virtual desktops can be provided in a pool on a first-come, first-served basis, or you can assign a specific desktop to a specific user.

- RD Web Access enables users to access RemoteApp and Desktop Connection through their computer's Start screen.

- RD Licensing is used to manage the RDS client access licenses. A license must exist for a user to connect to the RD Session Host server.

- RD Gateway enables users to access the internal enterprise network remotely from an Internet-connected device such as a tablet or laptop.

- RD Connection Broker helps manage session load balancing and reconnection. It also provides access to the RemoteApp programs and virtual desktops.

Beyond the reasons stated already are other reasons to use RDS:

- You can consolidate all apps to manage them more easily. When an app needs to be updated or otherwise serviced, you can perform the needed work on the RD Session Host server instead of on every client desktop.

- You can simplify deployment when applications are difficult to manage, perhaps because they are updated often or prone to problems.

- You can use fewer resources on client computers and simplify management by hosting rarely used applications.

- You can allow access to company applications remotely, for instance, from home, from tablets or other limited hardware, or while traveling on business.

Windows 8.1 Enterprise offers a Control Panel icon when you opt to view by large or small icons: RemoteApp And Desktop Connections. Users click this icon to access available remote desktops or remote applications. Figure 1-13 shows Control Panel and this icon (in the right column), the RemoteApp And Desktops Connections window, and the area where users type an email address or connection URL. (You can put icons on the desktop or tiles on the Start screen so that users can directly access virtualized apps.)

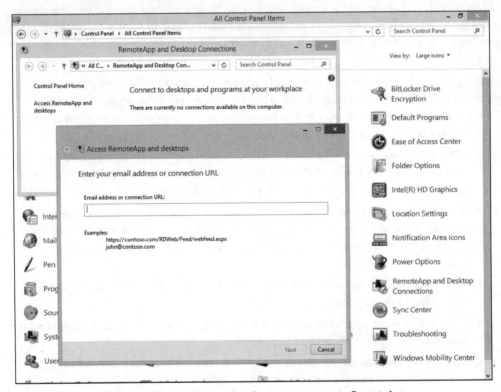

FIGURE 1-13 RemoteApp And Desktop Connections lets users connect to RemoteApp.

Understanding and supporting App-V

In some instances, you might need to run several applications side by side on a single computer. Doing so is generally okay, unless those applications conflict with one another. Such a conflict almost always occurs when you need to run multiple versions of the same application. This could certainly happen and is common in testing environments. In other cases, applications simply don't play well together; this might not have anything to do with versioning and could be caused by something completely different and difficult to diagnose. App-V helps you resolve these kinds of problems. Specifically, App-V lets you virtualize an application so that it remains independent of others but can still live on the same machine without causing conflict.

Application virtualization, as you've already learned, can also mean that users can access an application that's installed elsewhere from almost anywhere an Internet connection and compatible hardware can be used, and both users and administrators gain many benefits in doing so. Virtualization keeps applications off client machines, which means that the users' computers remain "clean" and administrators can manage the apps centrally (rather than have to manage every client in the enterprise). After App-V is set up and configured for use, a Windows 8.1 Enterprise user can install App-V client software to access and use the desired applications. As with other virtualization technologies, the running apps appear to the user to be installed and running on their own machines.

> **MORE INFO** **ADMINISTRATORS DETERMINE WHO CAN ACCESS VIRTUALIZED APPS**
>
> As soon as apps are virtualized, authorized users can access them through the App-V client application. If more than one app is available, a list appears from which they can select. Administrators set the required limitations on users and the apps they can access.

You must perform plenty of steps before end users can access virtualized applications. Setting up the actual infrastructure is beyond the scope of this book and is best left to experienced network administrators, but you must understand the fundamental task sequence and the hardware, software, and services required.

Using Microsoft Desktop Optimization Pack (MDOP)

App-V is available from Microsoft Desktop Optimization Pack (MDOP). MDOP is available as a subscription for Software Assurance (SA) customers, although you can download an evaluation to experiment with if you are an MSDN or TechNet subscriber. If you want to work through this part of the chapter, you'll want to download and install MDOP before continuing. Specifically, you need these elements, which are all part of App-V Server:

- App-V Management Server for managing App-V
- App-V Publishing Server to host virtual applications
- App-V Reporting Server to run and view applicable reports

- App-V Reporting Database Server to work with database deployments and report management

Beyond the required software, the hardware also must meet minimum requirements. The computer on which MDOP is installed must have the following:

- Microsoft .NET Framework 4.5
- Windows PowerShell 3.0
- Update for Windows KB2533623

Each element also must meet specific requirements. For example, the App-V client, Remote Desktop Services client, and the App-V server must all have the applicable Microsoft Visual C++ Redistributable Package installed. To see all requirements, refer to this article on TechNet: *http://technet.microsoft.com/en-us/library/jj713458.aspx*.

> **MORE INFO** **SOFTWARE ASSURANCE (SA)**
>
> Software Assurance is generally associated with an enterprise's ability to obtain the next version of Windows software as part of their enterprise agreement as a fee associated with qualified products. Some of the most popular additional benefits are free technical training, licenses for home users, online training, and 24x7 support. SA also provides deployment-planning services and other benefits.

Installing the App-V Sequencer and getting ready for sequencing

You should install MDOP and the App-V Sequencer on a 64-bit Windows 8.1 Enterprise computer. From the MDOP installation folder, navigate to App-V, Installers, 5.0_SP2 (or applicable version), and then run the setup program. As soon as it's installed, obtain the installer files for the application that you want to sequence. Copy those files to the computer that's running the sequencer. Create a new VM to use for the sequencing tasks, and make a backup copy of it before you start.

When you're ready, locate the Microsoft Application Virtualization Sequencer from the All Apps screen on your Windows 8.1 Enterprise computer. Click to open. Figure 1-14 shows the Microsoft Application Virtualization Sequencer as well as an open VM.

You can now do the following:

- Create virtual packages that can be deployed to computers that run the App-V 5.0 client.
- Upgrade and edit configuration information for packages you've already created.
- Convert virtual packages.

Creating a package also creates the following files:

- An .msi file that you'll use to install the virtual package on client computers
- A Report.xml file that contains all issues, warnings, and errors that were discovered during sequencing, in case you need to troubleshoot the package

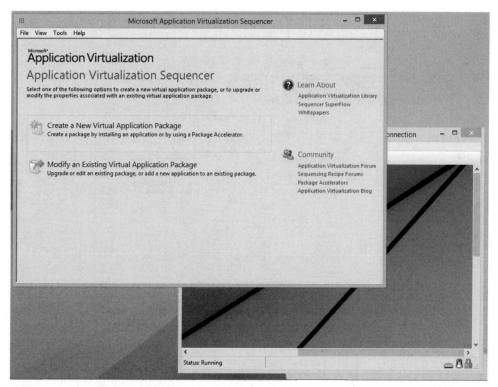

FIGURE 1-14 The Microsoft Application Virtualization Sequencer window helps you create or modify a new virtual application package.

- An .appv file, which is the virtual application file
- A deployment configuration file that regulates how virtual application is deployed
- A user configuration file that regulates how the virtual application runs

Sequencing an application

You can create virtualized application packages for standard applications, add-ons or plug-ins, and middleware. Creating packages for standard applications is the most common and what is detailed here. The following steps create one of the simplest types of packages. They don't configure every aspect available, including the option to stream the virtualized application; that experimentation is up to you. From the computer that has the sequencer installed, perform these steps:

1. At the Start screen, type **App-V**, and in the results click Microsoft Application Virtualization Sequencer.

2. Click Create A New Virtual Application Package. You can see this option in Figure 1-14.

3. Select Create Package (Default), and then click Next.

4. Resolve all listed issues that can cause the creation of the package to fail (see Figure 1-15).

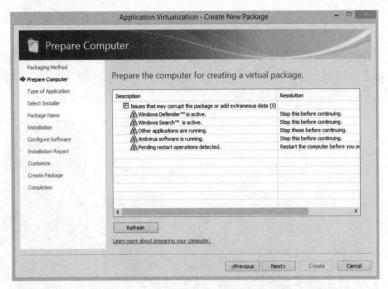

FIGURE 1-15 Prepare the computer for application sequencing.

5. Click Refresh and, if all problems are resolved, click Next.

6. Select the Standard Application (Default) check box, and then click Next.

7. Click Browse to find the installation file for the application. (If the application doesn't have an associated installer file, select the Perform A Custom Installation check box, and then click Next. Continue as prompted.)

8. Type a name for the package.

9. Click Browse to find the Primary Virtual Application Directory. Navigate to the location where the file would be installed by default, perhaps c:\ProgramFiles\<application name>. Note that you are navigating to this in the VM you already created.

10. Click Next three times. At the Create A Basic Package Or Customize Further page (see Figure 1-16), select Customize, and then click Next.

11. Click Next to bypass the option to run the program briefly.

12. Select Allow This Package To Run Only On The Following Operating Systems, and then select Windows 8.1 32-bit and Windows 8.1 64-bit. Notice the other options, such as the option to Allow The Package To Run On Any Operating System.

13. Click Next.

14. Click Create.

15. When the Package Completed page appears, click Close.

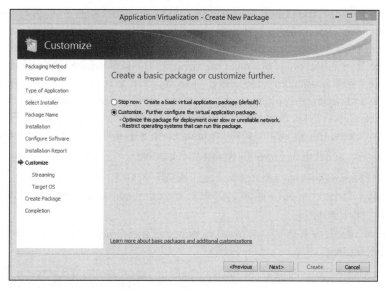

FIGURE 1-16 Opt to customize your package.

With the package created, you are now ready for deployment. You can deploy App-V packages by using an Electronic Software Distribution (ESD) solution. When you opt for an ESD, you eliminate the need for an App-V 5.0 management server, management database, and publishing server. Alternatively, you can use Windows PowerShell to deploy a virtualized application. You can, for example, also opt to install the virtual application on a single computer, deploy it through Group Policy, or use it with Configuration Manager.

> **MORE INFO** **DEPLOYING VIRTUAL APPLICATION PACKAGES**
>
> To learn more about deploying App-V packages via ESD, refer to this article on TechNet:
> *http://technet.microsoft.com/en-us/library/jj713482.aspx.*

Supporting installation and configuration of User Experience Virtualization (UE-V)

Users are more mobile than ever, and the trend will continue. Making the user experience the same no matter where the users log on—whether it's on a laptop, desktop, or tablet—would be valuable to users and enhance productivity. Network administrators have been doing so for quite some time by incorporating roaming user profiles, making the user's files and folders available offline, configuring syncing when a user reconnects to the network, and incorporating folder redirection. Quite a bit of this was covered in my previous book, *Exam Ref 70-687: Configuring Windows 8.1*. This exam doesn't focus on these technologies from what I've seen via the list of objectives; instead, it focuses on User Experience Virtualization (UE-V).

Microsoft UE-V monitors the Windows operating system, monitors apps and application settings that are applied when users are at their computers, and captures those settings. The information is saved to a defined storage location such as a network share folder. (This data isn't saved to OneDrive, a USB drive, or similar mechanism.) The settings are then applied (or can be applied) to the different computers and devices assigned to the user. What is synchronized (and where) and what apps and applications are included (or not) is determined by the settings location templates (XML files) that the network administrator creates and configures, in combination with what the applications' developers make available for synchronization.

Here are a few additional things to understand about UE-V:

- A user can change personal settings from any device included in the UE-V synchronization group. Those changes will be applied to the other computers the next time the user logs on to them.

- The user can use UE-V with a Windows 7 or Windows 8 computer. Applicable and compatible settings will sync automatically.

- Changes are saved to a file, and the file is synced on log on. Nothing is actually "virtualized."

- Application settings that can be synced can come from applications installed on the device, applications that are sequenced with App-V, and RemoteApp applications.

- Settings can be used as part of a recovery process when a machine is reimaged or reinstalled.

- You can incorporate Windows PowerShell and WMI to configure and deploy UE-V agents. Refer to this article to learn more: *http://technet.microsoft.com/en-us/library/dn458904.aspx*.

- UE-V includes application settings templates for various editions of Microsoft Office, Internet Explorer, Windows Accessories, desktop settings, ease of use settings, and more.

EXAM TIP

You might see exam questions with answers that include App-V, Roaming Profiles, Remote-App, UE-V, Windows Intune, Office 365, and similar technologies that you'll learn about in this chapter. These questions will include a scenario that includes something specific the user needs and that you want to provide (perhaps retrieving application settings from the cloud, with the ability to change those settings and sync them back as is possible with UE-V). You must be able to choose the ideal technology when you are asked to provide a specific option or feature for users.

Several elements must be in place for UE-V to work. A UE-V Agent must be used. This agent watches what changes and saves those changes as applicable. A settings package is also necessary to store the application and operating system settings and application template information. Finally, a UE-V Generator must exist where you can create your own custom templates. This might seem a little vague because it is. A lot of planning and resources are required to put this technology into place. Looking at it from a high level, deployment includes the following:

1. Deploy the Settings Storage Location.

2. Deploy the UE-V Agent.

3. Install the Group Policy templates.

4. Install the Agent Generator.

5. Deploy the Settings Template Catalog.

6. Deploy Settings Location Templates.

7. Administer UE-V, including but not limited to understanding how to

   - Manage frequency of scheduled tasks.
   - Restore application and Windows settings.
   - Configure applicable Group Policy objects.
   - Manage settings packages.
   - Incorporate App-V applications.
   - Incorporate Configuration Manager as applicable.

Deploying desktop apps by using Windows Intune

Not all companies have the money, time, or resources to set up and maintain an intricate server infrastructure, the ability or know-how to set up personal VMs, or the ability to set up a UE-V substructure to synchronize various user settings. However, those same companies might still want to virtualize applications. Keeping applications off users' desktops, especially with so many of them mobile and using multiple devices, can lighten the load required of network administrators (as well as support staff). This is where Windows Intune really shines. Any size company can use Windows Intune to virtualize applications.

In this section you'll learn just enough about Windows Intune to understand what it is and how you can use it. Later in this chapter and book you'll learn a lot more. Here are the highlights. With Windows Intune, a company can:

- Use a single web-based administrator console to manage computers and mobile devices via the cloud.
- Simplify the management of various devices, including Windows laptops, desktops, tablets, and phones—and even Apple iOS and Android devices.
- Make following company guidelines easier by using the cloud to manage all devices.
- Download Windows Intune client software when necessary, using a Microsoft account and password, from the administration page. (Client software can be deployed in many ways, including manually, through Group Policy and by using Configuration Manager.)

- Make software available to users, requiring all users to have the software or making it optional, while at the same time requiring no user interaction for installing it.

- Make software available through the company portal so that Windows RT users can install applications as needed.

- Create, upload, publish, and deploy software packages; configure and manage security policies; manage inventory; and create inventory reports when combined with Configuration Manager.

Unlike most of what you've seen so far in this objective, you can get a free 30-day trial of Windows Intune even if you don't have a Software Assurance plan or a subscription to TechNet or MSDN. After you set it up (and possibly install Microsoft Silverlight if you didn't have it already), go to *https://manage.microsoft.com/WindowsIntune*, log on, and work through the setup processes. Your logon name should look something like *administrator@ yourname.onmicrosoft.com*. Figure 1-17 shows the Windows Intune Administrator Console, with System Overview selected. Notice the alerts, system status, updates, agent health, and more, just from this one tab.

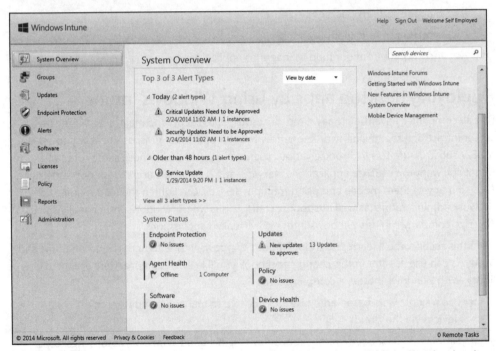

FIGURE 1-17 The Windows Intune Administrator Console consolidates the available tools and makes them easy to work with.

From the other tabs available in the Windows Intune Administrator Console, you can manage clients easily. Table 1-4 details the tabs available.

TABLE 1-4 Tabs available in the Windows Intune Administrator Console

Windows Intune tab	Available tools and options
System Overview	Read notices regarding the functionality of Windows Intune; view summaries of Alerts, Endpoint Protection, Agent Health, Policy, Device Health, Software, and Updates; view Computer Summary and Mobile Device Summary
Groups	Create groups; view hardware reports; see a Mobile Device Summary that includes Alerts, Update Status, Policy, Software Status, and Device Health Status; view information on available disk space, top five manufacturers, and top five operating systems used in your enterprise
Updates	View Update Status and Cloud Storage Status; perform update tasks; sort updates by type (Critical, Security, Definition, and so on)
Endpoint Protection	Review Malware Status and Computer Status to see if any issues exist; see Top Malware Instances
Alerts	See a list of Alerts that you can sort in various ways, including View By Date
Software	Review Software Status and Cloud Storage Status; manage cloud storage; perform tasks such as adding software and managing software deployment
Licenses	Review Licenses Overview specific to your organization; add agreements; create a License Group; view Purchase Report; view Installation Report
Policy	Configure policies to manage settings on computers and mobile devices (after it's configured, you can deploy the policy to groups of devices, or deploy mobile device policies to mobile users)
Reports	View various reports: Update, Detected Software, Computer Inventory, Mobile Device Inventory, License Purchase, and License Installation
Administrator	Access Administration Overview, including the name of the account, status, number of enrolled devices, and Cloud Storage Status; learn more about these items

If you've set up a free trial of Windows Intune, click the Software tab. Under Tasks, click Add Software. Download and install the Microsoft Intune Software Publisher, log on, and read the introductory screen. This should give you an idea of how to publish software with Windows Intune. Click Next; you see the screen shown in Figure 1-18, except the path to the location of the software setup files is blank. You learn how to complete this process later in the chapter.

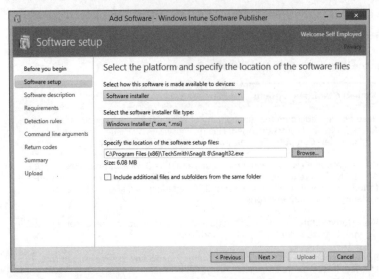

FIGURE 1-18 Use the Windows Intune Software Publisher to publish software.

 Thought experiment

Choosing the best method for hosting a desktop application

In this thought experiment, apply what you've learned about this objective. You can find answers to these questions in the "Answers" section at the end of this chapter.

You have been commissioned by a large organization to help prepare for an enterprise-wide rollout of Windows 8.1. Company employees use myriad desktop applications, two of which were written by a developer who's no longer in business. The company wants you to help test the applications to see whether they are or can be made compatible with Windows 8.1.

1. What tool will you choose to determine whether the applications in question are compatible?

2. What type of database must also be available for this technique to work successfully?

3. Several steps are involved in using this tool. What is the second step you'll take to use this tool to test the applications and determine compatibility, after performing the installation and setting up the applicable database?

4. After you create and deploy the appropriate collector package, what kind of package do you create and deploy next?

5. Where can you review the application compatibility reports?

Objective summary

- You can determine application compatibility and deal with problems that arise in many ways, including using ACT and creating shims.
- Applications can coexist with others that would usually cause compatibility issues or simply aren't compatible with the current operating system. The technologies to consider include Client Hyper-V, RemoteApp, and App-V. Each offers something unique and is used in specific circumstances to provide solutions.
- You can give users a consistent desktop and user experience with UE-V.
- You can use Windows Intune to host applications and manage computer inventory, even if you don't have a server structure in place.

Objective review

Answer the following questions to test your knowledge of the information in this objective. You can find the answers to these questions and explanations of why each answer choice is correct or incorrect in the "Answers" section at the end of this chapter.

1. You are planning for a Windows 8.1 deployment and have learned that one desktop application your company relies on heavily isn't compatible. The application vendor is still in business and promised an update soon, but you don't want to wait for that update. What can you do to make the application compatible until an update is available? Choose all that apply.

   A. Create a shim for the application.

   B. Create and deploy a runtime-analysis package.

   C. Run the program in Program Compatibility mode.

   D. Use RemoteApp for the application.

2. You have discovered that an application is incompatible with Windows 8.1 and the issue involves User Account Control. Which of the following tools can you use to resolve the issue?

   A. Create a shim with ACT.

   B. Use the Standard User Analyzer Wizard.

   C. Create a shim with App-V.

   D. None of the above; you can't resolve this kind of issue.

3. Which of the following lets you store and manage applications on your own network servers while also making them available to users?

   A. Client Hyper-V

   B. App-V

   C. RemoteApp

   D. Windows Intune

4. You try to enable Client Hyper-V on a workstation and can select Hyper-V and the Hyper-V Management tools, but you can't select Hyper-V Platform. Why?

   A. You aren't logged on as an administrator.

   B. The computer's processor isn't SLAT.

   C. The computer's architecture is 32 bit.

   D. The computer is running Windows 8.1, but not the Pro or Enterprise edition.

5. RemoteApp programs are stored on a(n) _____ and virtual desktops are hosted on a(n) _____.

   A. RD Virtualization Host server; RD Session Host server

   B. App-V Publishing Server; App-V Management Server

   C. App-V Management Server; App-V Publishing Server

   D. RD Session Host server; RD Virtualization Host server

6. You want to monitor Windows operating system, app, and application settings that are applied when users are at their computers. You want to capture those settings and then allow users to access those settings to provide a consistent user experience no matter where they log on. Which of the following are parts of the solution you will put into place to make this happen?

   A. A working Active Directory and network share

   B. A UE-V Agent

   C. A UE-V Generator

   D. A Settings Storage Location

   E. All of the above

   F. Only B and C

7. When you deploy UE-V, which of the following is the first thing you must do?

   A. Deploy the Settings Storage Location.

   B. Deploy the UE-V Agent.

   C. Install the Group Policy templates.

   D. Install the Agent Generator.

   E. Deploy the Settings Template Catalog.

   F. Deploy Settings Location Templates.

8. For Windows Intune, what does Endpoint Protection refer to?

   A. Malware

   B. Updates

   C. Policy

   D. Licensing

Objective 1.3: Support Windows Store and cloud apps

The previous objective covered supporting desktop apps. This objective covers supporting apps from the Windows Store and Office 365, sideloading apps, and managing the apps you want to use. You'll also see more about how to sync settings unique to a user by incorporating the cloud, specifically with a Microsoft account and a trusted PC.

> **This objective covers how to:**
>
> - Integrate a Microsoft account, including personalization settings and trusted PCs
> - Install and manage software by using Office 365 and Windows Store apps
> - Sideload apps into online and offline images
> - Sideload apps by using Windows Intune
> - Deep link apps by using Windows Intune

Integrating a Microsoft account

These days, almost all Windows 8 and Windows 8.1 users have Microsoft accounts that they use to log on to their personal Windows 8-based computers and tablets. These accounts enable them to sync certain settings related to their user experience, including but not limited to the Start screen layout, app data, account picture, web browser favorites, and some passwords. Settings are stored via OneDrive. Consumers can use their Microsoft accounts to manage billing for their Xbox accounts, the Store app, and even connect their Xbox gamer tags. Users also receive cloud services when they sign up for the account, including a calendar, contact list, and similar features and tools. They can decide what to sync by using PC Settings on their local computers.

EXAM TIP

If a scenario on the exam asks you to troubleshoot why a user can't sync passwords with other accounts and computers, make sure the scenario states that they are using a Microsoft account first. Local accounts can't be used to sync to the cloud. If a Microsoft account is in use, check to see whether the PC is a trusted PC (or if others are).

Network administrators can integrate users' Microsoft accounts into the workplace to help users incorporate what they've configured with these accounts with their domain accounts. Network administrators can also opt not to let users connect to their Microsoft accounts by setting limitations in Group Policy. This section looks at the Group Policy options first, followed by how users can tweak what they want to sync and how to trust various PCs, and then how users connect their Microsoft accounts to the domain account.

Exploring Group Policy settings

You configure Group Policy to allow or deny Microsoft accounts in a domain by using the \ or Group Policy Management Editor. You open the Group Policy Management Editor window, and then expand Computer Configuration, Policies, Windows Settings, Security Settings, Local Policies, Security Options. You also can use the Local Group Policy Editor to allow or block Microsoft accounts on local computers by navigating to Computer Configuration, Windows Settings, Security Settings, Local Policies, Security Options. Figure 1-19 shows the path to the latter.

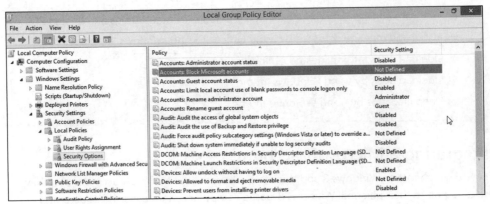

FIGURE 1-19 Navigate to the Local Group Policy setting Accounts: Block Microsoft Accounts.

Double-clicking the entry Accounts: Block Microsoft Accounts presents three options:

- **This Policy Is Disabled**   If you apply this setting or don't configure any others, users can use Microsoft accounts.

- **Users Can't Add Microsoft Accounts**   If you apply this setting, users can't create new Microsoft accounts, switch from local accounts to Microsoft accounts, or connect domain accounts to Microsoft accounts. This is the best option to choose if you want to limit the use of Microsoft accounts in your enterprise.

- **Users Can't Add Or Log On With Microsoft Accounts**   If you apply this setting, users who have existing Microsoft accounts can't log on to Windows. This can limit even the administrators' ability to log on.

Locating and managing what's synced with a Microsoft account

Users can change what items they opt to sync to and from the personal computers they log on to with their Microsoft accounts. Users can access the options on their personal computers via PC Settings, the OneDrive tab, and Sync settings (see Figure 1-20). (Press Windows logo key+C to access the charms and click Change PC Settings.) Users will encounter additional sync options when they connect with their domain accounts.

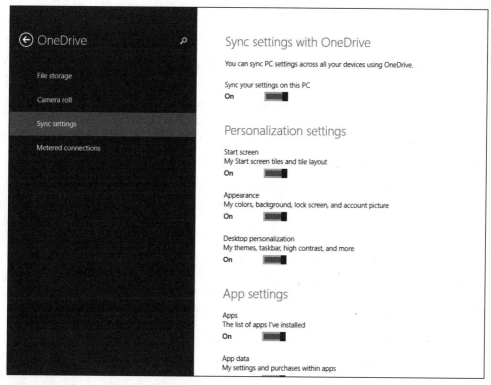

FIGURE 1-20 Change what syncs from PC Settings.

Configuring trusted PCs

User settings are synced via Microsoft accounts and OneDrive. OneDrive also enables users to configure and sync passwords with trusted PCs. You can use a configured trusted PC (sometimes called a *trusted device*) to synchronize passwords and to reset the Microsoft account password if it's forgotten or compromised. Users decide which of their devices should be trusted. Two scenarios are involved.

In the first scenario, users log on to a new computer with a new Microsoft account (or an account that's new to that computer). In this instance, users are prompted to enter a security code. Microsoft generates this code and sends it to a backup email address or cell phone number already configured for the account. After the users type the code, they can then opt to state that the PC being configured is one they log on to often and should thus be trusted.

In another scenario, users opt not to sync passwords while configuring a PC, for whatever reason. In this case, when they try to sync passwords later, they see a message that states the passwords can't be synced until the PC is trusted. When the users opt to trust the PC, the same process completes as noted before with the generation of a code they must type.

Finally, users can log on to their Microsoft account online via a web browser, navigate to Security info, and then gain access to options for recovering passwords and setting up additional trusted devices. Users can also remove all trusted devices associated with an account, should the account be compromised.

Connecting a Microsoft account with a domain account

If users have domain accounts in the workplace, they can connect their Microsoft accounts to them and see the same desktop background, browser history, and other account settings they've already configured on their home PCs. They also can use Microsoft account services from their domain PCs without signing in to them.

To connect a Microsoft account with a domain account, follow these steps:

1. Access the charms and click Change PC Settings.

2. Under PC Settings, click Accounts.

3. Click Connect To A Microsoft Account.

4. Clear the check boxes for items you don't want to sync, and click Next.

5. Enter the applicable email address and click Next.

6. Enter the password and click Next.

7. Complete the security information requirements and type in the generated code.

8. Click Next, and then click Finish.

Installing and managing software by using Office 365 and Windows Store apps

Network administrators who manage large enterprises of computers and users don't carry physical media from machine to machine to install software. Instead, they opt for more practical solutions. You've already learned about several of those options in this chapter. More ways are available than what's been covered so far, however; administrators can install and manage software using Office 365, and they can make their apps available from the Windows Store.

Installing software by using Office 365

Office 365 in its multiple editions is Microsoft Office. But it is Microsoft Office in the cloud, accessible via a user-based paid subscription. Because it's cloud-based, users can access the Microsoft Office products that are licensed to them on up to five compatible devices (with Office 365 ProPlus). Office 365 ProPlus is designed to run locally on PCs, so a persistent connection to the Internet isn't required.

Many compatible platforms are available, including Windows, Mac, and compatible mobile devices. With Office 365, updates are applied automatically, so enterprise administrators never have to worry about updating computers or other devices manually, although they are still in control of those updates and can decide how and when they'll be offered to users. Just about every other maintenance task you can encounter when you host Office 365 in your enterprise is also handled without any interaction from you (after Office 365 is set up). Beyond that, administrators can also decide where users' data should be stored: on a company's onsite data servers or private cloud, in the public cloud, or a combination of these.

The reality is that Office 365 is "application virtualization." And you know about virtualization, and that virtualized applications run in their own space. This means that users can run the latest version of Office in the cloud while at the same time leaving older versions installed and available on their own PCs. It also means that users can have the same user experience from wherever they log on while using the hosted apps.

You can get a free trial of Office 365 Small Business Premium or Office 365 Midsize Business here: *http://office.microsoft.com/en-us/business/compare-office-365-for-business-plans-FX102918419.aspx?tab=1*. Setting up Office 365 involves creating an account, creating an administrator logon and domain name, and requesting and then typing in a security code from Microsoft. Figure 1-21 shows the Office 365 Admin Center.

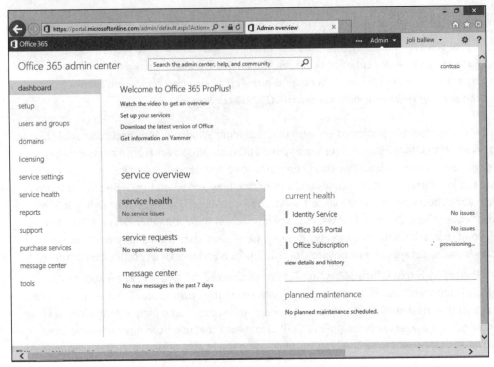

FIGURE 1-21 The Office 365 ProPlus Admin Center offers the tools you need in a single console.

Before you can go much further, you need to create at least one user account. That user will then log on to the Office 365 portal with a temporary password and create a new password. Then the user can download whatever parts of Office you want to license that user to use.

To perform the initial setup tasks and to create a user and assign a license (after signing up for a free trial, completing the administration requirements, and logging on to the portal at *https://portal.microsoftonline.com*), follow these steps:

1. Click the Settings icon in the top right corner and click Office 365 Settings.

2. Click Setup.

3. From the Quick Start section, click Start.

4. Choose the desired domain and click Next.

5. Click Add users and assign licenses.

6. Choose an option to add users. For this example, choose Add Users One At A Time. Click Next.

7. Input user details and click Next (see Figure 1-22).

FIGURE 1-22 Create a new user before deploying software.

8. Choose the new user's status (administrator or not) and set the user location. Click Next.

9. Leave Office 365 ProPlus selected under Assign Licenses, and then click Next.

10. Read the information on the final page and click Create.

11. Write down the temporary password (which is good for 90 days).

12. Click Finish.

The new user can now install Office Professional on one or more computers. The easiest way to do this is to let users install Office 365 directly from the Office 365 portal, as outlined here. You can also opt to download the software to a network share and deploy it to users in any applicable manner you prefer. An overview of how that's done comes later.

Before you start, though, you might want to explore the admin portal for a few minutes. Specifically, look at the Service Settings tab, where you can clear check boxes for Office products that you don't want users to have permission to install, if you have a software package that offers this as a feature. The list depends of the software package that the enterprise has obtained. Office 365 ProPlus includes Access, Excel, InfoPath, Lync, OneNote, Outlook, PowerPoint, Publisher, and Word, and installs as a single package. You can't select only one or two here. Whatever the case, you should check it out anyway.

EXAM TIP

If you don't want users to run a particular program but don't have the option to pick and choose what programs your users can install, as in the case of Office 365 ProPlus, you can use AppLocker to control it. You can also opt to deploy Office 365 ProPlus through App-V.

To let the new user install Office 365 ProPlus from the Office 365 portal, follow these steps:

1. Log on as an administrator to a local computer where you want to install Office 365.

2. With Internet Explorer, navigate to *https://portal.microsoftonline.com*.

3. Type the user ID and temporary password, and then click Sign In.

4. Type the old password, input a new password, and confirm it. Click Save.

5. Follow the applicable instructions to install the software and connect to Office 365.

6. Select the 32-bit version of Office 365 and the language to install. The 32-bit version is recommended. Click Install.

7. Click Run to start the installation, click Yes to continue, and click Next to start the wizard.

8. Select No Thanks to not send updates to Microsoft, and then click Accept.

9. Click Next in the Meet OneDrive screen.

10. Click Next to accept defaults, select No Thanks, and then click All Done.

EXAM TIP

When users install from the Office 365 portal, updates are installed automatically in the background. You can't change this behavior. Also, as an administrator, you can't control which computers the user installs the software on.

Other deployment options exist beyond this self-service method. For large organizations with a domain and Active Directory, administrators can save the installation files on a local network share. For this method to work, however, you need the Office Deployment Tool, available from the Microsoft Download Center. You can use this tool to create a Configuration.xml file that contains information about what language to download or what architecture to use. It can also include where the software is located on the network, how updates are applied after Office is installed, and what version of the software to install. As soon as the files are available, deployment can include Group Policy, startup scripts, or Configuration Manager.

MORE INFO **LEARN MORE ABOUT DEPLOYMENT**

To learn more about the different ways that you can deploy Office 365 ProPlus, visit *http://technet.microsoft.com/en-us/library/ee624360(v=office.15).aspx*.

On a high level, deployment via a network share involves these steps:

1. You create a network share, *yourservername**Officeversion**Source*, and the files are extracted there. The extraction command is *microsoftoffice.exe /extract:"pathtosourcefiles"*.

2. You download additional required files, such as template files and Office Customization Tool files.

3. You configure these files, complete installation, and copy the necessary data to the shared folder in a new folder called Admin.

4. You then start the Office Customization Tool, using the command *yourservername*\ *Officeversion**Source*\setup.exe /Admin, and customize Office. Changes are saved to a customization files (.msp). This is also saved to the shared folder.

5. Users log on to the Office 365 portal and run MicrosoftOffice.exe from the network share.

Managing software by using Office 365

When you set up Office 365, you are the Global Administrator. You have the power to create users who are administrators and users who aren't, and to perform any other task associated with Office 365. You can create several types of administrators, as outlined in Table 1-5. Creating these administrators and delegating responsibilities is part of managing Office 365. Each administrator has specific permissions.

TABLE 1-5 Administrator roles in Office 365

Permission	Admins who can manage	Admins who can't manage
View information related to the organization and users	Billing; Global; Password; Service; User Management	Not applicable
Manage support tickets	Billing; Global; Password; Service; User Management	Not applicable
Manage user passwords (reset)	Global; Service; User Management can reset passwords for Password and User Management admins	Billing
Manage billing and purchasing	Billing; Global	Password; Service; User Management
Manage user views	Global; User Management	Billing; Password; Service
Manage user licenses	Global; User Management with limitations (can't delete a global admin or create admins)	Billing; Password; Service
Manage domains	Global	Billing; Password; Service; User Management
Manage organization information	Global	Billing; Password; Service; User Management
Create and manage admin roles	Global	Billing; Password; Service; User Management
Use directory synchronization	Global	Billing; Password; Service; User Management

After you delegate responsibilities and roles to the various members of your administration team, you're ready to start managing the product. This involves many facets. To see these facets, click each tab in the Office 365 Admin Center. A few examples include the following:

- **Users And Groups tab**   From the Active Users tab (see Figure 1-23), you can set up single sign-on, set up Active Directory synchronization, create password policies, and configure multifactor authentication requirements. You can also add users, filter users, and search for users, as well as edit user information. The Delete Users, Security Groups, and Delegated Admins tabs each have their own available management tasks. (Click Learn More to the right of Single Sign-on to learn what this feature offers; you might be asked about this on the exam.)

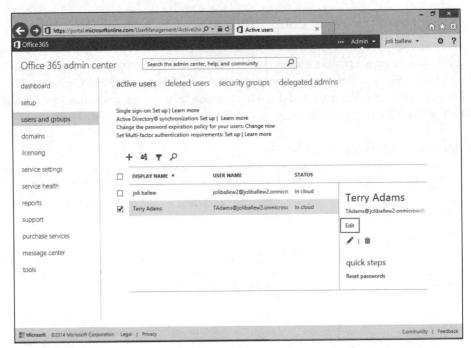

FIGURE 1-23 You can perform many management tasks from every tab and subtab in the Office 365 Admin Center.

- **Domains tab**   Use this tab to manage your domain, add a domain, buy a domain, and perform similar tasks.

- **Licensing tab**   Here, you can review your current subscription; view the number of licenses that are valid, expired, and assigned; and manage your subscription.

- **Service Settings**   Here, you can manage user software, including choosing which software your users can download directly from Office 365 (see Figure 1-24). You also can configure a password expiration policy.

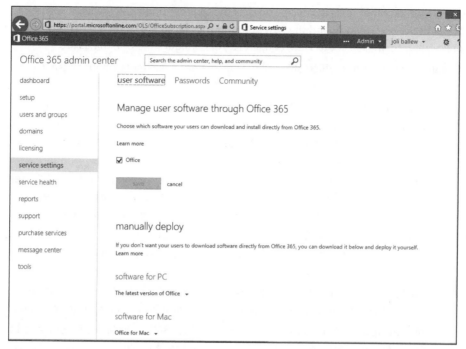

FIGURE 1-24 There are many options available from the Service Settings tab in the Office 365 Admin Center.

- **Service Health tab**   You can see the status of the Office 365 service in relation to use as categorized by day. You also can review planned maintenance.

- **Message Center tab**   You can access messages provided by Microsoft, including messages regarding new features in Office 365 and information about available upgrades.

As you can see, you can manage Office 365 in many ways. You should become familiar with how to perform certain tasks, such as resetting a user's password, configuring a password expiration policy, and creating new admins. Spend some time now exploring, and perform these tasks as time allows. Notice that the Dashboard tab, the first one on the left, offers access to videos for performing tasks as well as setting up services. For an introduction, the following steps walk you through one task: resetting a user's password.

To reset a user password, follow these steps:

1. From the Office 365 Admin Center, click Users And Groups.

2. Select the user you want to modify.

3. Click Reset Password.

4. Click Finish.

Performing other tasks is similar. You click the tab that offers the resource you need (perhaps Service Settings, and the Password tab you find there to set a password expiration policy), and then you click to view, edit, create, or configure the option desired.

Before you leave this Office 365 discussion, here are a few more things to familiarize yourself with:

- **Click-to-Run** Traditionally when you install Office, you have to wait until the whole Office product is installed before you can use it. Click-to-Run allows you to stream installations, which means users can open and start to use the product before the entire product is installed.

- **Other features** You might be familiar with features beyond Word, Excel, PowerPoint, and others. For example, large enterprises might also use Exchange Online, SharePoint Online, Lync Online, and opt to incorporate other services such as Yammer.

- **Windows PowerShell management** You can manage Office 365 with Windows PowerShell. Read this TechNet article to familiarize yourself with this: *http://technet. microsoft.com/en-us/library/dn568002.aspx*.

- **Desktop versions** Many Office 365 plans also include the latest desktop versions of Office. If your users can't always be online, this option is something to consider.

- **Mobile apps** Many mobile apps support Office 365, including but not limited to Office Mobile, Outlook Mobile, OneNote, and Lync Mobile.

EXAM TIP

In the past, Microsoft certification exams included questions that ask you to choose which Windows PowerShell command in a list of commands can be used to perform tasks. Whether you'll be asked this isn't known. To be on the safe side, read this article about performing common tasks with Windows PowerShell, such as licensing users, adding users, and adding domains: *http://technet.microsoft.com/en-us/library/dn568028.aspx*.

Installing software by using the Windows Store

You should know how to install software from the Windows Store as a consumer. You simply click the Store tile from the Start screen, navigate to the app to install, click it, and choose Install. These apps are also called packaged apps. If you aren't yet familiar with the Store, press the Windows logo key to access the Start screen, click the Store tile, and install a few apps before continuing here. Figure 1-25 shows the Store and the results that appear after searching for "Microsoft."

The Windows Store has the following characteristics and features:

- It's a central depository for publicly created apps available for free, as a trial, and for purchase.

- Users must have a Microsoft account to obtain Store apps.

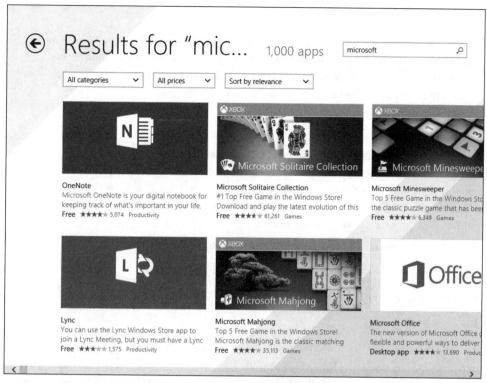

FIGURE 1-25 The Windows Store offers apps made available to the public.

- Publicly created apps must pass Microsoft's certification and compatibility tests before they can be published to the Store.

- Installed apps appear on the All Apps page. (They no longer appear automatically on the Start screen like they did in Windows 8.)

- Your enterprise can offer Line of Business (LOB) apps through the Store. You can certify your apps through Microsoft to make public, or choose not to certify them and make them private and available only to your employees.

- As an administrator, you need to configure Group Policy to define how you want your users to interact with the Store with devices you provide and those they bring to work ("bring your own device," or BYOD). See "Managing software by using the Windows Store," next.

Managing software by using the Windows Store

By default, all users can access the Windows Store. You might want to change this behavior. You can modify access in two ways. You can configure it so users can't access the Windows Store at all, or you can limit their use by allowing them to acquire only specific apps. If you opt to let users access the Store, you can disable app updates, if you want.

DISABLE APP UPDATES

You might opt to let users access Store apps but choose to disable app updates (they are installed automatically in Windows 8.1). You can do this by using Group Policy in a domain, via the Local Group Policy Editor in a workgroup, or from a single computer using the Store app options. First, look at how to achieve this on a single computer. This is really the only setting relevant to single users at a single PC.

To disable updates on a single client computer, follow these steps:

1. From the Start screen, click the Store app.

2. Press Windows logo key+I to open the Settings charm.

3. Click App Updates.

4. Move the slider under Automatically Update My Apps from Yes to No.

If you need to manage a group of computers in a workgroup or domain, you need to apply Group Policy. The location of the Group Policy setting is in the same place whether you use the Local Group Policy or the related Group Policy Management Console on your domain server. The path to the Local Group Policy setting (in gpedit.msc) is Computer Configuration, Administrative Templates, Windows Components, Store. If you enable the setting Turn Off Automatic Download Of Updates On Win8 Machines, updates are disabled (see Figure 1-26).

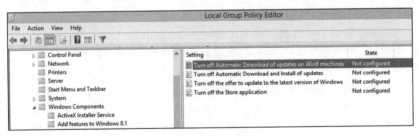

FIGURE 1-26 Use Group Policy to manage Store settings.

DISABLING ACCESS THROUGH GROUP POLICY

You can't disable access to the Windows Store from the Settings charm like you can when disabling app updates. To disable access, you must use the applicable Group Policy Editor. You might want to do this if your employees are downloading and installing games, for example. You might need to disable access to meet a company's security needs. You can disable the Store for computers, users, and/or groups. Whatever the case, to disable access to the Windows Store using the Local Group Policy Editor, follow these steps:

1. On the Start screen, type **gpedit.msc** and click it in the results. (You can also use the Run box on the desktop.)

2. In the Group Policy Editor, expand the following nodes: Computer, User Configuration, Administrative Templates, Windows Components, and Store.

3. Double-click Turn Off The Store Application.

4. Click Enabled.

5. Click OK.

EXAM TIP

The exam will have questions that ask how to open all manner of features, using various text-based shortcuts. For instance, rather than search for the Local Group Policy Editor on the Start screen of a workstation computer, you might be expected to know that you can also use Windows logo key+R, and in the Run box that opens, type **gpedit.msc**. So, as you work through this book and perform any task, know that likely other ways are available to do it.

Here are a few examples you can type in the Run box or on the Start screen to open a few of the popular Administrative Tools and Computer Management tools:

- File Signature Verification: Sigverif
- Group Policy Editor: gpedit.msc
- Local Security Settings: secpol.msc
- System Configuration Utility: msconfig
- Task Manager: taskmgr
- Computer Management: compmgmt.msc
- Event Viewer: eventvwr.msc
- Performance Monitor: perfmon.msc
- Disk Management: diskmgmt.msc

To find more, perform a web search for "List Run command for Windows 8."

Sideloading apps into online and offline images

Companies sometimes create their own apps. These apps have the same characteristics as the apps you find on the Start screen and from the Store (which aren't desktop apps). These apps are meant to be used by employees to do work. As noted earlier, enterprise administrators can make these apps available publicly if they want to go through the Microsoft certification process, or they can make them available to their enterprise users through a process known as *sideloading*. Tools such as DISM, Windows PowerShell, Configuration Manager, and Windows Intune help with sideloading.

As a new technology, sideloading can be used only with Windows Server 2012, Windows 8 and Windows 8.1 Enterprise, and Windows 8 and Windows 8.1 Pro. You can also do sideloading on Windows RT tablets, but with a few tweaks. Sideloading is easiest if the devices are also joined to an Active Directory domain, but you can work around this if you need to. Beyond that, you must enable a specific Group Policy setting, which you'll learn about shortly, and the app must be signed by a Certificate Authority (CA) trusted by the PCs on your network (at least the ones you want to offer the app to). If the PCs aren't domain-joined or are Windows RT devices, you'll also need a sideloading product activation key. You can get this key from Microsoft's Volume Licensing Service Center (VLSC).

Setting Group Policy

To set Group Policy so that computers can accept and install sideloaded apps that you created for your enterprise, on a Windows 8-based Enterprise or Pro machine, navigate to Computer Configuration, Administrative Templates, Windows Components, App Package Deployment. Double-click Allow All Trusted Apps To Install. Figure 1-27 shows this in the Local Group Policy Editor. When enabled, any LOB Windows Store app (signed by a CA that the computer trusts) can be installed. To perform this task for multiple computers in your enterprise, use the Group Policy Management Console (GPMC) and navigate to Computer Configuration, Policies, Administrative Templates, Windows Components, App Package Deployment.

> **MORE INFO** **CREATING A WINDOWS STORE APP**
>
> You create apps by using Microsoft Visual Studio Express 2012 for Windows 8 or something similar. If you're interested, you can find a tutorial to help you get started at *http://msdn. microsoft.com/en-us/library/windows/apps/dn631757.aspx*
>
> Another tutorial is at *http://technet.microsoft.com/en-us/windows/jj874388.aspx.*

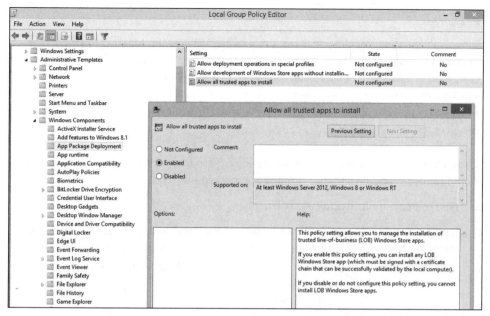

FIGURE 1-27 You must enable the applicable Group Policy setting Allow All Trusted Apps To Install to incorporate sideloading.

Activating a sideloading key

To enable sideloading on a Windows 8 or Windows 8.1 Enterprise computer that's not joined to a domain or on any Windows 8 or Windows 8.1 Pro computer, you must use a sideloading product activation key. To enable sideloading on a Windows RT device, you must also use a sideloading product activation key.

To add a sideloading product key and then activate it with the generic activation Globally Unique Identifier (GUID), follow these steps:

1. Open an elevated command prompt.

2. Type **slmgr /ipk *<sideloading product key>***.

3. Type **slmgr /ato ec67814b-30e6-4a50-bf7b-d55daf729d1e**.

Sideloading the app

After you configure the necessary Group Policy settings and create your app package, you're ready to sideload the app. You can do this manually, per user, or you can do it for multiple users at one time.

If you want to manually sideload the app to the current user, in Windows PowerShell you must add the appx module and then add the app package, as follows:

1. Type **Import-module appx**. Press Enter.

2. Type **Add-appxpackage "path and name of the app"** to add the app. Press Enter. Table 1-6 shows the available appx cmdlets. If you need to add app dependencies, the command should look more like this: *add-appxpackage C:\MyApp.appx –DependencyPath C:\appplus.appx*.

TABLE 1-6 Appx module cmdlets

Cmdlet	Desription
Add-AppxPackage	To add a signed app package to a single user account
Get-AppxLastError	To review the last error reported in the app package installation logs
Get-AppxLog	To review the app package installation log
Get-AppxPackage	To view a list of the app packages installed for a user profile
Get-AppxPackageManifest	To read the manifest of an app package
Remove-AppxPackage	To remove an app package from a user account

The app installs and then is available to the user. This must be done for each user if multiple users share a single computer. Figure 1-28 shows a Windows PowerShell session with two typed commands: *import-module appx* and *add-appxpackage*.

FIGURE 1-28 Use Windows PowerShell to sideload an app to the current user.

If you want to sideload the apps to multiple computers, use DISM. You can use DISM commands to manage app packages (.appx or .appxbundle) in a Windows image. The .appxbundle is new for Windows 8.1 and combines both app and resource packages to enhance the app experience. When you use DISM to provision app packages, those packages are added to a Windows image and are installed for the desired users when they next log on to their machines.

You should be familiar with the DISM syntax when servicing a Windows image, whether a computer is offline or online. Table 1-7 lists a few to keep in mind.

TABLE 1-7 DISM syntax for servicing a Windows image

Command	Purpose
*DISM.exe {/Image:<path_to_image_directory>	/Online} [dism_global_options] {servicing_option} [<servicing_argument>]*	To service a Windows image with DISM
*DISM.exe /Image:<path_to_image_directory> [/Get-ProvisionedAppxPackages	/Add-ProvisionedAppxPackage	/Remove-ProvisionedAppxPackage	/Set-ProvisionedAppxDataFile]*	To service an app package (.appx or .appxbundle) for an offline image
*DISM.exe /Online [/Get-ProvisionedAppxPackages	/Add-ProvisionedAppxPackage	/Remove-ProvisionedAppxPackage	/Set-ProvisionedAppxDataFile*	To service an app package (.appx or .appxbundle) for a running operating system

EXAM TIP

When you need to make a company app available to the public, you have to certify and publish the app to the Windows Store.

Other command-line service options include */Get-ProvisionedAppxPackages, /FolderPath, /PackagePath, /LicensePath*, and */Add-ProvisionedAppxPackage*. Becoming familiar with these is extremely important because you'll likely be tested on them. You can learn about all available commands and options at *http://technet.microsoft.com/en-US/library/hh824882. aspx*. Review this article and make sure that you can make sense of commands you might see, perhaps one that looks like

```
Dism /Online /Add-ProvisionedAppxPackage /FolderPath:C:\Test\Apps\MyUnpackedApp
/SkipLicense
```

or like

```
Dism /Image:C:\test\offline /Add-ProvisionedAppxPackage /FolderPath:c:\Test\Apps\
MyUnpackedApp /CustomDataPath:c:\Test\Apps\CustomData.xml
```

EXAM TIP

You must install an app package (.appx) on an operating system that supports Windows 8 apps. You can install an app bundle package (.appxbundle) on an operating system that supports Windows 8.1 apps. Apps aren't supported in Windows PE 4.0.

Sideloading apps by using Windows Intune

Windows Intune lets you sideload apps via the cloud and make them available to any authorized, compatible device that's connected to the Internet. You need to perform several steps to sideload apps (If you want to follow along, you can download Windows Intune for free and use it for 30 days without a subscription to TechNet or MSDN, or even without using a credit card):

1. Work through the available wizard to upload your software.

2. Add users and create groups, if applicable.

3. Choose the users, groups, computers, and devices that can download the software, and link them (user-to-device).

4. For the self-service model in this example, choose how to deploy the app. It can be available, or available and required.

5. Verify that the app is available in the Windows Intune Company Store.

NOTE **FORCING APP INSTALLATION**

Windows Intune is a self-service model. This means that you cannot use it to force apps to be installed on client machines. You can create groups and assign the apps to the groups, but the user will still need to approve the installation.

Adding a user

To get the full Windows Intune experience, you need to create a few users and, perhaps, add them to groups. From the Admin Overview page shown in Figure 1-29, click Add Users. Notice that the Admin page is selected at the top. Fill in the fields to create your new user. Type a first and last name, a display name, a user name, and any additional details you want to include. Assign the desired role, perhaps Billing Administrator or User Administrator, or simply create a new user. Finally, select the Windows Intune user group—by default, only one, Windows Intune (although you can create your own). Watch for an email that contains a temporary password for the new user.

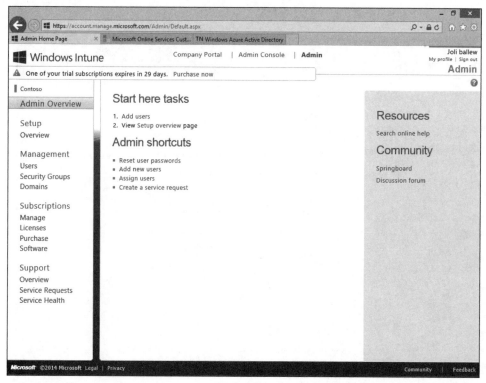

FIGURE 1-29 Add users and perhaps put them into groups before uploading software.

Uploading software

In the Windows Intune Admin page shown in Figure 1-29, click Admin Console at the top of the page. (Notice also a link to the Company Portal.) This opens a new window with many more tools and opportunities to personalize Windows Intune for your enterprise (see Figure 1-30). Click each tab in the left column, including System Overview, Groups (you might want to create a group now), Updates, Endpoint Protection, Alerts, Software, Licenses, Policy, Reports, and Administration. You'll be expected to be familiar with each tab when taking the exam. Now, click the Software tab.

To upload the desired software, follow these steps:

1. Click Add Software (on the Software Overview page).

2. If prompted, sign in with your Windows Intune Administrator account.

3. Read the information on the Before You Begin page and click Next.

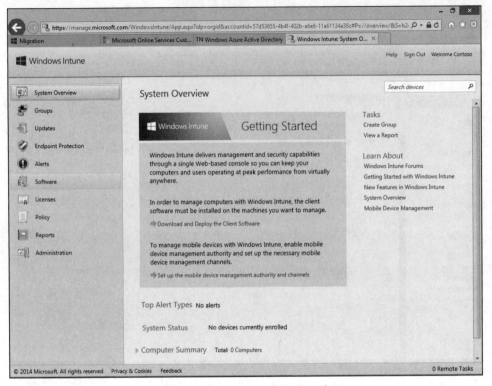

FIGURE 1-30 Review the options in the Windows Intune Admin Console page.

4. Make the desired choices from the Select The Platform And Specify The Location Of The Software Files page, including:

   A. How this software is made available to devices: Software Installer or External Link. Choose Software Installer here.

   B. The type of installer file type you'll use: Windows Installer (*.exe, *.msi) or Windows App Package (*appx, *appxbundle). Choose Windows Installer (*exe, *msi) here.

   C. Click Browse and locate the software file to install. You might browse to something like C:\Program Files as a start.

   D. Click Open.

   E. Click Next.

5. Continue to work through the wizard, adding information about the publisher, application name, architecture, operating system, and so on, clicking Next as applicable.

6. When you are at the end of the wizard, click Upload (see Figure 1-31).

7. Click Close.

8. Back on the Software Overview page, click Managed Software to see the uploaded file(s).

FIGURE 1-31 Upload software at the end of the wizard.

EXAM TIP

Detection rules let you specify how you want Windows Intune to determine whether the software already exists on the client. This ensures that the software isn't installed twice. You can opt for the default detection rules or create your own. The three rule types are File Exists, MSO Product Code Exists, and Registry Key Exists. If you are asked about these rules, first eliminate answers that don't have anything to do with those three things. Also, Registry key names that start with HKEY_LOCAL_MACHINE are okay to use in a detection rule, but other options aren't recommended because they aren't applied directly to the machine. Likewise, when using a path to create a rule, don't choose a path specific to a user; instead, choose a path that has to do with where program files are stored.

Selecting users and/or groups and deploying your app

With the software uploaded, you're ready to choose the users, groups, computers, and/or devices to which you want to deploy the application. You can use Active Directory synchronization to populate the account portal if you want. If you don't have that option, however, open the Windows Intune Admin Console, shown in Figure 1-30, click the Software tab and from Software workspace click Managed Software. From there you can manage deployment.

To use Windows Intune to manage a user's computer directly, you must first download and install (automatically or manually) the Windows Intune client software package on it. The computer can be a physical computer or a virtual machine. You can get this software from the Windows Intune Admin Console on the Administrator tab. The directions offered instruct you to wait 30 minutes before verifying that the computers appear in the Windows Intune Administrator Console.

Now you can select the users, groups, and computers that can access the software. If you are following along here, click Ungrouped Users and then click Add. Otherwise, select any group you've created or other applicable choices. From the Select The Deployment Settings For This Software page, shown in Figure 1-32, click the arrow beside each entry that shows Do Not Install and click Available Install or Required Install as applicable. Then, you can click Finish (not shown).

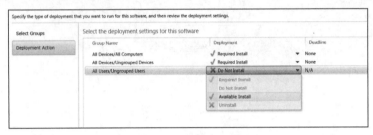

FIGURE 1-32 Make the software available to users.

Review the results. From the Managed Software page you can see how many users have this software available. Now, as an administrator you must link the users to a device (or devices) in your inventory. You do this from the Groups tab, from All Computers, and by clicking Link User. From there you select the desired device to link. The user is almost ready to log on and access your app. (You need to wait a half hour or so for all the information to sync.)

To test your new configuration, log on as the standard user you created at the Windows Intune Company Portal. If you created an administrator account, log on using either the Windows Intune Administrator Console or the Windows Intune Account Portal. All these links are available in the email the user received with his or her temporary password. After logon, users must click the option to enroll the device they're using. Following that, click All Apps to see the available app. Figure 1-33 shows the Windows Intune Company Portal.

Finally, you can review how many computers have installations pending and how many users have the deployed software available. Figure 1-34 shows the Managed Software tab in the Windows Intune Administrator Console, with a deployed application selected and the current status of the software showing at the bottom of the page.

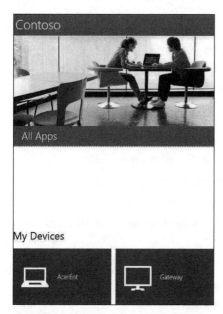

FIGURE 1-33 The user logs on to the Windows Intune Company Portal from an approved device to access the All Apps option.

FIGURE 1-34 Administrators can keep track of the status of their deployed software easily.

MORE INFO   USING WINDOWS INTUNE AND CONFIGURATION MANAGER

You can use Windows Intune to sideload apps in conjunction with System Center 2012 SP1 Configuration Manager by also incorporating the Windows Intune connector. This tool enables you to manage your apps with the Configuration Manager console. For more information, visit *http://technet.microsoft.com/en-us/windows/dn223286.aspx*.

Before moving on, you need to know a few more things about Windows Intune:

- You can embed Windows Intune in an operating system deployment image.
- After you install the Windows Intune client software, you must restart the PC.
- You can enroll mobile devices from the Administration tab.
- Windows Intune client software can be installed only on computers that are running the following:
    - Windows XP Professional, Service Pack (SP) 3
    - Windows Vista Enterprise, Ultimate, or Business editions
    - Windows 7 Enterprise, Ultimate, or Professional editions
    - Windows 8 Enterprise or Pro editions
    - Windows 8.1 Enterprise or Pro editions
- Windows Intune supports the following mobile devices:
    - Windows Phone 8
    - iOS
    - Android
    - Windows RT
- When you opt to deploy an application by using an external link, you can provide a link to an application on the Windows Store or to a web-based application that runs in a user's web browser.
- Users can contact IT from the Windows Intune Company Portal.
- After installing client software and performing other tasks, you might have to wait for a while before you see the changes in the Windows Intune Administrator Console.

Deep linking apps by using Windows Intune

You can make Windows Store apps available to your Windows RT users in your company portal by using Windows Intune as well as Configuration Manager. This section focuses on Windows Intune. You'll follow the same basic process as you did when deploying an app via the Installed Software option, but this time you choose External Link when you get to the Select The Platform And Specify The Location Of The Software Files page. Before you begin, decide which Windows Store app you want to deploy. For this example, choose OneDrive for Business.

The first part of the process requires you to obtain the link to the app you want to add to your company portal. To obtain the link for OneDrive for Business, follow these steps:

1. From the Start screen, click Store.

2. Search for OneDrive for Business, and then click it to access the installation page.

3. From the charms (Windows logo key+C), click Share.

4. Click Mail.

5. The email contains the link. Send this link to yourself, copy the link and paste it into Notepad, or otherwise make the link accessible for later.

The second part of the deep-linking process involves adding the app to add to Windows Intune:

1. Log on to the Windows Intune Administrator Console.

2. Click the Software tab, Managed Software, Add Software.

3. From the Select The Platform And Specify The Location Of The Software Files page, under Select How This Software Is Made Available To Devices, select External Link.

4. In the Specify The URL box, paste the link to OneDrive for Business. Click Next.

5. Carefully input the information to describe the software. What you input can be viewed by your employees. Click Next when finished.

6. Verify that the information is correct (see Figure 1-35). Click Upload.

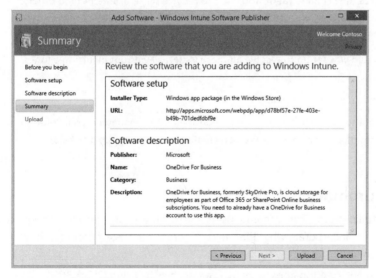

FIGURE 1-35 Add a Windows Store app to Windows Intune for deploying to users.

7. Click Close.

8. From the Managed Software screen, verify that OneDrive For Business is selected, and click Manage Deployment.

9. Click All Users, Add, and then click Next.

10. Under Approval, click the arrow and select Available Install.

11. Click Finish.

Your Windows RT users can now open their company portal app (which they've previously obtained from the Windows Store), log on, locate the deployed app, and install it.

Thought experiment

Managing Microsoft Office in a small business

In this thought experiment, apply what you've learned about this objective. You can find answers to these questions in the "Answers" section at the end of this chapter.

You manage a small business that has seven employees, and each employee has multiple devices that they use to perform work. You don't have an Active Directory domain. Sometimes the users are at the company, sometimes at home, and often in a hotel. Users don't always have Internet access.

Users complain that they can't always access their work documents and that when they use Microsoft Office on their devices, they get a difference user experience on all of them. Their settings and preferences continually need to be reset for each device as they change them. You want to resolve these problems (and others, including mandating Microsoft Office updates), but you don't have a lot of money to spend.

1. What should you set up to resolve all these issues, all without incurring a lot of expense?

2. Where would you store the users' data?

3. If you want to delegate some of the responsibilities for managing your solution, what types of administrator would you create to manage support tickets?

Objective summary

- Network administrators can integrate users' Microsoft accounts into the workplace to enable users to incorporate what they've configured with these accounts with their domain accounts.
- You can manage desktop apps in many ways, such as by using Office 365, Configuration Manager, DISM, and Windows Intune.

- You can sideload apps to offer them to your users without going through the Windows Store certification process.
- You can configure Group Policy settings to manage your desktop apps, to manage access to the Windows Store, and to enable sideloading.

Objective review

Answer the following questions to test your knowledge of the information in this objective. You can find the answers to these questions and explanations of why each answer choice is correct or incorrect in the "Answers" section at the end of this chapter.

1. Where can you configure a Group Policy that restricts the use of Microsoft accounts for a specific group of users in an Active Directory domain?

    A. In the Group Policy Management Editor window, by expanding Computer Configuration, Policies, Windows Settings, Security Settings, Local Policies, Security Options

    B. In the Group Policy Management Editor window, by expanding Computer Configuration, Policies, Windows Settings, Security Settings, Local Policies, User Rights Assignment

    C. In the Local Group Policy Editor, by navigating to Computer Configuration, Windows Settings, Security Settings, Local Policies, Security Options

    D. In the Local Group Policy Editor, by navigating to Computer Configuration, Windows Settings, Security Settings, Local Policies, User Rights Assignment

2. Where can users opt to connect a Microsoft account with a domain account?

    A. Users can't do this; an administrator must perform this task for them in Active Directory.

    B. From their local computer, in PC Settings, from the Accounts tab

    C. In the Group Policy Management Editor window, by expanding Computer Configuration, Policies, Windows Settings, Security Settings, Local Policies, Security

    D. From their local computer, in PC Settings, from the OneDrive tab

3. Which of the following can you manage in the Office 365 Admin Center?

    A. Active Directory synchronization

    B. Valid, expired, and assigned licenses

    C. User passwords, including resetting

    D. All of the above

    E. B and C only

4. You need to disable access to the Windows Store for one group of employees in your workgroup. How do you do this?

   A. Configure a Group Policy setting that disables the policy Turn On The Store Application.

   B. Configure a Group Policy setting that enables the policy Turn On The Store Application.

   C. Configure a Group Policy setting that disables the policy Turn Off The Store Application.

   D. Configure a Group Policy setting that enables the policy Turn Off The Store Application.

5. Which of the following tools and technologies can help you sideload company apps?

   A. DISM

   B. Windows PowerShell

   C. Configuration Manager

   D. Windows Intune

   E. All of the above

   F. Only C and D

6. What Group Policy setting do you have to enable before users can install apps you've sideloaded?

   A. None

   B. Allow All Trusted Apps To Install

   C. Allow Development Of Windows Store Apps

   D. Block Microsoft Accounts

7. When you offer a sideloaded app to a Windows RT device, which of the following commands must you run at an elevated command prompt?

   A. *slmgr /ipk <sideloading product key>*

   B. *slmgr /ato ec67814b-30e6-4a50-bf7b-d55daf729d1e*

   C. *import-module appx*

   D. *Add-AppxPackage*

   E. All of the above

8. True or false: You can make sideloaded apps mandatory and force their installation on to clients by applying the applicable settings in Windows Intune.

   A. True

   B. False

9. You want to manage a user's computer by using Windows Intune, on a computer running Windows 7 Professional. What must you do first?

   A. Install the Windows Intune client software package on it.

   B. Install the Windows Intune connector.

   C. Upgrade the computer to Windows 7 Enterprise or Windows 8 Enterprise.

   D. Install the company portal from the Windows Store.

10. Which of the following describes the purpose of deep linking an app?

    A. To push out specific Windows Store apps to your Windows RT users

    B. To make Windows Store apps available to your Windows RT users in your company portal

    C. To add your company apps to the Windows Store

    D. None of the above

Answers

This section contains the solutions to the thought experiments and answers to the objective review questions in this chapter.

Objective 1.1: Thought experiment

1. Native VHD.

2. Windows ADK. You can install this on another Windows 7 or Windows 8-based technician computer and use it to create the Windows PE disk.

3. DISM. You will use the Deployment Image Service and Management (DISM) tool to apply an existing Windows 8 image—in this case, the one you created.

4. 30 GB.

Objective 1.1: Review

1. **Correct answers:** A, C

   A. **Correct:** You must use a Windows 8-based computer, and you need the Windows 8-based installation files.

   B. **Incorrect:** The drive must be 32 GB or larger, not 64 GB.

   C. **Correct:** TPM protects a specific computer from unauthorized access, and Windows To Go is used on more than one.

   D. **Incorrect:** Resetting or refreshing isn't supported. Problematic drives should be reimaged.

   E. **Incorrect:** Windows To Go isn't supported on Windows RT or Mac computers.

2. **Correct answer:** A

   A. **Correct:** Because hibernation is disabled by default, leaving Not Configured or changing the policy to Disabled is correct.

   B. **Incorrect:** If you enable this policy, hibernation becomes enabled.

   C. **Incorrect:** Sleep and hibernate are different. Thus, the Group Policy for sleep isn't the proper policy to configure.

   D. **Incorrect:** Sleep and hibernate are different. Thus, the Group Policy for sleep isn't the proper policy to configure.

3. **Correct answer:** D

   A. Incorrect: Boot.ini is no longer used.

   B. Incorrect: BCDedit and BCDboot are command-line utilities used to configure and control the process.

   C. Incorrect: BCDedit and BCDboot are command-line utilities used to configure and control the process.

   D. Correct: Startup parameters are stored in the BCD Store.

4. **Correct answers:** B, D

   A. Incorrect: */import* is used to restore a store, using what you've obtained before using the */export* parameter.

   B. Correct: Use */create store* to create a new empty startup configuration store.

   C. Incorrect: */boot sequence* is used to configure a one-time startup sequence for the boot manager.

   D. Correct: */default* defines the default startup entry.

   E. Incorrect: */displayorder* sets the startup order in a multiboot system.

   F. Incorrect: */new* isn't a valid parameter.

5. **Correct answer:** C

   A. Incorrect: Although you could likely start to the Windows 7 DVD and begin an installation, you couldn't create a second partition or shrink the existing one while performing that installation.

   B. Incorrect: Before you can create a new volume from unallocated space, you must first make that space available by shrinking the existing partition.

   C. Correct: You must first open Disk Management and shrink the existing partition.

   D. Incorrect: Multibooting with an operating system older than Windows 7 required a specific order, but that is not a requirement now. Thus, there is no need to format the drive first.

6. **Correct answer:** B

   A. Incorrect: Thin images include little or no customization, and most of the device drivers, applications, and updates are installed by using another method on each client computer.

   B. Correct: Thick images are loaded with applications, drivers, and customizations and require a lot of planning, lots of bandwidth for rollout, and much more time to create and manage.

   C. Incorrect: Hybrid images are like thin images, but with a few more customizations. Hybrid images aren't thick images.

   D. Incorrect: A custom image might include only one device driver and one background image.

7. **Correct answer:** E
   - A. **Incorrect:** MDT is required, but so is Windows ADK, a network share, and a reference computer.
   - B. **Incorrect:** Windows ADK is required, but so is MDT, a network share, and a reference computer.
   - C. **Incorrect:** A network share is required, but so is a reference computer, MDT, and Windows ADK.
   - D. **Incorrect:** A reference computer is required but so is a network share, MDT, and Windows ADK.
   - E. **Correct:** All of the above are required.
   - F. **Incorrect:** You do need MDT.

8. **Correct answer:** B
   - A. **Incorrect:** MDT doesn't include DISM but does include tools needed to automate desktop deployments.
   - B. **Correct:** The Windows ADK includes DISM.
   - C. **Incorrect:** SIM, or System Image Manager, is used to create answer files and is available from the Windows Automated Installation Kit (AIK).
   - D. **Incorrect:** The Application Compatibility Toolkit (ACT) is used to verify compatibility of applications and computers with Windows 8.1.

9. **Correct answers:** A, B
   - A. **Correct:** *copype amd64 C:\WinPE_amd64* is a valid command for copying Windows PE files.
   - B. **Correct:** *copype amd32 C:\WinPE_amd32* is a valid command for copying Windows PE files.
   - C. **Incorrect:** *MakeWinPEMedia /ISO C:\winpe_amd64 c:\winpe_amd64\winpe.iso* is used to create an ISO file from the Windows PE files.
   - D. **Incorrect:** *Dism /Get-MountedImageInfo* is used when mounting an image.

10. **Correct answer:** F
   - A. **Incorrect:** DISM PowerShell cmdlets and all other choices are included in MDT.
   - B. **Incorrect:** DISM API and all other choices are included in MDT.
   - C. **Incorrect:** Windows System Image Manager (Windows SIM) and all other choices are included in MDT.
   - D. **Incorrect:** OSCDIMG and all other choices are included in MDT.
   - E. **Incorrect:** The Volume Activation Management Tool (VAMT) and all other choices are included in MDT.
   - F. **Correct:** All of the above are included in MDT.
   - G. **Incorrect:** Everything listed is included with MDT.

Objective 1.2: Thought experiment

1. ACT.

2. SQL Server (to create an ACT database).

3. Inventory the computers and applications in the enterprise.

4. First you create and deploy an inventory collector package, and then you create and deploy a runtime-analysis package.

5. The ACM.

Objective 1.2: Review

1. **Correct answers:** A, D

    A. **Correct:** A shim can be used as a short-term solution for application incompatibility.

    B. **Incorrect:** You create a runtime-analysis package to test compatibility, not to fix compatibility problems.

    C. **Incorrect:** You can use Program Compatibility Mode to manage compatibility issues by letting the applications run in an older operating system space, but you can't configure it to resolve compatibility issues in newer ones.

    D. **Correct:** This is an option, but would require a lot of work to set up. When you use RemoteApp, the application is run on a remote server and is made available for clients from there.

2. **Correct answer:** B

    A. **Incorrect:** Shims can fix quite a few types of problems but can't fix issues that are related to UAC.

    B. **Correct:** This tool lets you fix problems related to UAC.

    C. **Incorrect:** App-V is used to virtualize applications but can't be used to create shims.

    D. **Incorrect:** You can resolve the problem with SUA.

3. **Correct answer:** C

    A. **Incorrect:** Client Hyper-V lets you run and manage applications in a virtual machine that you manage.

    B. **Incorrect:** App-V lets you virtualize applications so that you can use the applications side by side on the same system.

    C. **Correct:** RemoteApp lets you access applications remotely through Remote Desktop Services, and the apps themselves are housed and managed on network servers.

    D. **Incorrect:** Windows Intune lets you manage apps in the cloud, not on your own network servers.

4. **Correct answer:** B

   A. **Incorrect:** If you can't provide administrator credentials you wouldn't have gotten as far as selecting the first two options.

   B. **Correct:** The computer's processor isn't SLAT.

   C. **Incorrect:** If the computer's architecture is 32 bit, you wouldn't see the first two entries at all.

   D. **Incorrect:** If the computer is running Windows 8.1 (not the Pro or Enterprise edition), you wouldn't see the first two entries at all.

5. **Correct answer:** D

   A. **Incorrect:** These two are required but are listed out of order.

   B. **Incorrect:** The required technology is RemoteApp, not App-V.

   C. **Incorrect:** The required technology is RemoteApp, not App-V.

   D. **Correct:** These two servers are required and are listed in the proper order.

6. **Correct answer:** E

   A. **Incorrect:** A working Active Directory and network share are required, but so are the other listed elements.

   B. **Incorrect:** A UE-V Agent is required, but so are the other listed elements.

   C. **Incorrect:** A UE-V Generator is required, but so are the other listed elements.

   D. **Incorrect:** A Settings Storage Location is required, but so are the other listed elements.

   E. **Correct:** All of the above are parts of the UE-V solution.

   F. **Incorrect:** All of the listed elements are required.

7. **Correct answer:** A

   A. **Correct:** Deploy the Settings Storage Location is the first thing you do.

   B. **Incorrect:** Deploy the UE-V Agent is the second thing you do.

   C. **Incorrect:** Install the Group Policy templates is the third thing you do.

   D. **Incorrect:** Install the Agent Generator is the fourth thing you do.

   E. **Incorrect:** Deploy the Settings Template Catalog is the fifth thing you do.

   F. **Incorrect:** Deploy the Settings Location Templates is the sixth thing you do.

8. **Correct answer:** A

   A. **Correct:** Endpoint Protection refers to malware.

   B. **Incorrect:** Endpoint Protection involves malware, not updates.

   C. **Incorrect:** Policy does refer to security, but it has more to do with creating security policies than it does with malware specifically.

   D. **Incorrect:** Licensing is an important element of Windows Intune, but Endpoint Protection refers to malware.

Objective 1.3: Thought experiment

1. Office 365.

2. Most likely using the cloud, with options that enable the user to sync that data even when they aren't online.

3. Billing; Global; Password; Service; User Management.

Objective 1.3: Review

1. **Correct answer:** A

    A. **Correct:** Options to restrict the use of Microsoft accounts for a group of users in a domain are in the Group Policy Management Editor window. Expand Computer Configuration, Policies, Windows Settings, Security Settings, Local Policies, Security Options.

    B. **Incorrect:** The User Rights Assignment node doesn't provide options for restricting Microsoft accounts.

    C. **Incorrect:** To restrict a group of users in an Active Directory domain you need to access Group Policy, not Local Group Policy.

    D. **Incorrect:** To restrict a group of users in an Active Directory domain, you need to access Group Policy, not Local Group Policy. Also, User Rights doesn't offer the options you need.

2. **Correct answer:** B

    A. **Incorrect:** Users can do this from their local computers.

    B. **Correct:** This is the correct answer; from their local computers, in PC Settings, from the Accounts tab.

    C. **Incorrect:** You can't connect a Microsoft account using Group Policy.

    D. **Incorrect:** This is achieved in PC Settings, but not from the OneDrive tab.

3. **Correct answer:** D

    A. **Incorrect:** Active Directory synchronization is one of the things can you manage in the Office 365 Admin Center, but others are correct here.

    B. **Incorrect:** Valid, expired, and assigned licenses is one of the things can you manage in the Office 365 Admin Center, but others are correct here.

    C. **Incorrect:** User passwords, including resetting, is one of the things can you manage in the Office 365 Admin Center, but others are correct here.

    D. **Correct:** All of the above can be configured in the Office 265 Admin Center.

    E. **Incorrect:** All the answers are correct, not just B and C.

4. **Correct answer:** D

   A. **Incorrect:** Access to the Store is on by default, and the policy listed here doesn't exist anyway.

   B. **Incorrect:** Access to the Store is on by default, and the policy listed here doesn't exist anyway.

   C. **Incorrect:** You need to enable this policy, not disable it.

   D. **Correct:** You need to configure Group Policy to enable the policy Turn Off The Store Application.

5. **Correct answer:** E

   A. **Incorrect:** DISM is only one of the correct options listed.

   B. **Incorrect:** Windows PowerShell is only one of the correct options listed.

   C. **Incorrect:** Configuration Manager is only one of the correct options listed.

   D. **Incorrect:** Windows Intune is only one of the correct options listed.

   E. **Correct:** All of the above

   F. **Incorrect:** "Only C and D" isn't correct because A and B are correct also.

6. **Correct answer:** B

   A. **Incorrect:** Special Group Polices are required.

   B. **Correct:** Allow All Trusted Apps To Install is the required Group Policy setting that must be enabled.

   C. **Incorrect:** Allow Development Of Windows Store Apps isn't the correct Group Policy setting to enable.

   D. **Incorrect:** You should not block Microsoft accounts; you should enable the Group Policy setting listed for answer B.

7. **Correct answers:** A, B

   A. **Correct:** *slmgr /ipk <sideloading product key>* loads the product key, which is required for Windows RT devices.

   B. **Correct:** *slmgr /ato ec67814b-30e6-4a50-bf7b-d55daf729d1e* is the second requirement, and the entry here is the GUID.

   C. **Incorrect:** *import-module appx* is a Windows PowerShell command used with sideloading, but isn't run at an elevated command prompt and isn't the correct answer here.

   D. **Incorrect:** *Add-AppxPackage* is a Windows PowerShell command used with side-loading, but isn't run at an elevated command prompt and isn't the correct answer here.

   E. **Incorrect:** All of the above isn't correct because C and D are incorrect.

8. **Correct answer:** B

   A. **Incorrect:** You cannot make sideloaded apps mandatory and force their installation on to clients by applying the applicable settings in Windows Intune.

   B. **Correct:** This statement is false.

9. **Correct answer:** A

   A. **Correct:** You must first install the Windows Intune client software package on it.

   B. **Incorrect:** To use Windows Intune to sideload apps in conjunction with System Center 2012 SP1 Configuration Manager, you must also incorporate the Windows Intune connector. It's not required in this scenario, though.

   C. **Incorrect:** You don't need to upgrade the computer to Windows 7 Enterprise or Windows 8 Enterprise; Windows 7 Professional is compatible.

   D. **Incorrect:** You don't achieve this by installing the company portal from the Windows Store.

10. **Correct answer:** B

   A. **Incorrect:** You don't use deep linking to push out specific Windows Store apps to your Windows RT users.

   B. **Correct:** To make Windows Store apps available to your Windows RT users in your company portal, you use deep links.

   C. **Incorrect:** You don't use deep linking to add your company apps to the Windows Store. It's used to make Windows Store apps available through the company portal.

   D. **Incorrect:** "None of the above" isn't correct. B is correct.

CHAPTER 2

Support resource access

Your employees must be able to access resources. That's what networking is all about, to be brief. Users access resources to do and save work. A resource can be a piece of hardware in an office, such as a printer, a removable drive, or a USB stick. A resource also can be data users store on their own computers, network-attached storage (NAS), or a storage location in the cloud. Users often need to access resources from external venues such as hotels, conference rooms, and home computers, and you must ensure that the applicable protocols are in place to secure and configure those connections for users.

Beyond that, a network administrator must make the resources users need available, and make sure that those who need access have access. You also must ensure that users can access only the resources they need and no more. That's a lot to consider and plan for. And after you create a plan, you can begin to configure and manage what you've decided on, and such management is a long-term, ever-changing commitment as technologies evolve. This chapter starts at the beginning, with network connectivity.

Objectives in this chapter:

- Objective 2.1: Support network connectivity
- Objective 2.2: Support remote access
- Objective 2.3: Support authentication and authorization
- Objective 2.4: Support data storage
- Objective 2.5: Support data security

Objective 2.1: Support network connectivity

Networks are what enable users to access resources. Small companies often create single networks that consist of a handful of computers configured as a workgroup. Larger enterprises generally create networks configured as domains. Corporations might create multiple domains and connect them by using various types of trusts. No matter what kind of network is used, though, the same TCP/IP addressing technologies are available and employed to define the computers on the network, the network itself, and any existing subnetworks. In this objective you'll learn how IPv4 and IPv6 are incorporated into networks, how resource names are resolved to IP addresses, how to support wireless networks, and how to apply network security.

Understanding IPv4 and IPv6

A protocol suite is a set of protocols that define the rules that must be used and incorporated for a specific group, technology, or other entity to function. Protocols are necessary so that all participants can use the same rules to work together and so that no one questions how or why something will and should happen. For networks, Transmission Control Protocol/IP Protocol (TCP/IP) is the suite of agreed-on protocols that is used over the Internet and within almost all kinds of computer networks. Internet Protocol (IP), the key protocol in this suite, is used to address data packets and to help get them to their destination. The TCP/IP suite, as a unit, defines the rules for how data packets are sent over a network. This includes rules for how data is packaged, formatted, sequenced, and so on, and also defines what happens when data packets are lost or incur errors in transmission.

Entire books, conferences, and training classes exist to fully explain TCP/IP. This objective can't offer such comprehensive information. However, you must have a firm grasp on the generalities of IPv4 and IPv6, and how they are applied and used in an enterprise. Beyond that, you need to understand the various transition technologies, when IPv4 and IPv6 are both used or required for network connectivity, and specific types of connections.

Exploring IPv4

An IPv4 address is a 32-bit number that consists of four octets of 8 bits each. It looks like this when written with the base 10 numbering system: 124.205.15.2, with the highest number in any octet 255 or less. The computer doesn't see this number; instead, it sees four octets of 1s and 0s: 01111100 011001101 00001111 00000010. The largest number in any octet is 255 because that's what 11111111 adds up to when you convert it from binary to base 10.

Although you shouldn't be asked to convert a binary octet to a base 10 number on the exam, you still must understand how a conversion would be calculated, so that you can fully understand how subnets are used (and named) to further define a network.

To get started, think about the base 10 numbering system. A number such as 3,253 can be broken up into 3000 + 200 + 50 + 3, which can be further expanded to $(3 \times 10^3) + (2 \times 10^2) + (5 \times 10^1) + (3 \times 10^0)$. To expand even further, consider $(3 \times 10 \times 10 \times 10) + (2 \times 10 \times 10) + (5 \times 10) + (3 \times 1)$. Here, you're thinking in terms of 10s.

With binary, you have to think in terms of 2s rather than 10s. So 124, which you already defined as 01111100 (used in the first paragraph in this section and in the first octet), is $(0 \times 2^7) + (1 \times 2^6) + (1 \times 2^5) + (1 \times 2^4) + (1 \times 2^3) + (1 \times 2^2) + (0 \times 2^1) + (0 \times 2^0)$. When you add this up, you get the following:

$(0 \times 2^7) = 0 \times 128 = 0$

$+ (1 \times 2^6) = 1 \times 64 = 64$

$+ (1 \times 2^5) = 1 \times 32 = 32$

$+ (1 \times 2^4) = 1 \times 16 = 16$

$+ (1 \times 2^3) = 1 \times 8 = 8$

$+ (1 \times 2^2) = 1 \times 4 = 4$

$+ (0 \times 2^1) = 0 \times 2 = 0$

$+ (0 \times 2^0) = 1 \times 0 = 0$

And when you add 0 + 64 + 32 + 16 + 8 + 4 + 0+ 0, you get 124. That's how 124 equals 01111100.

You must use these unique IP addresses to define specific devices on a network and the network on which it resides. The address given to the resource defines both and is used with a subnet mask. The default subnet mask defines the network by using 1s and 0s, as shown in Table 2-1. The three default subnet masks align with each of the three types of IPv4 addresses that you should be familiar with: Class A, Class B, and Class C. (Class D and Class E also exist but aren't relevant here.)

TABLE 2-1 TCP/IP v4 address classes

First octet is between	Subnet mask
1–127* (a Class A address)	255.0.0.0 (11111111 00000000 00000000 00000000)
128–191 (a Class B address)	255.255.0.0 (11111111 11111111 00000000 00000000)
192–224 (a Class C address)	255.255.255.0 (11111111 11111111 11111111 00000000)

* You can't use 0, 127, and 255 to define a specific computer or other resource because all 0s in any octet is used to designate the network (see the subnets discussed earlier). 127 is used for loopback testing to determine whether a resource's network stack is configured properly. 255 specifies broadcasting to all hosts on a network.

You can create your own unique subnet masks to define your address space by changing the subnet mask to meet your needs. If you define the subnet mask by changing 11111111 11111111 11111111 00000000 to 11111111 11111111 1111000 00000000, for example, the subnet mask becomes 255.255.240.0/20. The /20 defines the number of 1s in the mask. You might see a question related to this on the exam.

Beyond this, the IPv4 address defines the network ID and the host ID of the resource, as well as the number of networks and hosts available in that class of addresses. Although the mathematics is beyond the scope of this text, Table 2-2 defines these parameters.

TABLE 2-2 TCP/IP v4 network and host ID definitions

Class	Network ID	Host ID	Number of networks	Number of hosts
A	First octet	Second, third, and fourth octets	126	16,777,214
B	First and second octets	Third and fourth octets	16,384	65,534
C	First, second, and third octets	Fourth octet	2,097,152	254

Finally, you can use some reserved IP address spaces with network resources that don't directly connect to the Internet. Instead, they sit virtually behind a router that connects the intranet to an outside network such as the Internet. This requires the use of Network Address Translation (NAT). The purpose of this technology is to reduce the number of unique IP addresses needed for an organization. These private network ranges are as follows:

- The Internet Assigned Network Authority (IANA) has defined these reserved private network ranges:
    - 10.0.0.0 – 10.255.255.254
    - 172.16.0.0 – 172.31.255.254
    - 192.168.0.0 – 192.168.255.254
- The Automatic Private IP Addressing (APIPA) range is 169.254.0.1 to 169.254.255.254.

These addresses are never used on computers, routers, servers, or any other resource that connects directly to the Internet.

Understanding automatic IP address assignment

Network administrators can manually assign IP addresses for each resource on a network but don't generally do so. Instead, they use Dynamic Host Configuration Protocol (DHCP) to assign IP addresses to network resources. These addresses are assigned from a pool of available addresses, and DHCP can assign both IPv4 and IPv6 addresses. The DHCP server also provides the IP addresses of other important network resources, including the gateway and Domain Name Service (DNS) server. If you aren't familiar with how DHCP works or the command-line tools you can use to manage it (such as *ipconfig /release* and *ipconfig /renew*) read this TechNet article before continuing: *http://technet.microsoft.com/en-us/library/hh831825.aspx*. This chapter covers more on DHCP later as it applies to IPv6.

To find the IP address assigned to a host, and to see other entries such as the subnet mask and default gateway, type **ipconfig** at a command prompt or in a Windows PowerShell session (see Figure 2-1). Notice the entries, specifically the IPv4, IPv6, and Link-local IPv6 addresses as applicable.

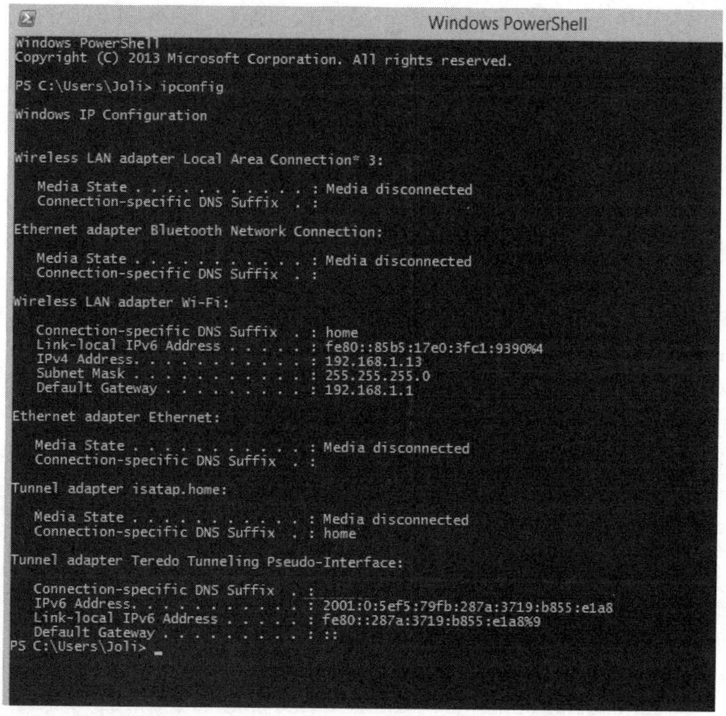

FIGURE 2-1 The command or cmdlet ipconfig shows IP addressing information.

Exploring IPv6

Unfortunately for the future of IPv4, IP addresses are running low because many more resources need their own address than was imagined when the addressing scheme was created.
In the beginning, even the most complex networks consisted only of desktop computers,
routers, gateways, and so on. Now, though, many more devices require unique IPv4 addresses,
including Internet service provider (ISP) servers that provide Internet access to consumers,
among other things. The future promises even more. Personal, wearable technologies and
medical data or GPS devices embedded under the skin are only a few things that will require
their own unique addresses. More than likely each of these personal items will also need a
"real" IP address, not one that's applied behind a router and offered via NAT or APIPA. Thus, a
larger IP address space was created.

An IPv6 address is a 128-bit number separated into eight blocks that are 16 bits each,
which is a lot larger than an IPv4 address, which is a 32-bit number separated into four octets
of 8 bits each. An IPv6 address can look something like this:

2001:db8:89a3::8a7e:370:7934

If two consecutive blocks are 0s, the address can be shortened by putting two colons
together with nothing in between. If you think about the number of bits available (16) and
how you would represent each of those unique bits, you can understand why the 16 bits must

be created from numbers 0–9, with the remaining 6 bits given letters A–F. Like the IPv4 address, the IPv6 address also defines the network ID and the host ID. However, those IDs aren't defined by subnet masks. Instead, the first 64 bits define the network, and the remaining bits define the host. The latter is created by using the host's Media Access Control (MAC) address. When DHCP is used to manage IPv6 hosts, it uses DHCP for IPv6 (DHCPv6).

> **MORE INFO** **UNDERSTANDING THE MAC ADDRESS**
>
> A MAC address is one assigned by the manufacturer of the device used to access the network, such as the Network Interface Card (NIC). Every unit has a unique MAC address hard-coded into it, which makes it a desirable number to use for addressing.

An important feature of IPv6 is that devices (hosts) can configure themselves autonomously. The ability to do this, especially when an enterprise supports many mobile devices such as smartphones and tablets, is essential to effective network management. Devices can maintain their existing connections while they go through the process required to change their location to your IPv6 network. Autoconfiguration comes in two types: stateful and stateless.

Stateful configuration uses DHCPv6 to centrally manage hosts on a network, and the DHCP clients use stateful DHCP to obtain IP addresses. The DHCPv6 server maintains information about the hosts, their current state, and the IP addresses available to them, as well as what addresses have been applied. It's similar to how DHCP works with IPv4. In the case of IPv6, the host (tablet, smartphone, and so on) uses its own autoconfigured link-local address (IPv6) to send out a multicast message to locate the applicable DHCP server. After it finds the DHCP server, it can obtain its own network IPv6 address. (If a request fails, subsequent requests are sent every 5 minutes.)

> **MORE INFO** **UNDERSTANDING LINK-LOCAL ADDRESSES**
>
> A link-local address assigned to a mobile device is the device's "home" address. This address (and subsequent connection) is always accessible from there. Link-local addresses in an IPv4 configuration start with 169.254.x.x; link-local addresses in an IPv6 configuration start with FE80.

Stateless configuration clients get both their link-local and non–link local addresses (the latter of which isn't an IP address) from a network that's configured to give this information to compatible clients. In essence, it enables each host to determine and configure its address from "advertisements" offered by nearby routers. A DHCP server configured as stateless doesn't give any host an IP address, but instead only the information the client needs to connect to the network. The parameters can include DNS servers and IPv6 prefixes.

Understanding transition technologies

You know that protocols define rules very specific to how data is sent over networks and to and from dissimilar networks. With TCP/IP, those rules can include how data packets are encapsulated, addressed, and moved among various systems. When you make changes to the underlying protocols, problems are bound to happen.

IPv6 is designed to replace IPv4, and someday that will happen. For now, though, IPv4 is still used on intranets and the Internet to facilitate the exchange of data. IPv6 is incorporated; in fact, when you look at the *ipconfig* results, notice that an IPv6 address is listed for the host (at least, on newer machines and devices). However, IPv4 is still the actual protocol.

IPv4 and IPv6 behave well together, assuming that IPv6 isn't required for the technology you want to use (and IPv4 can't be used). Consider this, for example: DirectAccess uses IPv6 with IP Security (Ipsec) to create a secure connection between DirectAccess clients and the internal enterprise network. This works well as long as the enterprise has an IPv6 infrastructure in place, but issues arise when the enterprise hasn't yet started deploying IPv6. In this case, you must use transition technologies. With the applicable technology in place, in this example, DirectAccess clients can access IPv6 resources across an IPv4-only network. Although DirectAccess is only one scenario—and note that there are many other reasons and scenarios for using IPv6—DirectAccess is mentioned here because it is specifically listed in the objectives for this exam. Whatever the case or condition though, a mechanism must be in place to enable IPv6 messages to move over IPv4 networks when it is a requirement for transmission.

Before you select a transition technology, decide what kind of network you have. Your network either has:

- No existing IPv6 infrastructure
- An existing Intra-Site Automatic Tunnel Addressing Protocol (ISATAP)–based IPv6 infrastructure
- A native IPv6 infrastructure

USING 6TO4 TUNNELING

When no existing IPv6 infrastructure exists, you can use 6to4 transition technology. These transmissions occur over the Internet (which uses IPv4), and 6to4 is applied when clients have a public IP address. A 6to4 tunnel adapter is configured automatically on the IPv6 client when necessary. The IPv6 messages are sent out through this adapter, and data packets are encapsulated with an IPv4 header.

USING THE INTRA-SITE AUTOMATIC TUNNEL ADDRESSING PROTOCOL (ISATAP)

If you have an existing ISATAP IPv6 infrastructure, you can use this protocol. This transition technology allows ISATAP hosts to communicate with one another using IPv6. This is achieved with an ISATAP tunnel adapter that has an IPv6 address bound to it. The data packets are then wrapped inside an IPv4 header so that the packets can be sent over the intranet. At the destination server, the IPv4 header is removed and the original IPv6 data packets are uncovered.

USING THE TEREDO TUNNELING TECHNOLOGY

Teredo is another type of transition technology. It is used when the client is sitting behind a NAT device and has been assigned a private IP address. Like other technologies, communications are sent through a tunnel adapter that's automatically configured on the client. With Teredo, the data packets are encapsulated with an IPv6 header first, and then encapsulated again with a User Datagram Protocol (UDP) header.

USING THE IP-HTTPS TRANSITION TECHNOLOGY

This transition technology, created by Microsoft, is used by clients who can't connect to a Forefront UAG DirectAccess server using any other IPv6 connectivity method. It is also used if force tunneling is configured. For example, this is applied when a DirectAccess client has been assigned a private IP address, and the NAT device or firewall is configured to allow only HTTP/ HTTPS outbound traffic. In these instances, the client will use IP-HTTPS.

Like other technologies, a tunnel adapter is created first. The messages are encapsulated with an IPv4 header, and then encapsulated in an HTTP header by using Transport Layer Security (TLS)/Secure Sockets Layer (SSL) encryption. This amount of overhead requires that many extra packets be created, and transmission rates will suffer for it. Using a web proxy server causes even more overhead because this server can't require authorization for multiple reasons (to begin with, the client doesn't have a way to enter authentication information that can be used by the web proxy server). The *netsh* command also must be used to configure the IP-HTTPS to use the applicable web proxy server.

SUMMARIZING THE FOUR TRANSITION TECHNOLOGIES

The four transition technologies can be summarized like so:

- **6to4**   Tunnels IPv6 traffic over IPv4 networks and is used by clients that are assigned public IP addresses.

- **ISATAP**   Tunnels IPv6 traffic over IPv4 networks and allows communication between ISATAP clients.

- **Teredo**   Tunnels IPv6 traffic over IPv4 networks and is used by clients that have been assigned private IP addresses and that sit behind a NAT device. Any client assigned a private IP address will try to use Teredo first. If it can't, it will use IP-HTTPS.

- **IP-HTTPS**   Tunnels IPv6 traffic over IPv4 networks and is used by clients that can't use the other transition technologies. This incurs the most overhead and should be used as a last resort.

Supporting names resolution

You know that every computer or network resource that's connected directly to the Internet must have a unique IP address. Resources on local networks must also have one unique to their network. DNS is used in TCP/IP networks to enable users to type a resource name to access it, such as *http://www.microsoft.com* or *RWDCO1_Server01.contoso.com*, instead of the actual IP address. DNS servers handle the task of resolving names to addresses in both scenarios. On a personal or enterprise network, internal DNS servers exist for this purpose; in fact, the first server that you promote to a domain controller is often a DNS server.

DNS servers function by routing data to the appropriate top-level domain first, then to any subdomains, and then to the applicable host. When fully qualified domain names are mapped to IP addresses, the process is called *DNS name resolution* and is referred to as "resolving an IP address." Table 2-3 lists the top-level domains you'll find on the Internet. Note that companies have their own domain names, such as contoso.com.

TABLE 2-3   Common top-level Internet domains

Domain	Purpose
COM	Public commercial websites
NET	Public network websites
ORG	Public, non-profit organization websites
EDU	Restricted, for schools and educational organizations
MIL	Restricted, for the U.S. military
GOV	Restricted, for the U.S. government
UK, RU, and other two-letter country/region codes	Used to identify a specific country/region

> *NOTE* **ROOT DOMAIN MANAGEMENT**
>
> The root domain is managed by the Internet Corporation for Assigned Names and Numbers (ICANN) and is under the auspices of the U.S. Department of Commerce. Root servers have a "zone file" that maintains a list of the names and IP addresses of the DNS servers for the top-level domains.

So if .com is a top-level domain name, Microsoft.com is an extension of that. Addresses also include subdomains. To continue the example, a website name could include something like this: *technet.microsoft.com*. Finally, the leftmost name in an address is the host name.

Many hosts are named www, mail, www2, and so on. DNS servers dissect this information a piece at a time to route data to the applicable host.

DNS servers are usually offered to the general public by an ISP. Enterprises maintain and manage their own DNS servers and then depend on outside DNS servers to manage outside DNS tasks. When DNS is applied at a high level, resolving a friendly name to an IP address is achieved like so:

1. If the name that needs to be resolved lies on the same domain as the resolution request, the local DNS server attempts to resolve it by using its own database of names and IP addresses.

2. If the local DNS server doesn't have the domain name and IP address in its database, it contacts another DNS server such as a forwarder. That DNS server might continue the process, forwarding requests to other DNS servers until the name is resolved.

3. Generally, the address is resolved and the connection is made. However, sometimes it can't be resolved because the name was typed incorrectly or doesn't (or no longer) exists.

4. If after a reasonable amount of time the name can't be resolved, the DNS server returns an error (and possibly a suggestion). Figure 2-2 shows the error received after typing www.bing.gom instead of www.bing.com.

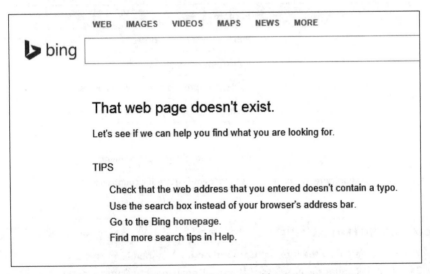

FIGURE 2-2 When a name can't be resolved to an IP address, an error occurs.

In both the TCP/IPv4 and TCP/IPv6 properties dialog boxes, no DNS servers are specifically named. For both, like DHCP, the option Obtain DNS Server Address Automatically is selected. However, if you need to name a specific DNS server to use, or perhaps two or three, you can.

To name a specific DNS server to use, follow these steps:

1. Open the Network And Sharing Center.

2. Click Change Adapter Settings.

3. Right-click the default connection and select Properties. (You might have to repeat this step for other optional connections.)

4. Choose either Internet Protocol Version 6 (TCP/ IPv6) or Internet Protocol Version 4 (TCP/IPv4) and click Properties.

5. On the General tab of the TCP/IPv4 Properties page, type the desired DNS addresses. You can configure alternate connections from the Alternate Configuration tab.

6. On the General tab of the TCP/IPv6 Properties page, type the desired DNS addresses. (To add others, click Advanced, and on the DNS tab, click Add. Type the DNS server to use.)

Figure 2-3 shows the applicable dialog boxes for IPv6.

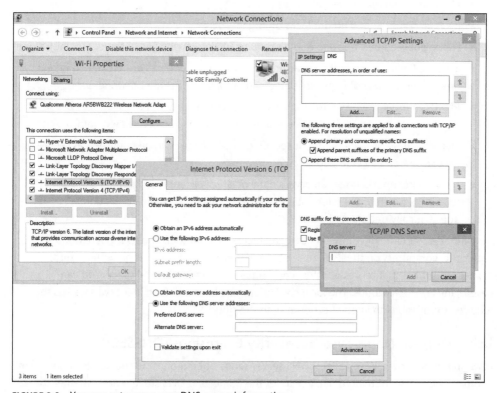

FIGURE 2-3   You can enter your own DNS server information.

Although you should try to learn quite a bit more about DNS, this exam specifically calls out two types of name resolution with which you should be familiar: Peer Name Resolution Protocol (PNRP) and Domain Name System Security Extensions (DNSSECs).

Using Peer Name Resolution Protocol (PNRP)

In peer-to-peer environments, name resolution is handled by peers that rely on other peers to resolve addresses, protocols, and ports. The process is complicated partly because of DNS limitations and connectivity issues. The Windows peer-to-peer networking platform is included with Windows Server 2012 R2 and previous server versions, as well as Windows 8.1, Windows 7, and previous Windows editions. It helps address the current issues with DNS. The solution includes Peer Name Resolution Protocol (PNRP), a name-resolution solution that's scalable (to the billions), secure (uses public key cryptography), and dynamic (instantaneous publication). Here are a few of the advantages of PNRP over previous name-resolution configurations:

- PNRP uses minimal server resources.

- It's fault-tolerant, and no gridlocks or logjams occur.

- Name publication is free and doesn't require any interaction with a server administrator.

- Because PNRP doesn't rely on caching like DNS does, updates are processed in real time, eliminating problems associated with addresses that are no longer valid.

- PNRP is a great way to access mobile devices, computers, and even services because the information includes an address, a port, and perhaps more related data.

- Names can be protected against spoofing because they can be published as secure or non-secure and include public cryptography.

- Networking applications can access data via an application programming interface (API). Much of the information required to access the name and address is automatically determined.

PNRP uses "clouds" of computers that can locate one another. The sole *global cloud* represents computers on the IPv6 Internet. A *link-local address cloud* is generally a local, connected subnet that represents IPv6 computers in an IPv6 link-local space. You can have many link-local clouds. The local computer must have a default identity as well as the required permissions to interact properly with the cloud.

Using Domain Name System Security Extensions (DNSSECs)

DNS isn't ultra-secure. When a local DNS server sends out a request for name resolution from another DNS server, nothing is in place to let the requesting DNS server know whether the answer it receives is coming from a trusted, valid DNS server or from somewhere else. The resolver simply accepts the first answer it receives. Something had to be done to ensure that the server sending the response back could be trusted. This is how Domain Name System Security Extensions (DNSSECs) came to be.

To sum up the technology, DNSSEC allows for a DNS zone and all records in it to be cryptographically signed. Thus, when a DNS server that hosts a signed zone receives a name-resolution inquiry, that DNS server returns digital signatures along with the requested records. A name resolver or another server can validate that the responses are accurate and haven't been altered using these signatures. It does this by obtaining the public key of the public/private key pair. Signing is important because DNS is often subject to spoofing attacks (and other attacks, such as man-in-the-middle), and managing this issue is a critical part of securing enterprise networks as well as the Internet.

> **MORE INFO** **DNSSEC**
>
> You might see one or two questions on the exam regarding DNSSEC. You might be asked about the technology in general terms or asked something specific about security requirements, the types of resource records used, example DNS queries, or even DNSSEC scenarios. The best I can offer here is to recommend that you read, in its entirety, the TechNet article "Overview of DNSSEC," published in February 2014 and found at *http://technet.microsoft.com/en-us/library/jj200221.aspx*.

You should be familiar with a few terms:

- **DNS servers**   These servers perform name-resolution tasks. DNS servers support DNSSEC. This technology has been greatly enhanced on the latest version of Windows Server 2012 R2. For more information about DNS servers, visit *http://technet.microsoft.com/en-us/library/dn593674.aspx*.

- **DNS clients**   Clients running Windows 7 and later are DNSSEC-aware and can be configured to require DNSSEC validation. Previous operating systems weren't. For more information about DNS clients, visit *http://technet.microsoft.com/en-us/library/dn305899.aspx*.

- **DNS zones and signing zones**   A *zone* is a group of computers. It can be large or small. For example, *secure.contoso.com* is a zone that might contain only 100 computers. A root zone is very large. Signing a zone with DNSSEC protects it from all kinds of attacks, including spoofing attacks. To sign a zone, you must specify various options and parameters with Windows PowerShell or the Zone Signing Wizard provided in the DNS Manager console. For more information about DNS zones, visit *http://technet.microsoft.com/en-us/library/dn593642.aspx*.

- **Trust anchors**   A trust anchor is a public cryptographic key that enables a DNS server to validate DNS responses. Trust anchors must be updated every time you sign a zone. For more information about trust anchors, visit *http://technet.microsoft.com/en-us/library/dn593672.aspx*.

- **The NRPT**   The Name Resolution Policy Table (NRPT) contains namespaces and other settings stored in the Windows Registry. This information is used to determine how the DNS client will behave when it asks for and receives responses. This way, you can create security-aware DNS clients that will require validation of DNS responses before accepting those responses. For more information about the NRPT, visit *http://technet.microsoft.com/en-us/library/dn593632.aspx.*

EXAM TIP

To guarantee that communications are secure, DNSSEC uses SSL. This enables the DNS client to verify, by validating the server's certificate, that the DNS server is trustworthy. Also, if you have a domain IPsec policy in place, you have to exempt TCP/UDP port 53 traffic (DNS traffic) from it. Otherwise, the domain IPsec policy is applied and the authentication of certificates isn't performed.

Supporting wireless networks and connections

More and more workers are mobile than ever before. Their mobility doesn't just occur when users are out of the office on a cellular or Wi-Fi connection. Mobility occurs in offices too, via your enterprise's Wi-Fi configuration. Supporting wireless networks and connections in an organization involves many things, including configuring encryption, selecting an infrastructure option, and managing compatibility among devices and technology standards.

Connecting users and managing Wi-Fi connections

Users can join a wireless network from a Windows 8.1 client in several ways. If they're configured to do so, mobile devices such as Windows 8.1 phones and Windows 8.1 tablets will prompt users to join available networks. On laptops, desktops, and similar devices, if users aren't prompted, they can join an available network from the Settings charm. The network must be broadcasting its Service Set Identifier (SSID) to be accessed here. If the network isn't broadcasting its SSID, users can manually join it, again from the Settings charm or from the Network And Sharing Center. Users can also disconnect from these places. Finally, users can connect and disconnect from wireless networks from PC Settings, from the Network tab, and view information about the network to which they are joined.

First look at the Settings charm. You access the charms by pressing Windows logo key+C, by flicking in from the right side of a touch-compatible device, or by moving the cursor to the bottom or top right corner of the screen. Click Settings to see what's shown in Figure 2-4. Here, device is connected to a network named 4B7QL.

FIGURE 2-4 The Settings charm offers information about the connected network.

If you click the icon for the connected network (or a similar icon that shows you're not connected to any network), a list of nearby networks appears. You can then click the appropriate network name from the list and click Connect. (You can also check Connect Automatically if you desire.) Optionally, if you are connected, you can click the network to which you're connected and click Disconnect. When joining a secure network, you need to type the password before you can join.

Another way to manage connected networks is from PC Settings. From the charms, click Settings and then Change PC Settings. When PC Settings opens, click any back arrows that appear first and then click Network. From the Network list, click Connections. Now, click the network to which you are connected to see the statistics shown in Figure 2-5. From here you can see such settings as the SSID, the protocol used, the security type, and the IPv4 and IPv6 addresses. (Take note of the protocol and security type if you're following along on your own computer. I'll talk about both of those things shortly.)

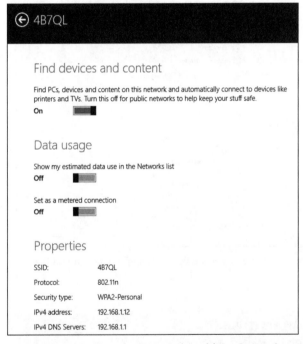

FIGURE 2-5 PC Settings, from Network, and from Connections, offers information about the connected network.

Finally, look at the Wi-Fi Properties dialog box to see even more information about the connected Wi-Fi network:

1. From the taskbar's Notification area of the Desktop, right-click the Network icon and click Open Network And Sharing Center.

2. Click Change Adapter Settings.

3. Double-click the icon that represents the connected Wi-Fi network.

4. From the Wi-Fi Status dialog box shown in Figure 2-6, click Wireless Properties.

5. Note what is shown on the Connection tab of the Wireless Network Properties dialog box and then click the Security tab. The Security tab is shown in Figure 2-6.

6. Note the security type and the encryption type. Leave this dialog box open while you read the next section.

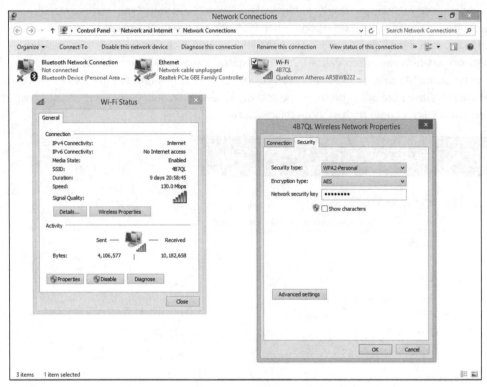

FIGURE 2-6   Wi-Fi Status and Wireless Network Properties dialog boxes offer information about the connected network.

NOTE   **CONFIGURING ADVANCED WI-FI SETTINGS**

From the Wi-Fi Status and Wireless Network Properties dialog boxes you can disable a Wi-Fi adapter, diagnose a problematic connection, view advanced security settings (to enable Federal Information Processing Standards (FIPS) compliance for the connected network), opt to look for other wireless networks while connected to the present one, and connect even if the network isn't broadcasting its SSID, among other things. Explore each of these dialog boxes carefully before continuing.

You can also view detailed information about the network connection by clicking Details in the Wi-Fi Status dialog box (where you clicked Wireless Properties in step 4 of the preceding steps). From there you can access even more information, including but not limited to:

- Connection-specific DNS Suffix value
- Description of the wireless network adapter, which includes the manufacturer and model number
- The MAC address
- Whether the connection is enabled for DHCP and when the lease was obtained and expires
- The IPv4 and IPv4 subnet mask, default gateway, DHCP server, DNS server, and so on
- The IPv6 default gateway and DNS server, as applicable
- Any other pertinent information regarding the connection

EXAM TIP

You might be asked how to connect to a wireless network that's not broadcasting its SSID. You do this from the Network And Sharing Center, from Set Up A New Connection Or Network. From there, click Manually Connect To A Wireless Network. You'll need to input the network name, choose a security and encryption type (detailed in the next section), and type the security key. You can also configure options to start the connection automatically or to connect even if the network isn't broadcasting its name.

Understanding Wi-Fi technology standards

You saw in the last section that clients that connect to a wireless network are configured with a type of security (such as No Authentication or Open) and a type of encryption (such as None). What can be configured and/or used on any client depends on how your wireless network is configured, what kind of equipment you're using, what kinds of technologies and standards the network and the client are compatible with, and more. Thus, you must be careful when designing a wireless network from scratch and must make sure that what you implement will support and be compatible with every element of your network.

These types of wireless technology standards are available to you and your clients:

- **802.11b**   This technology standard supports transmission rates of up to 11 Mbps, the slowest of the available Wi-Fi standards, and uses the 2.5 gigahertz (GHz) frequency. However, because this frequency is also used with cordless phones, microwaves, and other electronic devices, interference from them can cause problems. This standard can be used with the Wireless Equivalent Privacy (WEP) and Wireless Protected Access (WPA) encryption protocols, as detailed in the next section.
- **802.11a**   This technology standard is faster than 802.11b, up to 54 Mbps, and uses the 5 GHz frequency. Thus, 802.11a and 802.11b are incompatible. Although this frequency reduces the chance of interference with household devices such as cordless phones and microwaves, you should note that the higher a frequency is, the shorter

the transmission can travel. The transmission also has a harder time traveling through objects such as walls. Like 802.11b though, 802.11a is WEP and WPA compatible.

- **802.11g**   This technology standard is backward compatible with 802.11b. It uses the 2.5 GHz frequency and supports transmission rates (bandwidth) of up to 54 Mbps, combining the two strengths of 802.11a and 802.11b. It is WEP and WPA compatible.

- **802.11i**   This technology standard is compatible with 802.11a, 802.11b, and 802.11g and provides enhanced encryption for improved security. The standard supports new protocols as well: Temporal Key Integrity Protocol (TKIP) and Advanced Encryption Standard (AES). You saw AES in Figure 2-6.

- **802.11n**   This technology standard is slated to replace 802.11a, 802.11b, and 802.11g, and supports Wi-Fi Protected Access version 2 (WPA v2), as detailed in the next section. It can be used to replace the listed previous standards because it uses two frequencies: 2.5 GHz and 5 GHz. It supports transmission rates of up to 200 Mbps.

- **802.1x**   This technology standard supports all 802.11 networks that also use Remote Authentication Dial-In User Service (RADIUS) for authentication. The RADIUS networking protocol provides centralized authentication, authorization, and accounting for users who connect remotely. It's often used by ISPs and enterprises to secure all kinds of connections: Internet, intranet, wireless networks, integrated email services, and so on.

- **802.11ac**   This technology was approved in January 2014 and provides throughput of up to 1 gigabit per second on the 5 GHz band. This band resolves issues of wireless inter-ference common to 2.4 GHz bands that so many other devices use. It offers something new called beamforming, which can improve communications in crowded areas because of the ability to target signals in a specific direction. To use the new technology both user devices and Wi-Fi access points must be equipped with 802.11ac chips.

Understanding encryption protocols

In addition to technology standards for wireless connections are encryption protocols. Three types of encryption secure and protect data sent over wireless connections:

- **WEP**   This type of encryption is easily broken. Initially created to provide the same data protection afforded to wired networks, it was at one time widely accepted and implemented but has since been found to permit even simple attacks, like brute-force password attacks. WPA is preferred over the outdated WEP. WEP supports two methods of authentication: Open System and Shared Key. WEP uses a stream cipher which includes plain text digits and an encryption scheme called RC4. Encryption keys are not changed automatically or on a schedule. You can learn more about WEP on TechNet or MSDN.

- **WPA**   The successor to WEP and predecessor of WPA2, this encryption protocol protects data by using TKIP and AES to provide integrity and encryption. It also incorporates Extensible Authentication Protocol (EAP) to enhance the WEP authentication mechanism. EAP supports passwords that can be used only one time, certificates, smart cards, public-key encryption, and forwards authentication requests to a RADIUS server (which authenticates the user) for even more security and protection.

- **WPA2** This encryption protocol is widely accepted and currently used. It incorporates an improved AES and doesn't use TKIP, which was found to have security issues of its own. Encryption keys are changed automatically. WPA2 is compatible with 802.11a, 802.11b, 802.11g, and 802.11n.

Exploring connection options and modes

You can enable devices to connect to wireless networks in various ways. One is quite common: Infrastructure mode. With this mode, you can configure a wireless network access point that broadcasts the wireless signal, which clients in turn use to connect. This type of connection is used in homes, small businesses, and large enterprises. This network includes a router to connect it to other networks, perhaps the Internet or subnetworks in an organization. When a Windows 8.1 device is within range of the access point (and thus the network) and is authorized to connect to it, users can connect and have the encryption settings automatically configured for them.

The other type of network is ad hoc. In this scenario, devices connect to each other wirelessly and don't require a router or wireless access point to do so. This type of connection is generally used with very small groups of computers and mobile devices to share a connection to the Internet. To begin to configure a shared, ad hoc network, one user in the group must share an Internet connection with others from the Sharing tab of the Wi-Fi Properties dialog box, shown in Figure 2-7.

FIGURE 2-7 You can create an ad hoc network to share an Internet connection.

Now, from the computer that shared the connection, work through the following steps to complete the setup of the ad hoc network:

1. Open an administrator command prompt.

2. Type the following command and press Enter (see Figure 2-8):

   ```
   netsh wlan set hosted network mode=allow ssid=<network name: use "hosted">
   key=<8-63 character key: use 123c1s45>
   ```

FIGURE 2-8 Manually creating an ad hoc network.

3. At the command prompt, type the following and press Enter:

   ```
   netsh wlan start <network name>
   ```

   Notice that the network has been started.

4. From any nearby compatible wireless device, try to connect to the new hosted network. Figure 2-9 shows the network "hosted" from a Windows 8 phone. (You'll also see the new network listed in the host's Network Connections window.)

You also need to consider two modes when creating a network when you use WPA devices: Personal and Enterprise. With WPA-Personal (WPA-PSK or "preshared key") mode, a password, or a master or preshared key, is used to secure the access point. Users are provided this key, which they use to connect. After the connection is made, the client computer uses that key to generate its own key, called a session key, which changes automatically and regularly to maintain the security of the connection. No authentication server is needed for this option, and it's suitable for small and home networks. This is the type of network with which you are already familiar.

FIGURE 2-9 Connecting to the new network from a mobile device.

The other mode is WPA-Enterprise (WPA-802.1x, RADIUS). This is like Personal mode in that a master key and a session key are used. The difference here is that both keys are changed regularly and are generated automatically. This improves security greatly. If you opt for Enterprise mode, you need to use EAP, 802.11x, and a RADIUS server. The RADIUS server is used as a central database to add users. This mode is complex and suitable for larger enterprises.

EXAM TIP

I'm not sure how much you'll need to know about protocols, RADIUS servers, modes, and so on, but being overprepared is better than being underprepared. TechNet hosts many articles that deal with the various encryption protocols outlined here, as well as the various requirements and uses of WPA-PSK and WPA-802.11x modes.

Supporting network security

You already know that securing a network involves more than just choosing an encryption type, setting up a router and wireless access point, and giving users the password. It also involves securing the network perimeter, perhaps with several lines of defense to provide protection from outside hackers. One defense built into Windows 8.1 is the Windows Firewall.

Briefly, a firewall creates a virtual barrier between a computer and the network to which it's connected for the purpose of protecting the computer from unwanted incoming data and to protect the network from unwanted outgoing data. The firewall allows specific types of data to enter and exit the computer and blocks others, and settings are configured by default for each network option—Domain, Private, and Public—to make using the firewall under typical circumstances easy (but the settings can be changed).

Monitoring the Windows Firewall

You can monitor the state of the Windows Firewall in Control Panel. You can easily tell whether the firewall is on or off, what incoming connections are blocked by default, the active network, and how you are currently notified when the firewall takes action. It's all available in the main window. To make basic changes to the state of the firewall, in the left pane click Turn Windows Firewall On Or Off. From there you can change settings for both private and public networks. Two options are available for the private and public settings:

- Turn On Windows Firewall (this is selected by default)
  - Block All Incoming Connections, Including Those In The List Of Allowed Apps
  - Notify Me When Windows Firewall Blocks A New App (this is selected by default)
- Turn Off Windows Firewall (not recommended)

> **NOTE** **FIREWALL SETTINGS IN A DOMAIN**
>
> If you are a member of a domain, some firewall settings are likely unavailable. This happens because your network administrator is controlling them through Group Policy. You can see the Domain Profile using the Windows Firewall with Advanced Security on a local computer though, by clicking Advanced Settings in the Windows Firewall window. By default that profile is set to On, with inbound connections that do not match a rule blocked and with outbound connections that do not match a rule blocked. You can make changes to the domain profile with Windows Firewall with Advanced Security, as you'll learn later in this chapter.

Although Control Panel and the Windows Firewall window is a good place for general home users to manage the firewall or to ensure that it's enabled, what you'll be most interested in as a network administrator are the options available in the left pane—specifically, Allow An App Or Feature Through Windows Firewall and Advanced Settings. Allowing an app through the firewall is covered in the book, *Exam Ref 70-687: Configuring Windows 8.1*, as is turning on or off the firewall, creating exceptions, and performing other tasks.

Exploring filters and rules

Although you can configure a few options in the main Windows Firewall window, the real power lies with Windows Firewall with Advanced Security, shown in Figure 2-10. You can open this window in various ways, one of which is to click Advanced Settings from the Windows Firewall window detailed in the previous section. Here you can, for example, create filters (rules) for the kinds of data that can pass through the firewall. The filters are generally based on IP addresses, ports, and protocols:

- **IP Address** IP addresses are assigned to every computer and network resource connected directly to the network. The firewall can block or allow traffic based on an IP address of a resource (or a scope of addresses).

- **Port** Port numbers identify the application that's running on the computer. For example, Port 21 is associated with the File Transfer Protocol (FTP), Port 25 with Simple Mail Transfer Protocol (SMTP), Port 53 with DNS, Port 80 with Hypertext Transfer Protocol (HTTP), and Port 443 with HTTPS (HTTP Secure). You can create filters to allow or disallow these kinds of data and others. As you work through this book, notice that some features require a specific port be opened. This is where you do it.

- **Protocol** Protocols define the type of packet being sent or received. Common protocols are Transmission Control Protocol (TCP), Telnet, FTP, HTTP, HTTPS, Post Office Protocol 3 (POP3), Internet Message Access Protocol (IMAP), and User Datagram Protocol (UDP). You should be familiar with the most common protocols before taking the exam.

Although plenty of rules (that filter data) are already configured for the firewall, you can create your own inbound and outbound rules based on whatever ports, protocols, programs, and more that you feel you need to configure. Thus, you can uniquely construct the firewall to suit your exact needs.

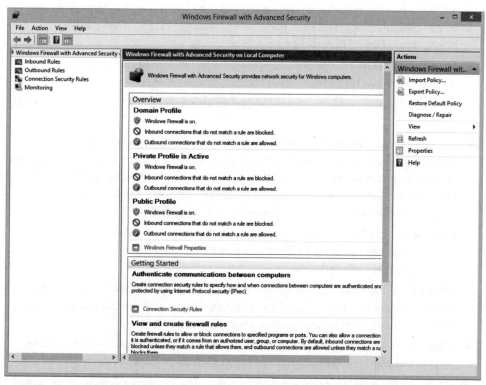

FIGURE 2-10 Windows Firewall with Advanced Security offers many more options than the Windows Firewall.

The left pane contains the following (and the items in the middle and right panes change based on what you select here):

- **Inbound Rules** This lists all configured inbound rules. You can double-click any item in the list and reconfigure it as desired. Some app rules are predefined and can't be modified much, but they can be disabled. You can also right-click Inbound Rules in the left pane and create your own custom rule. Rule types include Program, Port, Predefined, and Custom. *Exam Ref 70-687: Configuring Windows 8.1* explains how to create these rules.

- **Outbound Rules** This offers the same options as Inbound Rules, but these options apply to outgoing data. You can also right-click Outbound Rules in the left pane and create your own custom rule. Rule types include Program, Port, Predefined, and Custom. *Exam Ref 70-687: Configuring Windows 8.1* explains how to create these rules.

- **Connection Security Rules** Connection security rules that you create manually appear here. These rules establish how computers must authenticate before any data can be sent. IPsec standards define how data is secured while it's in transit over a TCP/IP network, and you can require a connection use this type of authentication before computers can send data, if you want. *Exam Ref 70-687: Configuring Windows 8.1* covered how to create this type of rule.

- **Monitoring** This offers information about the active firewall status, state, general settings, and more for both private and public profile types.

The right pane displays the following (what you see depends on what you select in the left pane):

- **Import/Export/Restore/Diagnose/Repair Policies** This section enables you to manage the settings you've configured for your firewall. Polices use the .wfw extension. A common task is to export policies from one computer and import them to another. Exporting is a simple task and involves only saving the policy file. Importing is more difficult but can be achieved by importing it to a Group Policy Object (GPO).

- **New Rules** This section enables you to start the applicable Rule Wizard to create a new rule. You can also do this from the Action menu when Inbound Rules or Outbound Rules is selected in the left pane.

- **Filter By** This section enables you to filter rules by Domain Profile, Private Profile, or Public Profile. You can also filter by state: Enabled or Disabled. Use this section to narrow the rules listed to only those you want to view.

- **View** This section enables you to customize how and what you view in the middle pane of the Windows Firewall With Advanced Security window.

When you opt to create your own inbound or outbound rule, you can choose from four rule types. A wizard walks you through the process, and the process changes depending on the type of rule you want to create:

- **Program** A program rule sets firewall behavior for a specific program you choose or all programs that match the rule properties you set. You can't control apps, but you can configure traditional programs whose file format ends in .exe. You can't change items distributed through AppLocker either. After you select the program to create the rule for, you can allow the connection, allow the connection but only if the connection is secure and has been authenticated using IPsec, or block the connection. You can also choose the profiles the rule will be applied to (domain, private, or public) and name the rule.

- **Port** A port rule sets firewall behavior for TCP and UDP port types and specifies which ports are allowed or blocked. You can apply the rule to all ports or only ports you specify. As with other rules you can allow the connection, allow the connection but only if the connection is secured with IPsec, or, block the connection. You can also choose the profiles the rule will be applied to (domain, private, public) and name the rule.

> **NOTE CREATING RULES AND IPSEC**
>
> When you create inbound and outbound rules, and when you opt to allow the connection only if the connection is secured by authenticating the connection with IPsec, the connections are secured by using the settings in the IPsec properties and applicable rules in the Connection Security Rules node.

- **Predefined** A predefined rule sets firewall behavior for a program or service that you select from a list of rules already defined by Windows.
- **Custom** A custom rule is one you create from scratch, defining every aspect of the rule. You use this if the first three don't offer the kind of rule you need.

> **NOTE CONFIGURING INACTIVE PROFILES**
>
> When you are working inside the Windows Firewall With Advanced Security window and subsequent dialog boxes, you have access to and can configure rules for every profile, even if they aren't active. This includes Private, Public, and Domain.

You can explore other areas by selecting Windows Firewall With Advanced Security in the left pane and using the Overview section of the middle pane, click Windows Firewall Properties. From there you can make changes to the firewall and the profiles, even if you aren't connected to the type of network you want to configure.

EXAM TIP

You might be asked how to administer Windows Firewall with Advanced Security via Windows PowerShell. You can find more information about that at *http://technet.microsoft. com/en-us/library/hh831755.aspx*.

In Figure 2-11 and Figure 2-12, the Domain Profile tab and IPsec Settings tab are selected. On the Domain Profile tab you can configure the firewall to be turned off when connected to a domain network. On the IPsec Settings tab you can configure IPsec defaults, exemptions, and tunnel authorization. You'll learn a little bit more about this later. You also can strengthen the settings for the public profile and customize settings for the private profile.

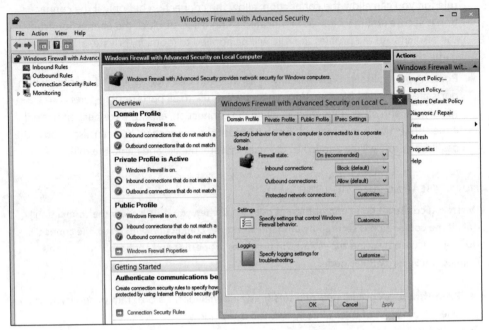

FIGURE 2-11   You can change the domain profile defaults from the Windows Firewall With Advanced Security dialog box.

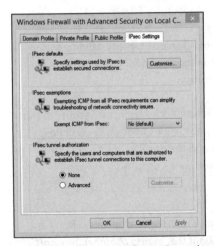

FIGURE 2-12   You can configure IPsec rules on the IPsec Settings tab.

MORE INFO   **USING THE IPSEC SETTINGS TAB**

Before going further, read this TechNet article on what you can achieve from the IPsec Set-tings tab shown in Figure 2-12: *http://technet.microsoft.com/en-us/library/cc753002.aspx*. Although this article refers to its use in Windows 7, the information is also applicable here.

Understanding IPsec

IPsec ensures private, secure communications over IP networks. To achieve this, it uses available cryptographic security services. You create IPsec policies to configure these services, and those policies consist of settings and rules that determine the key exchange settings and methods. IPsec rules also determine what kinds of traffic IPsec must examine and how that traffic is handled, among other things. Policies you create can be applied to a domain, an Organization Unit (OU), or locally.

You can review the options set as defaults for IPsec by clicking Customize in the IPsec Defaults area of the Windows Firewall With Advanced Security dialog box shown earlier in Figure 2-12. The options there are configured with defaults separated into three sections:

- Key Exchange (Main Mode)
- Data Protection (Quick Mode)
- Authentication Method

CONFIGURING KEY EXCHANGE (MAIN MODE)

Before two computers or devices can exchange secured data, a trust must be established between them. This *security association* is an agreement between the two regarding how they will exchange the data securely. A key (created via a mathematical algorithm) is used for this purpose in this example. For Key Exchange (Main Mode), a shared master key is generated that the two parties can use to exchange additional keying information securely.

You can dive deeper into the options for configuring Key Exchange (Main Mode) settings and click Advanced and then Customize (see Figure 2-13) to get an idea of how complex key exchange is. The encryption methods include SHA-1 AES-CBC 128 Diffie-Hellmann Group 2 and SHA-1 3DES Diffie-Hellmann Group 2. You can add your own algorithms, too. For more information, refer to the article at *http://technet.microsoft.com/en-us/library/cc731752.aspx*.

EXAM TIP

You must be familiar with the terms you see here. Be sure to review these terms via TechNet or other sources before taking the exam.

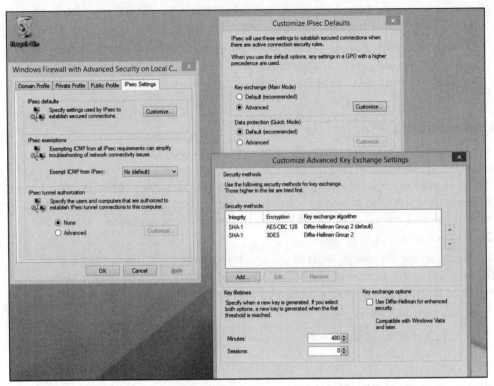

FIGURE 2-13 Key Exchange settings are configured by using defaults, but you can add your own.

CONFIGURING DATA PROTECTION (QUICK MODE)

Data Protection settings are used by connection security rules to protect network traffic. You can opt to require encryption for all connection security rules that use the configured settings here if desired, but that's not the default setting. You need to review two areas in this section of the Customize IPsec Defaults dialog box when you opt to customize: Data Integrity Algorithms and Data Integrity And Encryption Algorithms. You can add your own to both areas. The protocols you'll be required to know here include Authentication Headers (AH) and Encapsulating Security Payload (ESP).

AH is a member of the IPsec protocol suite and ensures the integrity and authentication of the entire IP packet. ESP is also a member of the IPsec protocol suite and ensures the authenticity, integrity, and confidentiality protection of IP packets. ESP also supports encryption-only configurations (which are discouraged) and authentication-only configurations. Unlike AH, though, ESP doesn't provide security for the entire IP packet unless in tunnel mode (where the entire original IP packet is encapsulated).

UNDERSTANDING AUTHENTICATION METHODS

You should have an idea of what each of the listed Kerberos v5 Authentication methods offer. You can choose from three options: Computer And User (Kerberos V5), Computer (Kerberos V5), and User (Kerberos V5). Also, an Advanced option includes Kerberos options and settings.

The Kerberos V5 authentication protocol uses "tickets" to allow devices to communicate over nonsecure networks. The tickets help the nodes identify themselves, and the client/server model provides for mutual authentication. Kerberos protects against eavesdropping and other security risks, uses cryptography, and requires a trusted third party. It is the default security method for Windows 8.1. To learn more about Kerberos, refer to the TechNet article at *http://technet.microsoft.com/en-us/library/hh831553.aspx*.

Configuring connection security rules (IPsec)

Because IPsec deals with connections, to configure an IPsec rule, you need to create a connection security rule. You can do so in Windows Firewall with Advanced Security. You can create inbound and outbound rules that use the settings you've configured and opt to allow the connection only if it's secured with IPsec. To begin, you right-click Connection Security Rules (located just below Outbound Rules) in the left pane and click New Rule (see Figure 2-14).

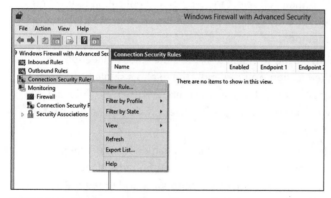

FIGURE 2-14   Create a new connection security rule.

Creating a rule involves several steps, and a wizard is available to guide you. The wizard pages that appear depend on the choices you make on the prior page. For instance, if you choose an Isolation rule type on the first page, you have to work through four additional steps: set the requirements, choose the authentication method, choose the profiles to apply the rule to, and name the rule. However, if you choose to create an Authentication Exemption rule, you'll be prompted to add the remote computers you want configure authentication requirements for, before you can continue.

There are many types of connection security rules:

- **Isolation**   Used to create a rule restricting connections based on credentials, such as domain membership, computer status or health, or compliance with policies. You can opt to request authentication for inbound and outbound connections, require authentication for inbound and request for outbound, or, require authentication for all connections. Following that, you select the type of authentication to use. You can choose from the defaults already configured or use the appropriate Kerberos or advanced authentication method.

- **Authentication Exemption**   Used to create a rule to state what connection types can be excluded from authentication. You can apply the rule to a single IP address, a subnet, an IP address range, or a predefined set of computers (such as DHCP or DNS servers). With that done, you can choose the profiles to apply the rule to (domain, private, or public) and name the rule.

- **Server-to-server**   Used to create a rule that applies to named IP addresses or all IP addresses; to request authentication for inbound and outbound connections; to require authentication for inbound and request for outbound; and to require authentication for all connections. You also choose the authentication method, which can be a certificate from a certificate authority or a health certificate issued from Network Access Protection (NAP). You can do this to protect specific servers from interacting with each other.

- **Tunnel**   Used to create a rule that authenticates connections between two computers by using tunnel mode in IPsec, perhaps between two computers such as client-to-gateway or gateway-to-client. You also can opt to exempt IPsec-protected connections and choose the authentication requirements.

- **Custom** Used to create a custom rule if the previous options don't offer what you need.

> **NOTE   ALLOW A CONNECTION**
>
> Connection security rules specify how and when authentication occurs, but they don't allow those connections. To allow a connection, you must create an inbound or outbound rule. When creating the inbound or outbound rule, you choose the required conditions for the connection, including requiring that the connections have been authenticated by using IPsec. When you do, connections are secured by using the settings in the IPsec properties and rules in the Connection Security Rules node.

EXAM TIP

This book covers the exam objectives that Microsoft posts on the exam website. However, the Microsoft certification page for this exam clearly states, "Please note that the questions may test on, but will not be limited to, the topics described in the bulleted text." This means that you'll see questions on items that aren't addressed here, and no one can even guess at what those might be. However, as an example, you might see questions that ask you about the different types of Wi-Fi authentication, including Temporal Key Integrity Protocol (TKIP), Advanced Encryption System (AES), and the various WPA options. Likewise, you might be faced with questions that require you know a specific file extension, such as .wfw, which is the file type used when you export a Windows Firewall policy. You also might be expected to know a little about BranchCache or DirectAccess.

Because a single book can't address all these things, you must study and prepare for aspects other than what's offered here. To find out where to access additional resources, visit *http://www.microsoft.com/learning/en-us/exam-70-688.aspx* and click Show All under Skills Measured. For each objective is a list of additional preparation resources. Review that list and become familiar with the options presented.

Here are two more articles to review before you move on to the next section:

- "Windows Firewall with Advanced Security Design Guide" at *http://technet.microsoft.com/en-us/library/jj721516.aspx*
- "IP Security (IPsec)" at *http://technet.microsoft.com/en-us/network/bb531150.aspx*

Thought experiment

Configuring network security

In this thought experiment, apply what you've learned about this objective. You can find answers to these questions in the "Answers" section at the end of this chapter.

You manage the wireless network for a small company. Currently the company has a router that connects to the Internet, and it's configured to share its connection with the network clients. For now, that connection is shared via a 16-port Ethernet switch. You plan to install a wireless access point and position it in the middle of the building, and you also want to secure this network against eavesdropping and hacking. In fact, the owner wants you to secure this network using the best means possible. The mobile devices are all Windows 7 or later, except for one very old netbook that is running Windows XP.

1. Which of the three wireless standards detailed in this section offers the best protection, including improved AES and the elimination of TKIP?

2. After using the standard selected in question 1 to configure the network, you attempt to connect the mobile clients. Everyone can connect except the netbook. The netbook supports only one very old standard, WEP. What should you do?

3. You've read about RADIUS servers and how they can be used to further secure a network. Should you consider a RADIUS server in this instance?

Objective summary

- To identify network resources, a DHCP server is generally used to dole out IP addresses. DHCP can be used to offer IPv4 and IPv6 addresses.

- The IPv4 address space is broken up into classes. Each class has a default subnet mask that further defines it.

- Private IP addressing is used for resources behind a router that don't connect directly to the Internet.

- When IPv6 must be used over an IPv4 network, transition technologies are used.

- Names can be resolved to IP addresses in various ways, including using DNS. Improvements to DNS have been made with PNRP and DNSSEC.

- Various Wi-Fi standards support wireless clients in different ways and at different speeds and frequencies. Not all standards are compatible with one another or all resources or clients.

- Encryption and authentication protocols help secure a network.

- You can use Windows Firewall and Windows Firewall with Advanced Security to fine-tune network security.

Objective review

Answer the following questions to test your knowledge of the information in this objective. You can find the answers to these questions and explanations of why each answer choice is correct or incorrect in the "Answers" section at the end of this chapter.

1. An IPv4 address is a _____ number that consists of ____ octets that are ____ bits each.

   A. 32-bit; 4; 8

   B. 64-bit; 4; 16

   C. 32-bit; 8; 16

   D. 128-bit; 8; 16

2. In a Class B IPv4 address, which part of a resource's IP address represents the network ID?

   A. First octet

   B. First and second octets

   C. First, second, and third octets

   D. You can't tell from the octets; you must convert all the numbers in the address to 1s and 0s and use the 1s to determine the network ID.

3. Which of the following are true statements when discussing DHCP servers that run on Windows Server 2012?

   A. They can assign both IPv4 and IPv6 addresses to hosts on a network.

   B. They can provide clients the necessary IP addresses of the applicable DNS server and gateway.

   C. DHCP must be used in large enterprises for all resources.

   D. All of the above

4. Which of the following transition technologies can be used to allow DirectAccess clients that use a public IP address to transmit data via the Internet?

   A. 6to4

   B. ISATAP

   C. Teredo

   D. IP-HTTPS

   E. None of the above

5. DNS servers handle the task of resolving names to addresses but _____ is a name resolution solution that's better because it's scalable (to the billions), secure (uses public key cryptography), and dynamic (instantaneous publication).

   A. DNS zones

   B. trust anchors

   C. NRPT

   D. PNRP

   E. DNSSEC

6. Which Wi-Fi technology standard matches this description: Is meant to replace 802.11a, b, and g but doesn't support other standards like 802.1x; is compatible with (supports) Wi-Fi Protected Access version 2 (WPA v2); uses two frequencies, 2.5 GHz and 5 GHz; supports transmission rates of up to 200 Mbps?

   A. 802.11a

   B. 802.11b

   C. 802.11n

   D. 802.11i

   E. 802.1x

7. You want to set up an ad hoc network from your Windows 8.1 laptop so that you can share its Internet connection with another device you own. You've shared the Internet connection from the adapter's Properties dialog box. What do you do next?

   A. Open an administrator command prompt and enter the following command:

   ```
   netsh wlan start hosted network
   ```

   B. On the second device, work through the steps to connect. The shared connection is ready.

   C. Create an inbound rule in Windows Firewall with Advanced Security to allow the second device access.

   D. Open an administrator command prompt and enter the following command:

   ```
   netsh wlan set hosted network mode=allow ssid=<networkname> key=<password>
   ```

8. Which of the following are types of inbound and outbound rules you can create to further secure Windows Firewall?

   A. Program

   B. Port

   C. Predefined

   D. Custom

   E. All of the above

9. Which encryption method(s) describe(s) what's included with IPsec Key Exchange (Main Mode) custom settings?

   A. SHA-1 AES-CBC 128 Diffie-Hellmann Group 2 and SHA-1 3DES Diffie-Hellmann Group 2

   B. Data Integrity Algorithms and Data Integrity And Encryption Algorithms

   C. Kerberos V5

   D. None of the above

Objective 2.2: Support remote access

Your users will need to connect to internal resources when they are away from the office. You can set this up in several ways, and you must initiate the process. You can create and manage VPNs, use DirectAccess, and manage users remotely, among other things.

> **This objective covers how to:**
>
> - Construct a virtual private network (VPN), including Connection Manager Administration Kit (CMAK)
> - Understand Remote Desktop Protocol (RDP), including Remote Desktop Services Gateway access
> - Configure and manage DirectAccess
> - Explore remote administration
> - Support Network Access Protection (NAP)

Constructing a virtual private network (VPN)

Exam 70-687, Configuring Windows 8.1, includes two objectives related to creating virtual private networks:

- Configure virtual private network (VPN) connections and authentication
- Enable VPN reconnect

Because those objectives were covered there, they aren't repeated here. However, you need to know how to create a VPN and have a client connect, so if you've never done it before review the information at *http://technet.microsoft.com/library/jj613767.aspx*. This section will cover the objective listed for VPNs for the 70-688 exam, specifically how to construct a VPN with CMAK.

Understanding VPN and authentication protocols

Before diving into the objective itself, you need to review the VPN protocols. You might see questions about these on the exam. Windows 8.1 supports many protocols, and the ones listed here are used with VPNs (loosely listed from oldest to newest and least secure to most secure):

- **Point-to-Point Protocol (PPP)**   When a dial-up connection is used to connect a client to a server, a dedicated link is used, and that connection is maintained throughout the session. This PPP link is a notably secure connection because dial-up makes it difficult to hack into. You can also use PPP with a VPN over the Internet. This is less secure than a dial-up connection, because a hacker can more easily get to the data transmitted over the Internet. This isn't a recommended VPN protocol for these reasons and more, and should be used only when no other options exist.

- **Point-to-Point Tunneling Protocol (PPTP)**   Another of the less-secure VPN protocols, PPTP doesn't require the use of certificates to ensure security. It's a better option than PPP, however, because the packets are encapsulated via tunneling technologies and are better protected during transmission. PPTP supports only the Microsoft Challenge Handshake Authentication Protocol version 1 and version 2 (MS-CHAP v1 and MS-CHAP v2), Extensible Authentication Protocol (EAP), and Protected Extensible Authentication Protocol (PEAP).

- **Layer 2 Tunneling Protocol (L2TP)**   This protocol uses IPsec for encryption and encapsulation. It encrypts with Data Encryption Standard (DES) or Triple DES (3DES) with keys obtained from Internet Key Exchange (IKE) from IPsec. L2TP/IPsec uses preshared keys or certificates and offers data integrity checks. L2TP/IPsec is supported by Windows XP, Windows Vista, Windows 7, Windows 8, Windows 8.1, Windows Server 2003, and Windows Server 2008.

- **Secure Socket Tunneling Protocol (SSTP)**   This protocol encapsulates PPP traffic through the SSL protocol, and uses certificates for authentication. Authentication involves Extensible Authentication Protocol-Transport Layer Security (EAP-TLS) and provides integrity checks. SSTP is supported on Windows Vista SP 1, Windows 7, Windows 8, Windows 8.1, Windows Server 2008 R2, and Windows Server 2012. SSTP uses port 443.

- **Internet Key Exchange, Version 2 (IKEv2)**   This protocol supports IPv6 and VPN Reconnect, authentication with EAP, PEAP, EAP-MSCHAPv2, and smart cards. It doesn't support Password Authentication Protocol (PAP) and CHAP as authentication methods. IKEv2 is useful when a user moves from one type of connection to another (wireless to wired, for example) and in many other scenarios. Windows 8.1 clients try to use this protocol first when connecting to remote servers. IKEv2 is supported on Windows 7, Windows 8, Windows 8.1, Windows Server 2008 R2, and Windows Server 2012.

Clients must be authenticated before they can access network resources. Here are the most common authentication protocols:

- **PAP** This protocol—the least secure—uses plain-text passwords and is used as a last resort when other authentication methods can't be negotiated. It's not enabled by default on a Windows 8-based client.

- **CHAP** This protocol uses a three-way handshake between the client and server, using a key for encryption. This is best used for legacy connections, and is better than PAP, but other methods are preferred.

- **MS-CHAP v2** This protocol uses a two-way mutual authentication and is stronger than CHAP. Still, better protocols exist, including EAP.

- **EAP-MS-CHAPv2** This protocol authenticates using EAP, which offers the strongest and most flexible security option. With it, authentication can be negotiated using something other than passwords, including certificates and smart cards. This is the default selection for new connections on Windows 8-based machines.

Installing and using Connection Manager Administration Kit (CMAK)

Clients use Connection Manager (not CMAK) on their own computers to connect to available VPNs. Connection Manager is available from the Network And Sharing Center on any Windows 8-based machine (click Set Up A New Connection Or Network, and then click Connect To A Workplace to connect to a VPN). Connection Manager uses profiles to assist clients with connections and to make managing those VPN connections easier for everyone involved. The profiles contain the settings necessary to allow the clients to connect. You use CMAK to create those profiles and make them available to users, and users install the profiles you create.

Here are some facts to remember regarding CMAK:

- CMAK is a tool that you can use to create predefined connections to remote servers and networks for your clients. To do this you use the CMAK Wizard. You can create profiles for Windows server-based operating systems and Windows client-based operating systems. Connection profiles you create must match the architecture (32-bit or 64-bit) of the client that will use them to connect.

- You save the profile to a location you name, perhaps C:\Program Files\CMAK\Profiles\ Windows Vista And Above.

- The profile is an executable (.exe) file.

Using a profile and making a connection on a client machine

The user profiles you create in CMAK are executable files. This means that a client can install the profile in many ways, including but not limited to:

- Removable media
- Network share

- Email
- Website download
- Software distribution system

MORE INFO **UNDERSTANDING CMAK**

For more information on CMAK, read this TechNet article at *http://technet.microsoft.com/ en-us/library/hh831675.aspx.*

Clients can opt to create a desktop icon for the profile during its installation and use that shortcut to start the connection process. Another common way to connect is through the Connection Manager. Briefly, the process is as follows:

1. From the Network And Sharing Center, click Set Up A New Connection Or Network.

2. Select Connect To A Workplace, click Next, and then click Use My Internet Connection (VPN).

3. Enter the address of the Remote Access server and the name of the destination and click Create.

4. Locate the new VPN connection from the Settings charm (click the Network icon). It's listed under Connections (see Figure 2-15).

5. Enter credentials and click OK.

FIGURE 2-15 You can locate the VPN from the Settings charm.

You can also view the connection's properties. When you do, you'll see five tabs, as shown in Figure 2-16:

- **General** Host name, IP address of VPN server
- **Options** Credentials, idle time, PPP settings
- **Security** Data encryption, authentication, tunneling and protocols
- **Networking** IPv6, IPv4, File and Printer Sharing, Client for Microsoft Networks
- **Sharing** Share the connection

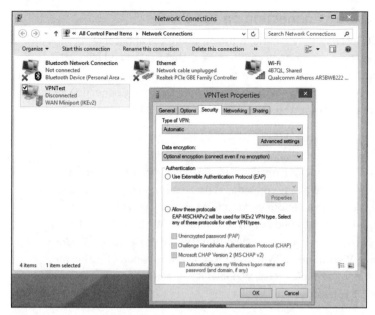

FIGURE 2-16 The VPNTest Properties dialog box offers a way to configure the connection.

EXAM TIP

You can create and manage VPN connections and clients using Windows PowerShell. You might see questions about this on the exam, and you'll be asked to identify the proper Windows PowerShell command to use to perform a task, perhaps to retrieve a specific VPN profile or to change the configuration settings of an existing VPN connection. There is an excellent list of cmdlets at *http://technet.microsoft.com/en-us/library/jj554820.aspx*.

Understanding Remote Desktop Protocol (RDP), including Remote Desktop Services Gateway access

Remote Desktop Services (RDS) lets users connect to remote servers for the purpose of accessing remote desktops and applications. You learned about this in the Objective 1.2 section titled "Supporting desktop application coexistence." In this section you'll learn about one part of RDS, Remote Desktop Protocol (RDP), and the Remote Desktop (RD) Gateway.

NOTE **RD GATEWAY**

One element that makes RDS work is the RD Gateway, which enables users to connect securely from any device connected to the Internet, assuming it can run the Remote Desktop Connection (RDC) client. RD Gateway uses the Remote Desktop Protocol (RDP) over HTTPS to establish a secure, encrypted connection between the client and server.

Opening Remote Desktop Connection on the client

For users to access the RD Gateway, they (or you) must configure the applicable settings on their computers. When they have access, they can then be authenticated and allowed access to the features and settings you've made available to them. You configure these settings from the Remote Desktop Connection window. To open the Remote Desktop Connection window, type **mstsc.exe** at a command prompt. You can see both in Figure 2-17.

> **NOTE   MORE USES FOR REMOTE DESKTOP**
>
> Remote Desktop is used by network administrators to remotely administer computers and servers, often from another company computer in the same building or in another one close by. Users can connect to a remote desktop from almost any type of computer, including those running Windows XP, Windows Vista, Windows 7, Windows 8, Windows 8.1, or Windows RT. The host computer must be running Windows XP Professional, Windows Vista Enterprise, Windows Vista Ultimate, Windows Vista Business, Windows 7 Ultimate, Windows 7 Enterprise, Windows 7 Professional, Windows 8 Pro, Windows 8.1 Pro, Windows 8 Enterprise, or Windows 8.1 Enterprise.

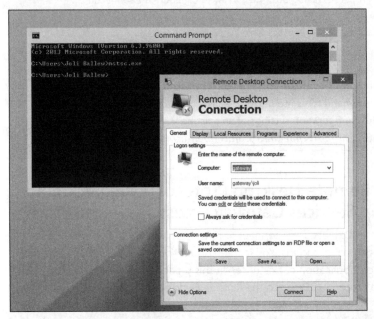

FIGURE 2-17   Use the command-line tool Mstsc.exe to open the Remote Desktop Connection window.

As a side note, here are parameters you can use with the command Mstsc.exe when using Remote Desktop:

- **<connection file>**   Specifies the name of an .rdp file for the connection.
- **/edit <connection file>**   Opens the specified .rdp file for editing.

- **/v:<Server[:<Port>]**   Specifies the remote computer and (optionally) the port number to which you want to connect.

- **/admin**   Connects you to a session for administering the server.

- **/f**   Starts Remote Desktop Connection in full-screen mode.

- **/w:<Width>**   Specifies the width of the Remote Desktop window.

- **/h:<Height>**   Specifies the height of the Remote Desktop window.

- **/public**   Runs Remote Desktop in public mode. In public mode, passwords and bitmaps aren't cached.

- **/span**   Matches the Remote Desktop width and height with the local virtual desktop, spanning across multiple monitors if necessary.

- **/migrate**   Migrates legacy connection files that were created with Client Connection Manager to new .rdp connection files.

Entering RD Gateway server settings and connecting

You configure the RD Gateway server settings from the Remote Desktop Connection window, from the Advanced tab, as follows:

1. With the Remote Desktop Connection window open, click the Advanced tab.

2. Under Connect From Anywhere, click Settings.

3. To input RD Gateway server settings manually, select Use These RD Gateway Server Settings (see Figure 2-18).

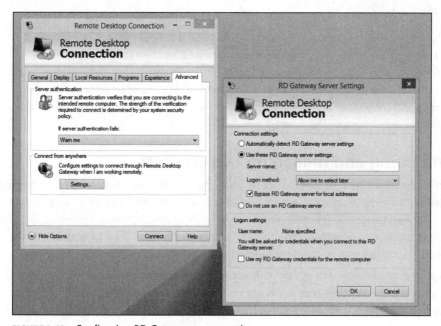

FIGURE 2-18   Configuring RD Gateway server settings.

4. Input the desired settings by selecting from the following options and then click OK:

- **Automatically Detect RD Gateway Server Settings** (default)   Use this option if the RDS client should attempt to use the Group Policy settings you've preconfigured to make the connection.

- **Use These RD Gateway Server Settings**   Select this option if an RD Gateway server is available and you want to specify the name of the server to use. Use a fully qualified domain name (FQDN).

- **Bypass RD Gateway Server For Local Addresses** (default)   Use this if you want the RDS client to automatically detect when an RD Gateway is required. If computers are always connected to your local network, RD Gateway isn't used. If computers aren't on the local network and need to connect to it, RD Gateway is used. For mobile computers, use this option to enhance performance and minimize latency.

- **Do Not Use An RD Gateway Server**   Select this option if you know you won't need to use an RD Gateway. This might be because the computer is always connected to the LAN or is on this side of the internal network firewall.

5. To connect, click Connect. Enter credentials when prompted.

EXAM TIP

You might be expected to know what's new in Remote Access for Windows Server 2012 R2. To prepare, read the article at *http://technet.microsoft.com/en-us/library/dn383589.aspx*.

> **MORE INFO**   **UNDERSTANDING RDP**
>
> RDP is a proprietary protocol developed by Microsoft. It provides your clients with a way to connect easily to another computer over a network. The client uses the RDP client software, and the other computer must run the RDP server software. You can learn more about RDP and Remote Desktop Services in general at *http://blogs.msdn.com/b/rds/archive/2013/03/14/what-s-new-in-windows-server-2012-remote-desktop-gateway.aspx*.

Configuring and managing DirectAccess

DirectAccess allows remote users to access your internal network securely without connecting to it through a VPN. When they are connected and authenticated, users can access whatever they're allowed to, including but not limited to network shares, intranet websites, applications, virtual desktops, personal files, and printers. You learned a little about DirectAccess earlier in Objective 2.1, in the section "Understanding transition technologies."

After the initial connection is made, DirectAccess clients establish a connection with the internal network every time they connect to the Internet. As a result, users don't have to manage the connection (or worry about it in any way), and administrators can manage the computers from virtually anywhere. For administrators, this means they can apply Group Policy, install updates, and perform similar tasks just about anytime they like.

The objective for DirectAccess appears under the heading "Support," which you can take to mean a few specific things: understanding how DirectAccess works, what's new, how it can be deployed in an enterprise, and how Windows 8.1 users access the connections you create.

Understanding how DirectAccess works

Domain clients that run Windows 7 Enterprise, Windows 7 Ultimate, and Windows 8 Enterprise and later can use DirectAccess. It can also be configured to work on Windows Server 2008 R2 and Windows Server 2012 machines. For clients that aren't compatible, traditional VPNs are used.

DirectAccess originally established two tunnels to connect the user to the DirectAccess server, and those tunnels used IPsec to protect the transmission. One tunnel accessed the network's DNS server to obtain authentication requirements from the AD DS domain controller; the second tunnel handled the actual network authentication and access to intranet resources such as websites, network shares, and other application servers. The Windows Server 2008 R2 DirectAccess server required two network adapters to handle this load. One was used to connect to the Internet, the other to the intranet. These adapters also needed two consecutive public IP addresses and sat at the network edge. Now though, a DirectAccess server can be deployed behind a Network Address Translation (NAT) device, using only a single network interface and without a public IP address. This is just one improvement from the older version of DirectAccess.

DirectAccess also uses a network location server (NLS) to detect whether DirectAccess client computers are located in the enterprise network (this is discussed in more detail later). Clients on an enterprise network don't use DirectAccess to reach network resources; instead, they connect to those resources directly. Clients not located on the enterprise network use DirectAccess to connect. The network location server can be installed on the DirectAccess server or on another server.

Finally, DirectAccess uses IPv6. When clients must communicate over IPv4-only networks, data is encapsulated by using the application transition technologies discussed earlier. By default, only certain network traffic (data) can be transported through a DirectAccess tunnel; however, you can use force tunneling to change this behavior.

> ***NOTE*** **DIRECTACCESS AND VPNS**
>
> DirectAccess doesn't use a traditional VPN connection. However, a VPN connection is created for clients that can't use DirectAccess, such as third-party VPN clients, nondomain clients, and legacy clients. Routing and Remote Access Services (RRAS) can be incorporated when this is the case.

Seeing what's new in DirectAccess for Windows Server 2012

Since the release of Windows Server 2012, DirectAccess and RRAS have been combined so that they create a combined Remote Access role. (It used to be that both couldn't reside on the same server.) The reasons they couldn't be combined before is complex, but briefly it was because DirectAccess relied on IPv6 and RRAS implemented IKEv2 IPsec. This caused problems with the DirectAccess traffic being blocked when a single server was configured. That problem has been resolved in Windows Server 2012.

In Windows Server 2008 R2, a Public Key Infrastructure (PKI) was required to issue the certificates that were used to manage server and client certificate-based authentication. Windows Server 2012 no longer requires this. Now, client authentication requests are sent to a Kerberos proxy service, which then sends requests to domain controllers. Windows Server 2008 R2 didn't have complete support for scripting either. Windows Server 2012 offers full Windows PowerShell support. You can now use Windows PowerShell to set up, configure, manage, monitor, and even troubleshoot remote access.

Here are a few more enhancements:

- Support for a DirectAccess server behind a NAT device, which means that only one network interface is required and no public IP address is necessary.

- Load-balancing support for better scalability and network availability.

- Support for multiple domains to allow remote clients from different domains to connect.

- Support for multiple sites so that you can configure multiple entry points. Users can access the device closest to them.

- Support for One-Time Password (OTP) (token-based authentication) for enterprises that require a specific security level such as RSA SecurID or a domain policy that requires multifactor authentication.

- Automated support for force tunneling via a setup wizard.

- User and server health monitoring to obtain data related to the number of clients and users connected, totals for active DirectAccess and VPN clients, total amount of data transferred, and more.

Choosing deployment options

Planning for DirectAccess involves three areas to consider: where you'll place the DirectAccess server (behind or in front of a firewall/router/NAT device); where you'll install the NLS (on the DirectAccess server or another server); and what users you want to have access. You'll have additional options for deployment if you have multiple sites or domains to connect and manage, need OTP Authentication, or need to force clients to meet "health requirements" before they can connect to your network (NAP).

Understanding what Windows 8.1 users needs to know

Your end users understand the problems that occur with VPNs (if they've used them in the past). They are responsible for initiating the connection; they must log on, and sometimes connections can be blocked inside hotels or similar places. Connections can also be dropped and must be reconnected. Users might also have to change their passwords often. Administrators have their own set of problems, one of which is supporting these users when they can't connect. Another problem is not having any way to initiate a connection to a remote user when it's necessary.

As soon as DirectAccess is set up and configured on a client computer, these problems go away. After that, users are connected each time they establish a connection to the Internet. Users might also be required to insert a Smart Card or virtual PIN, but they generally know how to do this and rarely have problems with it. When connected to the corporate network via DirectAccess, users can access the network just as they would if they were onsite. When connected to the Internet, they can:

- Use Federated Search. This allows them to search for items from their computers and get results from local network resources.

- Access their personal work folders via Folder Redirection and not worry about syncing manually on their return to the office.

- Get a replacement computer quickly, if necessary, and get it up and running in a matter of minutes.

If users want more information, the Microsoft DirectAccess Connectivity Assistant (DCA) is available for free download from the Microsoft Download Center. This requires .NET

Framework 3.5, which users will be prompted to install during the DCA installation if it isn't already available on their computers. When installed, a DCA icon appears in the taskbar's Notification area. This also makes tools available for end users if problems occur with the connection. It also offers connection status. You can use CMAK (discussed earlier in this objective) to create the profiles the clients need.

For more information on Connection Manager, refer to this TechNet article and the links to the left of it: *http://technet.microsoft.com/en-us/library/hh831583.aspx*.

Exploring remote administration

As an administrator, you can remotely manage your DirectAccess clients from a Windows Server 2012 machine. This enables you to perform all kinds of management tasks, including upgrading features or applying security updates even if the machine isn't on site. Some of these advanced tasks (like updating) require you also have System Center Configuration Manager or something similar.

Many prerequisites must be met by the server and the client for you to successfully manage remote clients, and they are outlined at *http://technet.microsoft.com/en-us/library/ jj574200.aspx*. You'll possibly see exam questions that ask why a client can't be administered remotely or why DirectAccess can't be used on a client (or some similar scenario). The answer is probably that one of these prerequisites hasn't been met. Thus, you must read through the preceding link. Here are some of the highlights:

- Windows Firewall must be enabled on all profiles.

- ISATAP in the enterprise network isn't supported. You must use native IPv6.

- DirectAccess clients must be installed with Windows 8.1, Windows 8, and Windows 7. Remember, legacy clients use VPNs. They all must be domain members. Because Windows RT machines can't join domains, they can't be included here.

- DirectAccess and VPN clients are managed in the same console.

- When you change policies, you must use the DirectAccess management console or Windows PowerShell cmdlets.

- If you don't want to use self-signed certificates for IP-HTTPS or the network location server, a CA server is required. This is also required if you want to use client certificates for client IPsec authentication. However, you can request certificates from a public CA, if you'd prefer to go that route.

- A DNS server is required. That server must be running Windows Server 2008 SP2, Windows Server 2008 R2, or Windows Server 2012.

- The Remote Access server must be a domain member, and the server can be deployed at the edge of the internal network or behind an edge firewall or similar device.

When all these and other prerequisites are met, you can remotely manage the clients through the DirectAccess connection. You'll learn about two ways you can do this next: using Remote Server Administration Tools (RSAT) and using Windows PowerShell.

Using Remote Server Administration Tools

You can remotely manage computers in your enterprise from a Windows 8.1 computer using the applicable Remote Server Administration Tool (RSAT). This allows you to manage servers and clients from your own laptop or personal desktop computer and reduces the number of servers that you have to connect to via RDP.

This free download, when installed, offers Server Manager, Microsoft Management Console (MMC) snap-ins, consoles, and Windows PowerShell cmdlets and command-line tools, among other things. RSAT for Windows 8.1 can be installed only on computers running Windows 8.1 Pro or Windows 8.1 Enterprise and are compatible with x86- and x64-based editions. Remote Server Administration Tools can't be installed on computers running Windows RT 8.1.

> **MORE INFO** **INSTALLING RSAT**
>
> Quite a bit of information is available about how to install RSAT, important notes regarding installation, and how to get started with the available tools at *http://technet.microsoft.com/ en-us/library/hh831501.aspx*. Because this book has only a limited number of pages to devote to this topic, I suggest that you read this article before taking the exam, along with the supporting papers also available at this link.

After you install RSAT, you might notice that it doesn't appear on the Start screen. Instead, you'll find it in Control Panel, under Administrative Tools. You might want to create a shortcut to RSAT if you plan to use it often.

> **NOTE** **USING RSAT TOOLS**
>
> You can't use the RSAT tools for Windows 8.1 to manage the local computer on which the tools are installed. Instead, you must specify what server(s) you want to manage.

You can start Server Manager on the client from the Administrative Tools folder by double-clicking Server Manager. As shown in Figure 2-19, a Quick Start section is available to help you connect to a server to manage, add roles and features, and create a server group that contains multiple servers. To add a remote server, click Add Other Servers To Manage. Your computer must be domain-joined. From the Active Directory tab, select the server to manage, click the right arrow to add it, and click OK. You can now begin managing that server from your Windows 8.1 computer.

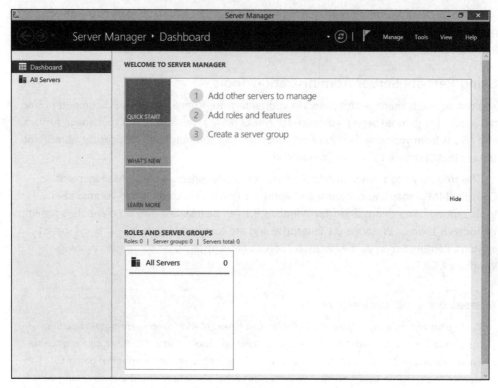

FIGURE 2-19 Server Manager is one tool you can use to manage computers remotely.

If possible, explore the other areas of Server Manager—specifically, the Manage and Tools options listed at the top. From there you can add and remove roles and features and access other tools including Event Viewer, Active Directory Administrative Center, and Hyper-V Manager.

Using Windows PowerShell

When you install RSAT, you also install the tools necessary to run Windows PowerShell cmdlets and command-line commands. Remotely managing computers with PowerShell is called Windows PowerShell Remoting. This means you can run PowerShell commands on remote computers just as you would if you were sitting in front of them.

> **MORE INFO** **PERFORMING REMOTE TASKS WITHOUT ESTABLISHING A REMOTING SESSION**
>
> You can perform a lot of remote administration tasks without remoting, using Windows PowerShell cmdlets. These cmdlets can be directed at a remote computer without establishing a remoting session first. You can find more information about this from Ed Wilson, "The Scripting Guy," at *http://technet.microsoft.com/en-us/scriptcenter/dd901334.aspx*.

To get started, at the Windows 8.1 computer you want to manage remotely, open an elevated Windows PowerShell session, type **Enable-PSRemoting**, and then type **A** to enable the required Windows Remote Management configuration tasks to run, as shown in Figure 2-20. (Windows PowerShell Remoting is enabled by default on Windows Server 2012 computers. Also, you don't need to run this command on a Windows 8.1 computer that's sending the commands.)

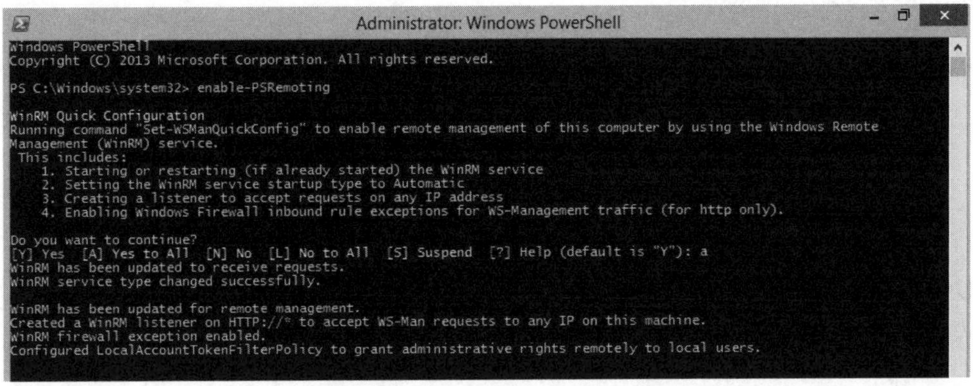

FIGURE 2-20 Enabling Windows PowerShell Remoting from an elevated Windows PowerShell session.

Now you can begin managing a remote computer with Windows PowerShell using one-to-one remoting. To get started, type **enter-pssession –computername -<*computername*>**. For example

```
PS c:\>enter-pssession –computername DC003
```

When you press Enter and make the connection, the prompt changes to look like this

```
[DC003]: PS C:\>
```

Finally, you can use dozens of core cmdlets. Related commands include *Get-Command*, *Out-Default*, and *Exit-PSSession*. You can view these commands and others, as well as their available parameters, at *http://technet.microsoft.com/en-us/library/hh849695.aspx*. You can also manage multiple computers at one time by using one-to-many remoting. However, this is much more complex; TechNet has many articles about this.

MORE INFO   **THE SCRIPT CENTER**

You'll find a ton of information about remoting and Windows PowerShell from The Scripting Center at *http://technet.microsoft.com/en-US/scriptcenter/default*.

Supporting Network Access Protection (NAP)

Network Access Protection (NAP) was mentioned earlier, albeit briefly. This section expands on that topic. To summarize, NAP lets you enhance network security by requiring that remote clients meet the "health requirements" you've previously set before they can connect to your protected internal network. Health requirements might include up-to-date virus protection and a running firewall. When you incorporate NAP, you can verify the remote computer's health before the client is granted access to your network and, if a problem is found, offer a solution to remediate it. Generally, this involves letting the computer into some kind of quarantined area of your network where remediation can be achieved. When the computer is considered healthy (perhaps its firewall is now enabled), it's then deemed compliant, and network access is granted.

EXAM TIP

Microsoft has stated in the TechNet article at *http://technet.microsoft.com/en-us/library/ dn303411.aspx* that NAP has been deprecated in Windows Server 2012 R2, and you can assume that it will be deprecated in future editions of Windows. But because NAP is listed as an objective on this exam, you need to be sure you understand it.

Using NAP on the server

When enterprise administrators decide to incorporate NAP, they first have to decide what a healthy computer is. Health requirements can include the items listed earlier (firewall and antivirus) but they can also require that the computer has installed the latest critical updates from Microsoft, has the latest malware definitions, or has the updates you've provided for your own clients via your own enterprise. When the requirements are known, the infrastructure can be built.

Here are a few of the requirements and items to consider:

- **NAP Agent** This collects and manages health information on the NAP client computers.
- **NAP client computer** This computer has the NAP agent installed, running, and reporting. This type of computer runs Windows Server 2008 and higher, Windows XP with SP3, Windows Vista, Windows 7, and Windows 8.
- **Compliant computer and noncompliant computer** These computers meet the health requirements or don't meet the health requirements, respectively.
- **Health status** A NAP client computer provides health status updates called *statements of health* (SoH) to the server that manages computer compliance.
- **NAP health policy server** A server that runs the Network Policy Server (NPS) role, it evaluates the health of NAP client computers when they request network access, and knows when their health state changes based on the SoH it receives. This server's job is to determine whether a computer is healthy enough to join the network.

As the enterprise administrator, you can also decide how to enforce the health rules. The decision you make determines what type of infrastructure you'll have to build and maintain. For instance, if you want to use NAP with IPsec enforcement, you'll need an AD DS domain controller, a Network Policy Server, a Certification Authority, and a Health Registration Authority, and the computer must have the required IPsec certificate. You must also configure NAP health registration authority settings when you deploy IPsec-based enforcement.

If you want to use NAP with 802.1X enforcement, you'll have to build an infrastructure that includes compliant 802.1X wired Ethernet switches and compliant wireless access points.

You'll also need an NPS, server certificates, and EAP or EAP-Tunneled Transport Layer Security (EAP-TTLS) authentication.

If you want to use NAP with VPN enforcement, you'll need to configure Routing and Remote Access as a VPN server running the NPS role, or the server must be able to communicate with an NPS. The Network Policy Server needs to be configured as the primary RADIUS server, and you'll need to configure related policies, configure system health agents, and so on.

If you want to use NAP with DHCP enforcement, you'll need a DHCP server, and the various policies configured.

Finally, based on these options, a computer that isn't compliant with a network you've configured will be handled as follows:

- **NAP with IPsec enforcement** The computer might be allowed to communicate with the resources it needs to become compliant on the network, but nothing else. Like with other options, you choose not to restrict access, not to create a remediation zone, and so on. You can simply use the associated reports to manage remediation yourself. Of course, you can also deny access.

- **NAP with 802.1X enforcement** The computer can be restricted to a remediation zone.

- **NAP with VPN enforcement** The computer also can be restricted to a remediation zone.

- **NAP with DHCP enforcement** The computer can be assigned an IP address that allows it to enter the remediation zone but not the protected network.

> *MORE INFO*   **NETWORK POLICY AND ACCESS SERVICES OVERVIEW**
>
> To learn more, read the TechNet article at *http://technet.microsoft.com/en-us/library/hh831683.aspx.*

Using NAP on the client

Before you can use NAP on your client computers, you need to configure their NAP settings through the NAP Client Configuration console. This console helps you configure the desired user interface settings, enforcement settings, and Health Registration Authority (HRA) settings. You can use other options, though; you can configure settings with the applicable *netsh* commands or you can use the Group Policy Management Console (GPMC). If you use Group Policy, the settings you apply are automatically configured on all your domain-joined, NAP-capable client computers the next time Group Policy is refreshed.

If you can't use Group Policy, don't like to use *netsh*, or want to manage only a small number of computers, you should opt for the NAP Client Configuration console. Group Policy is better for larger organizations, though, and *netsh* can certainly be incorporated.

USING THE NAP CLIENT CONFIGURATION CONSOLE

You can open the NAP Client Configuration console by typing **napclcfg.msc** at the Start screen or in a Run window. Figure 2-21 shows the dialog box and the three steps required to completely configure the interface for clients.

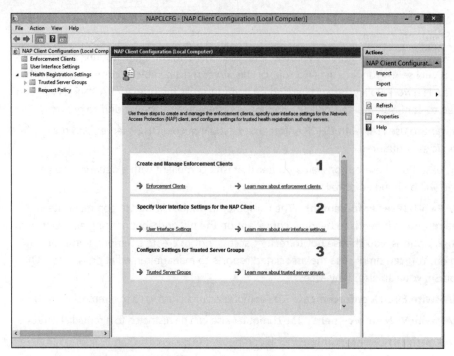

FIGURE 2-21 Configure the NAP clients using the NAP Client Configuration console.

One of the simpler things to do is change the properties of the user interface. To do this, click User Interface Settings in the left pane; in the middle pane, right-click User Interface and then click Properties. From there you can type a title, description, and add an image (see Figure 2-22).

FIGURE 2-22 Personalize the User Interface settings on the NAP Client Configuration console.

You can configure the NAP Client Configuration console using *netsh*. For example, to set a title for the interface, type this at a command prompt:

```
netsh nap client set userinterface title = <title>
```

Be sure to familiarize yourself with the available *netsh* commands as outlined in the following section, because you'll likely see something about *netsh* on the exam.

Here are some other things you can do inside this interface:

- Enable and disable NAP enforcement clients, including the built-in clients and any compatible non-Microsoft clients.
- Identify the HRA servers you want your NAP clients to use.
- Specify how you want to secure communications from the client to the HRA server by configuring a request policy. You can specify only one asymmetric key algorithm, hash algorithm, and cryptographic service provider on a client computer.
- Enable and disable NAP tracing.
- Specify the level of detail you want to capture in a tracing log file.
- Import and export NAP client settings. You can do this with an .xml-based configuration file.

A NAP client configuration checklist is available on TechNet at *http://technet.microsoft.com/en-us/library/cc732527.aspx*. From here, you can find links to guide you through processes such as how you could:

- Import a NAP configuration file.
- Configure NAP clients.
- Configure a NAP client request policy.
- Configure trusted server groups for clients.
- Configure NAP tracing.
- Export NAP configuration settings.

MORE INFO   LEARNING MORE ABOUT NAP

TechNet offers a full spectrum of papers on NAP configuration. You can access the first of those at *http://technet.microsoft.com/en-us/library/cc754803.aspx*. Use the links on the left side of the page to access related documents. You'll find "Export NAP Client Configuration Settings" at *http://technet.microsoft.com/en-us/library/cc732315%28v=ws.10%29.aspx* and "Import NAP Client Configuration Settings" at *http://technet.microsoft.com/en-us/library/cc753594%28v=ws.10%29.aspx*.

USING NETSH

As noted earlier, you can use *netsh* at a command line to perform many of the tasks associated with NAP. Table 2-4 details the commands you should be familiar with that are associated with *netsh nap client*. For the parameters these commands offer, type the command in full and press Enter. For example, you could type **netsh nap client show**, and the resulting list would offer available parameters, including but not limited to *show configuration*, *show hashes*, *show state*, and *show trustedservergroup*. The parameter *add* would offer these two parameter options: *add server* and *add trustedservergroup*. Finally, a command like *netsh nap client import* would produce an error, and you'd be prompted to correct the command by adding a parameter: *filename=<path to filename.xml>*.

TABLE 2-4 Commands for *netsh nap client*

Command	What it does
? or help	Displays a list of commands
add	Adds a configuration
delete	Deletes a configuration
dump	Displays a configuration script
export	Exports configuration settings
import	Imports configuration settings
rename	Renames a configuration
reset	Resets a configuration
set	Sets a configuration
show	Shows configuration and state information

Explore the *netsh nap client* command as follows:

1. Open a command prompt.

2. Type **netsh nap client help** and press Enter. Note the list of commands.

3. Type **netsh nap client add** and press Enter. Note that you are prompted to add a parameter to specify what to add.

4. Type **netsh nap client rename** and press Enter.

5. Continue until you've typed each of the entries in Table 2-4 (see Figure 2-23).

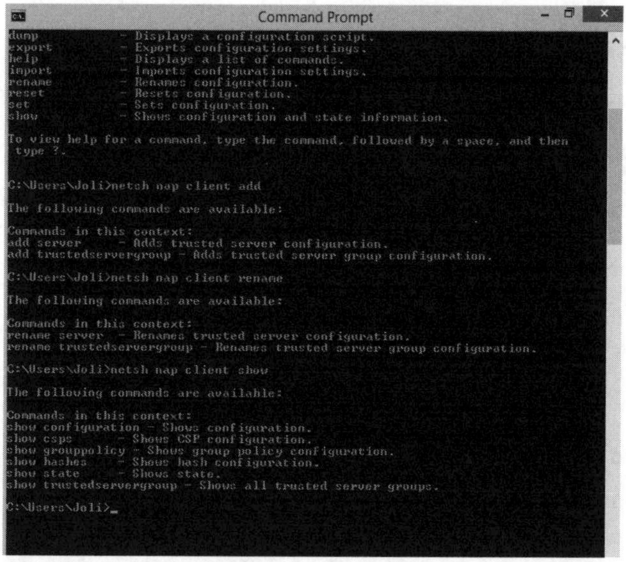

FIGURE 2-23 Exploring the *netsh nap client* command.

CONFIGURING GROUP POLICY SETTINGS IN THE GPMC

Finally, you can manage NAP from the applicable Group Policy settings. You do this in the GPMC on the appropriate domain controller. The following steps configure the NAP client service to start automatically on NAP client computers:

1. In the applicable GPMC, open Group Policy Objects, right-click the name of the GPO you want to edit, and click Edit.

2. Navigate to Computer Configuration, Policies, Windows Settings, Security Settings, System Services.

3. In the details pane, double-click Network Access Protection Agent.

4. In the Network Access Protection Agent Properties dialog box, select Define This Policy setting, choose Automatic, and then click OK.

Many other settings are available, as you can imagine. You can configure trusted server groups here:

Computer Configuration, Policies, Windows Settings, Security Settings, Network Access Protection, NAP Client Configuration, Health Registration Settings, Trusted Server Groups

You can configure wireless authentication settings here:

Computer Configuration, Policies, Windows Settings, Security Settings, Wireless Network (IEEE 802.11) Policies

Even more settings are available, so take a moment to explore them.

Thought experiment
Designing a remote connection

In this thought experiment, apply what you've learned about this objective. You can find answers to these questions in the "Answers" section at the end of this chapter.

You want to design a remote connection for your remote clients that enables them to connect to your network automatically. You don't want to field troubleshooting calls from users who can't connect because of a limiting hotel firewall or any other common problem associated with VPNs. All your clients run Windows 8.1 Enterprise and you have a Windows Server 2012 domain controller on a domain named Contoso.

1. What type of connection would you design that will enable clients to connect to your internal network automatically anytime they connect to the Internet?

2. The required authenticating server sits on the network side of your enterprise firewall. Will you need to obtain one public IP address, two public IP addresses, or none at all?

3. What type of device will you need to help you determine whether clients are on the enterprise network or away from it?

4. If at a later date you add to your network clients that can't be connected via DirectAccess, what do you need to incorporate to let those clients connect via VPN?

Objective summary

- Many types of VPN and authentication protocols are available, each offering different levels of features and security. You should use the protocol with the most security for your network infrastructure.

- You use CMAK to create VPN profiles and make them available to users, and users install the profiles you create.

- Remote Desktop Services (RDS) lets users connect to remote servers for the purpose of accessing remote desktops and applications. A Remote Desktop Gateway helps you manage those users and their access to resources.

- DirectAccess allows remote users to securely access your internal network without connecting to it through a VPN. It also lets them connect automatically anytime they connect to the Internet.

- DirectAccess has been improved from its first emanation in Windows Server 2008 and includes many new features.

- You can remotely administer clients and servers through RSAT and Windows PowerShell.

- NAP lets you assess a computer's health before letting it connect to your network. Noncompliant computers can be quarantined and remediated.

Objective review

Answer the following questions to test your knowledge of the information in this objective. You can find the answers to these questions and explanations of why each answer choice is correct or incorrect in the "Answers" section at the end of this chapter.

1. Which of the following protocols supports the use of a preshared key for authentication?

   A. PPP

   B. SSTP

   C. L2TP

   D. EAP

   E. RDP

2. How does a client computer connect to a VPN?

   A. CMAK

   B. Connection Manager

   C. Via the Windows PowerShell command *Get-VpnConnection*

   D. RSAT

3. The RD Gateway uses which of the following to establish a secure, encrypted connection between the client and server?

   A. Internet Key Exchange, Version 2 (IKEv2) protocol

   B. Secure Socket Tunneling Protocol (SSTP) protocol

   C. Applicable and compatible transition protocols

   D. Remote Desktop Protocol (RDP) over HTTPS

4. DirectAccess clients can run which of the following operating systems? (Choose all that apply.)

   A. Windows 7 Enterprise

   B. Windows 7 Ultimate

   C. Windows 8 Enterprise

   D. Windows 8.1 Enterprise

   E. Windows XP with SP3

   F. Windows Vista Business

5. You want to administer your DirectAccess clients remotely. Which of the following requirements must be met before you can do this? (Choose all that apply.)

   A. Clients must be joined to the domain or a local workgroup.

   B. Windows Firewall must be enabled on all profiles.

   C. You must install and configure a DNS server.

   D. All of the above.

6. Which Windows PowerShell command lets you start a remote, interactive PowerShell session by using one-to-one remoting?

   A. *enter-pssession*

   B. *enable-psremoting*

   C. *start-job*

   D. *set-pssessionconfiguration*

7. You want to use NAP with IPsec enforcement. Which of the following must your network infrastructure include? (Choose all that apply.)

   A. Active Directory domain controller

   B. Network Policy Server

   C. Certification Authority

   D. RRAS

8. Which *netsh* command lets you display a configuration script for a NAP client?

   A. *netsh nap client reset*

   B. *netsh nap client set*

   C. *netsh nap client dump*

   D. *netsh nap client show*

Objective 2.3: Support authentication and authorization

Authentication is the process of entering the credentials required to gain access to a computer, device, or network. What happens after that is called authorization. Users must be authenticated to access a computer or network before they can be authorized to access the resources on it. In the first section, you'll learn about this first part, authentication.

Understanding and supporting multifactor authentication

For the most part, the concepts on this exam are fairly difficult to grasp, and you must have had experience in the field to really understand what's going on with all the features discussed so far. This section isn't like that; for the most part, the concepts we review next and how you configure them are pretty straightforward. For example, configuring a picture password for a client who uses a stand-alone computer isn't difficult, nor is connecting a biometric device (such as a fingerprint reader) and configuring it for use.

Understanding multifactor authentication

Multifactor authentication requires two (or more) types of authentication to gain access to a device or network. Most often, one type is a password, and the other is something else, such as a smart card, fingerprint, or digital certificate. This section focuses a little more on certificates as a means for achieving authentication, but this book has covered this topic in various places and you should review those entries when you can. (For the most part, certificates have been associated with apps, because apps must be signed to ensure that they can be trusted.)

A digital certificate is issued by a Certificate Authority (CA) such as Verisign or Active Directory Certificate Services (AD CS) in Windows Server 2012 R2. The certificate can be used to provide proof that the identity asking for authentication is trusted and true, and that the identity offering it is also. Authentication with certificates involves a public key and a private key that can be matched up to provide that authentication. If no match occurs, no authentication (access) is provided. (You can learn more about Certificate Authorities at *http://technet. microsoft.com/en-us/library/cc732368.aspx*.)

AD CS can issue and manage public key infrastructure (PKI) in a domain, provides public key cryptography and the ability to create digital certificates, and offers digital signature capabilities. For the purposes here, AD CS provides authentication by associating certificate keys with computers, users, and device accounts on a network. This is called *binding*.

For the exam you might be asked how to allow users to access a network resource and be
given a specific scenario. A scenario that includes AD CS will note that the network has its own
PKI infrastructure. You must understand that the required certificates must be available to the
computer and the user, and they must be stored in the proper location for authentication to
be granted. Client certificates are stored in the personal certificate store for the applicable
user account on the client's computer. Computer accounts need trusted root certificates to
be stored in the Trusted Root Certification Authorities store, again on the client's computer.
You can explore many other certificate folders as well. To view these stores on a local computer,
type **certmgr.msc** in a Run dialog box and click OK. Open this console and review the available certificate folders before moving on. Figure 2-24 shows a local computer, not connected
to a domain, and the related personal certificates. You'll see more certificates than this,
generally.

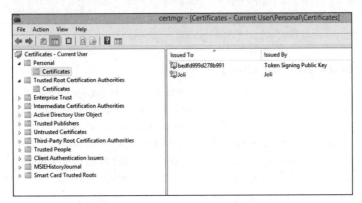

FIGURE 2-24 Use CertMgr to review certificate stores and the certificates in them.

Note that certificates are also associated with secure, encrypted communications.
ActiveSync, Exchange Server, Outlook Web App, and Internet Information Services use SSL
certificates to authenticate the server's identity to the mobile devices that need access. You'll
find other uses for certificates elsewhere and as you work as a network administrator.

> **NOTE**   **USING WINDOWS POWERSHELL CMDLETS TO BACK UP AND RESTORE A CA**
>
> You can use two new Windows PowerShell cmdlets to back up and restore a CA database: *Backup-CARoleService* and *Restore-CARoleService*.

Understanding virtual smart cards

You've already learned a little about smart cards in this book. A virtual smart card works in the same general manner as a physical smart card does but doesn't require a connected or installed smart card reader. Instead, the virtual smart card works with a Trusted Platform Module (TPM) chip installed on the computer that's used to protect the virtual card information through encryption. As with other more advanced security options, you'll need a PKI domain infrastructure, complete with certificates and the ability to create and manage them, to incorporate this technology. Virtual smart cards offer the following:

- Authentication protection
- Confidentiality of the machine and its contents
- Private keys for security
- Encrypted card information that can't be mined or removed (that is, it can't be exported)
- Protection from rogue software that attacks at startup
- Multifactor protection (smart card and PIN)

To use virtual smart cards, you must meet more requirements than when you opt to use physical ones. These requirements include but aren't limited to the following:

- Computers must be running Windows 8 or higher and Windows Server 2012 or higher.
- A compatible TPM must be installed on those computers that adheres to TPM 1.2 or higher standards.

- A limit of 10 smart cards (virtual or physical) can be used on a single computer.

- The PIN and the PIN Unlock Key must be a minimum of eight characters. These can include numbers, letters, and special characters.

One very important thing to know for the exam is Tpmvscmgr.exe, the command-line tool you use to configure a virtual smart card. You can use the command locally or remotely. Parameters you can use include *Create* and *Delete*. Examples include */name* (the name of the smart card), */admin key* (administrator key), */PIN* (the PIN), */generate* (to create the files in storage necessary for the card to function), and others listed at *http://technet.microsoft.com/en-us/library/dn593707.aspx*.

To configure a virtual smart card environment from scratch in a domain, you must follow these steps:

1. Create a certificate template, a 16-step process performed on a Windows server in a domain that's installed with and running a CA, as outlined at *http://technet.microsoft.com/en-us/library/dn579260.aspx#BKMK_Step1*.

2. Create the virtual TPM smart card, a four-step process that uses the *Tpmvscmgr.exe* command with parameters such as the following, as outlined at *http://technet.microsoft.com/en-us/library/dn579260.aspx#BKMK_Step2*:

   ```
   tpmvscmgr.exe create /name tpmvsc /pin default /adminkey random /generate
   ```

3. Enroll the certificate on the TMP virtual smart card, a six-step process, by using the CertMgr.msc console (refer to Figure 2-24) to add the certificate to the Personal store as outlined at *http://technet.microsoft.com/en-us/library/dn579260.aspx#BKMK_Step3*.

> **MORE INFO** **VIRTUAL SMART CARDS**
>
> Learn more about virtual smart cards and be sure to explore the additional links on the left side of this page: *http://technet.microsoft.com/en-us/library/dn593708.aspx*

To configure a Windows 8.1 virtual smart card on a stand-alone computer if you have the required technology and credentials available follow these steps:

1. Open an elevated command prompt.

2. Type **TPM.msc**.

3. Verify that a compatible TPM can be found that's at least a 1.2 or later. If you receive an error instead but are sure a compatible module is available, enable it in the system BIOS before continuing.

4. Close the TPM management console.

5. At the command prompt, enter

   ```
   TpmVscMgr create /name MyVSC /pin default /adminkey random /generate
   ```

   To provide a custom PIN value when creating the virtual smart card, use */pin prompt* instead.

Configuring a picture password

A picture password is a way to log on to a computer by using a series of three movements consisting of lines, circles, and/or taps. You can pick any picture you want. Picture passwords can't be used to log on to domains; they are used to log on only to stand-alone computers. Picture password combinations are limitless because the pictures that can be used are limitless. Although picture passwords are considered more secure for stand-alone computers than typing a PIN or password, a hacker can get into a device by holding the screen up to light to see where most of the gestures are (by following the smudges on the screen). This is especially true if the user touches the screen only to input the password and rarely uses touch for anything else.

You create a picture password (or a 4-digit PIN) from PC Settings:

1. Open the charms by swiping in from the right or pressing Windows logo key+C.

2. Click Settings, and then click Change PC Settings.

3. If applicable, click any back arrows and then click Accounts.

4. Click Sign-in Options.

5. Under Picture Password, click Add.

6. Input your current password, and then click Choose Picture to browse to and select the picture to use.

7. Follow the instructions in the resulting wizard to configure the picture password.

Exploring biometrics

Biometrics, like picture passwords, provides infinite possibilities for securing a computer and can be used as part of a multifactor authentication plan (using it on its own isn't recommended). Biometric options are generally configured by incorporating a person's fingerprint and using a fingerprint reader (you "enroll" the user when configuring this), but you can also use a person's face, eye, or even their voice. Biometrics usually aren't configured as the only form of authentication, though, because the technology isn't that reliable yet. You might have experienced the flaws if you've ever configured a smartphone to unlock using face recognition; often almost any face will unlock it.

Microsoft has made using biometric   er than ever by including native support for biometrics through the Windows Biometric Framework (WBF), which includes an option in PC Settings for configuring the device on Windows 8.1 and Windows RT machines. Windows now also includes Group Policy settings related to biometrics, and you can enable or disable this feature as desired. I doubt you'll see much on the exam regarding this, but you should review the information at *http://technet.microsoft.com/en-us/library/dn344916.aspx* and locate the available Group Policy settings just in case. You can find Local Group Policy options here (and follow the same general path in Group Policy): Computer Configuration, Administrative Templates, Windows Components, Biometrics, as shown in Figure 2-25.

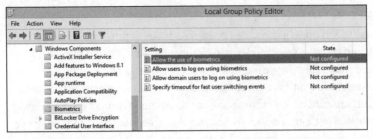

FIGURE 2-25 Using Group Policy to enable, disable, or limit the use of biometrics.

Distinguishing among workgroup vs. domain, homegroup, computer, and user authentication

In this section, you'll learn more about the differences among some similar technologies and network configurations, such as workgroup versus homegroup, workgroup versus domain, and credential caching versus Credential Manager.

Distinguishing among homegroups, workgroups, and domains

In almost all instances and scenarios, using a computer to complete tasks involves connecting to a network of some sort, even if it's just to access the Internet or to back up your work someplace other than your own PC. In homes, networked computers are often configured as homegroups. In a small business, the configuration is generally a workgroup. The purpose of both of these types of networks is frequently to share an Internet connection as well as files, folders, printers, and other resources. Domains are used in larger enterprises, which require more control and good protection of resource access. Domains are the only one of these three that employ AD DS to manage users, computers, and resources.

UNDERSTANDING HOMEGROUPS

A homegroup lets home users easily share documents, printers, and media with others on their private, local network. This is the simplest kind of network sharing and is limited in what permissions and restrictions can be placed on the data shared. By default, all users that join a homegroup (only one per network) have read-only access to what's already shared by others. Users can reconfigure this, however, allowing both read and write access, if desired.

When opting for a homegroup, users can:

- Create or join a homegroup from the prompt offered by Windows, assuming the network is configured as Private.

- Create or join a homegroup from the Network And Sharing Center, assuming the computers that want to join are Windows 7-based or Windows 8-based.

- Work through the applicable homegroup wizard to create or join a homegroup. Windows generates a random password other users will need to use to join.

- Share files from their original locations and their default libraries.

- Grant read-only or read/write access to the data they've shared.

- Limit access to only those network users who also have an account and password on their computers.

- Configure the same permissions for all network users, or set different permissions for individual users.

> ***NOTE*** **UNABLE TO CREATE OR ENABLE A HOMEGROUP?**
>
> A homegroup might not be able to be created or enabled for several reasons, and one reason is that IPv6 isn't enabled on a particular network computer. If a network is created, a user successfully types the password and joins, but if that user can't access any shared resources, more than likely the time set for the user's computer isn't the same as other homegroup computers. You resolve this problem by configuring the time properly.

Because you can create and join a homegroup using a wizard, detailing the steps in this text isn't really necessary. However, you should create a homegroup on your own local network and let other computers join it just so that you are familiar with the process. Note that users might already be joined to a homegroup because Windows detects and will prompt you to join existing homegroups automatically during setup.

UNDERSTANDING WORKGROUPS

In businesses where a little more control is required and a homegroup isn't the ideal configuration, a workgroup is used. A workgroup is a manual grouping of computers (almost any operating system will do, including Windows RT) that doesn't include an Active Directory domain controller but still offers security options. A workgroup exists on a single network segment. Securing data here is a distributed concept similar to a homegroup; each user decides what to share, how to share it, and with whom to share. Note that Windows doesn't create a password for joining the workgroup, nothing is shared automatically by default (except possibly the Public folders), and users join the workgroup from the System Properties dialog box from the Computer Name tab (see Figure 2-26). Click Change in System Properties and then enter the workgroup name in the Computer Name/Domain Changes dialog box.

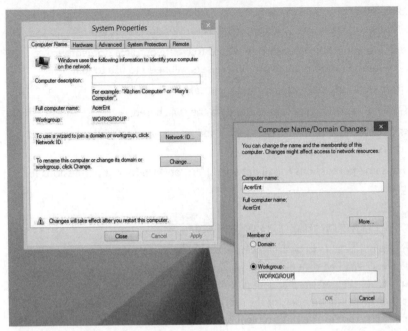

FIGURE 2-26 Joining a workgroup from the Computer Name/Domain Changes dialog box.

Because this section is about authorization, you need to consider that concept with regard to a workgroup. Users decide what to share, and then share it. The person who wants access to shared items must have an account on the sharing computer (or be given one). Accounts are stored in the sharing computer's Security Account Manager (SAM) database. Because each computer maintains its own local database, users who need to access resources on multiple workgroup computers must be authenticated on each. The problem with this is that as the network grows, so does the amount of work required to maintain and manage these accounts.

Here is an overview of how authorization works:

1. The first time a user tries to access a shared resource, he or she is asked for a user name and password.

2. The user name and password that are entered must be from an approved account on the sharing computer and must be listed in the SAM database. The user can opt to have Windows remember the password for next time.

3. The Local Security Authority (LSA) looks to the SAM database to see whether the account that was entered is valid.

4. If the account is valid, the user is granted access.

5. The same user who wants to access another shared resource on the same computer during the same session can do so without reentering the password.

6. If this same user wants to access a shared resource on another computer in the workgroup, the process must be repeated.

UNDERSTANDING DOMAINS

Companies and enterprises configure networks as domains. You couldn't successfully manage 100 computers by using a homegroup or workgroup, so a domain is an obvious choice for enterprise networks. Domain computers must be running a compatible Windows Professional, Business, Ultimate, or Enterprise edition to join the domain (for Windows 8.1, that's Windows 8.1 Pro or Enterprise). Windows RT devices can't join a domain.

Domains are configured with at least one AD DS domain controller that authenticates users centrally and secures network resources. These larger networks can contain additional servers that manage data storage, email, faxes, and printers; maintain database replications; and so on. Managing all resources as a whole is important to keeping everything secure and available for users and enables a simpler management solution for administrators. A large enterprise can have more than one domain. When multiple domains exist, a Global Catalog is used to locate objects on other domains.

EXAM TIP

No one's sure just how much you'll need to know about multiple domain configurations. To be safe, you should be familiar with what trees and forests are and how trusts can be created among the forests and domains.

Authentication in a domain is handled by AD DS, a database that contains objects such as user accounts, computers, groups, and so on. In this case, a network administrator creates user accounts, almost always puts those accounts into groups, and then assigns the desired permissions to the group. This makes managing users simpler than trying to manage users one at a time, and it enables administrators to deal with newly hired or recently fired employees. The authentication process includes and uses the Kerberos v5 authentication protocol to identify the user or the host. The Kerberos Key Distribution Center (KDC) uses the domain's AD DS as its security account database. AD DS is required for default Kerberos implementations within the domain or forest. If you aren't familiar with Kerberos v5, the TechNet article "Kerberos Authentication Overview" at *http://technet.microsoft.com/en-us/library/hh831553.aspx* offers a good explanation of how this works and offers links to additional resources.

Distinguishing between computer authentication and user authentication

The previous section discusses AD DS and authentication with regard to user accounts. Network administrators create these accounts. Users input their account credentials to log on to the domain, and authentication is handled by the applicable AD DS server and Kerberos v5. Computers that join domains automatically acquire a computer account. Like user accounts, computer accounts are used to authenticate the computer to allow it to access network and domain resources. Each computer account must be unique. A user doesn't have to do anything to cause the computer to be authenticated. Note that computers have passwords, that passwords are automatically managed, and if a computer password on a client is out of sync with AD DS then the computer can't authenticate.

Computer accounts are necessary for auditing, for control, and for grouping purposes. You can apply changes to computer accounts that affect whoever logs on to the computer and not the individual users. For instance, you can force policies regarding the desktop appearance, how updates are applied, and so on, and those policies will affect the computer and anyone who uses it.

Administrators can manage computer accounts in the same way they can user accounts— by adding, deleting, resetting, and disabling them in the Active Directory Users And Computers snap-in.

Understanding Secure Channel

When applications need network or Internet access, you have to ensure that the connection is secure. This is especially true if you are transmitting data over an untrusted network. You can use Transport Layer Security (TLS)/Secure Sockets Layer (SSL) security to authenticate servers and client computers and then use it to encrypt messages between them. These two protocols are included in the Secure Channel set of security protocols. TLS and SSL aren't interchangeable and SSL is the predecessor to TLS, but both protect against tampering and eavesdropping.

Secure Channel can authenticate an identity as well as provide a secure and private connection to another host by using encryption. It's also called Schannel and is mostly used for applications that require secure HTTP communications. Schannel is a Security Support Provider (SSP), and the TLS/SSL protocol uses a client/server model that's based on certificate authentication. This means you must also have a Public Key Infrastructure configured and available.

> **MORE INFO** **DISCOVERING SECURE CHANNEL**
>
> You can learn more about this feature on TechNet at *http://technet.microsoft.com/en-us/ library/hh831381.aspx*.

Exploring account policies

The weakest link when protecting computers that use a password as part of the authentication process is most often the password itself. The password could be nonexistent (not likely, especially with the advent of the Microsoft account for stand-alone computers), too short, too simple, too predictable, or the user might simply never change it. Often, users create and use the same password for multiple user IDs. This is a secondary weak link. To protect authentication in both workgroups and domains, you can create local policies and GPOs defining how passwords should be created, how often they can or must be changed, and what happens when a user fails to log on after attempting a specific number of times that you set. You can configure account policies in the Local Security Policy for a stand-alone computer or computers in a workgroup, and in Group Policy for domains. In Local Security Policy, Account Policies is listed first; click it and click Account Lockout Policy to see the options.

You can consider three account lockout policies, and in most instances they must be configured together:

- **Account Lockout Duration**   If you've configured an account lockout threshold and if that threshold is met, this setting defines how long (in minutes) the user will be locked out of the computer. A setting of 5 to 15 minutes is usually fine.

- **Account Lockout Threshold**   You must configure this to use the other options. This setting defines how many times a user can try to log on to the computer and fail before being locked out.

- **Reset Account Counter After**   This setting defines the number of minutes that must pass after a failed logon attempt before the failed logon attempt counter is reset to zero. If an account lockout threshold is defined, this must be less than or equal to the number of minutes set there.

Understanding credential caching

Read-only domain controllers (RODCs) host replicated read-only copies of a domain's AD DS database and the contents of the SYSVOL folder. RODCs aren't writable domain controllers. One purpose of an RODC is to selectively cache credentials to resolve issues that can arise when users try to authenticate from remote offices or behind perimeter networks. You need to be able to let users authenticate from a branch office if the writeable domain controller isn't available over a WAN link or other connection. You might also opt for cached credentials to resolve security issues that can occur in branch offices and over WAN links.

By default, an RODC doesn't store user credentials or computer credentials, except for its own computer account and one specialty account. If you want to use an RODC to cache credentials, you must configure it to do so. To do this, you configure a Password Replication Policy (PRP) for the RODC to allow for passwords to be cached. When cached, the RODC can authenticate those users when they can't authenticate in another way. To cache the credentials for the first time, a user must request authentication, and the RODC must get those credentials from the AD DC (to cache them).

Here is how it works:

1. When a user needs to authenticate with an RODC, the RODC can't perform the validation by default.

2. The RODC forwards the request to a writeable domain controller.

3. If the proper PRPs are configured, the RODC obtains the credentials from the authenticating domain controller.

4. The user is authenticated.

5. The next time the same user requests authentication, the RODC can authenticate from the cached credentials.

> **NOTE CACHED CREDENTIALS**
>
> Note that, by default, user account credentials are cached on the applicable computer. This is configurable via Group Policy. In high security environments, policy can dictate that users cannot sign into their computers unless they can contact a domain controller (thus no credential caching allowed).

Exploring Credential Manager

Using user names and passwords is a common way to authenticate users. Windows 8.1 comes with Credential Manager to help manage and maintain those passwords. Credential Manager saves the credentials users enter when they use their own computers to access network servers and resources on local networks (Windows Credentials) and can be used to back up and restore them. When prompted, users have to check the box Remember My Credentials, though, or else the credential won't be saved. Credential Manager also offers Credential Locker, which saves usernames and passwords associated with websites and Windows apps (Web Credentials). It saves all of these in an area called the Windows Vault.

> **NOTE SAVING CREDENTIALS**
>
> Credentials are saved in encrypted folders on the computer under the user's profile. Applications that support this feature, such as web browsers and Windows 8 apps, can automatically offer up the correct credentials to other computers and websites during the sign-in process.

If the username or password has been changed since the last time it was saved and access is unsuccessful, the user is prompted to type the new credentials. When access to the resource or website is successful, Credential Manager and Credential Locker overwrites what was there.

The saved usernames and passwords follow users when they move from one computer to another in a workgroup or homegroup, presuming they log on with their Microsoft accounts. However, this feature isn't enabled on domains for security reasons. You can open Credential Manager from Control Panel. Figure 2-27 shows Credential Manager.

Here are a few more things to know about Credential Manager:

- You can program Windows Store apps to use Credential Locker.
- Credential roaming requires the Microsoft account for synchronization.
- Credential roaming is enabled by default on non-domain–joined computers, and it is disabled on domain-joined computers.
- Credential Locker supports seamless sign in by using Windows Store apps that use Web Authentication Broker and remember passwords for services such as Twitter and LinkedIn.

FIGURE 2-27 Using Credential Manager to cache passwords.

Notice in Figure 2-27 that options exist to back up and restore credentials, but these options are available only when Windows Credentials is selected. When you click Back Up Credentials, you are prompted first to browse to a location to save the credentials to, name the file (it has a .crd extension), and then to press Ctrl+Alt+Del to continue the backup process on the Secure Desktop. There, you create a password for the file so that only you can access it.

To back up a single certificate, right-click the certificate, click All Tasks, and then click Export. Work through the wizard to select the format to use. This is the only way to back up a certificate and have the options shown in Figure 2-27 available. If you select more than one certificate, you'll have to choose from Personal Information Exchange or Microsoft Serialized Certificate Store.

Certificate import and export operations support four file formats:

- **Personal Information Exchange (PKCS #12)** This format supports secure storage of certificates, private keys, and all certificates in a certification path. The PKCS #12 format is the only file format that you can use to export a certificate and its private key.

- **Cryptographic Message Syntax Standard (PKCS #7)** This format supports storage of certificates and all certificates in the certification path.

- **Distinguished Encoding Rules (DER)-encoded binary X.509** This format supports storage of a single certificate. It doesn't support storage of the private key or certification path.

- **Base64-encoded X.509** This format supports storage of a single certificate. It doesn't support storage of the private key or certification path.

Knowing when to use a local account vs. a Microsoft account

The Microsoft account (what used to be called Windows Live ID) is a new way to log on to a Windows 8-based computer. This type of account enables users to sync specific settings to the cloud for the purpose of having access to those settings from other computers that they can log on to using that same Microsoft account. With a Microsoft account, users can also access their own cloud space, called OneDrive. Windows 8.1 comes with a OneDrive app, and OneDrive can be accessed from compatible applications, various web browsers, and File Explorer.

Users are prompted to create a Microsoft account when they set up their Windows 8-based computers. They can opt to do that, or they can decline and create a local account instead. A user might also create a local account if the computer can't access the Internet during setup (because they can't create or confirm the Microsoft account if no Internet access is available). Child accounts can also be created. Users generally opt to create a Microsoft account later even when they start with a local account, because many apps are inaccessible if the user is logged on with a local account. Users also can't get apps from the Store without a Microsoft account.

After a Microsoft account is created, users don't need to be connected to the Internet to log on in subsequent sessions. The account information is saved locally. If an Internet connection isn't available, the last saved settings are also applied because they are cached locally. You can switch from a local account to a Microsoft account from PC Settings.

A Microsoft account can be used in a domain, if it isn't restricted through Group Policy. If possible at your place of business, when connected, users will see the same desktop background, app settings, browser history, and so on that they see on their main computers at home (or in another office). Again, you make the change through PC Settings. There, you'll opt to connect your Microsoft account and work through the setup process.

Configuring Workplace Join

Personal devices have become part of the enterprise landscape, and if you don't already, at some point you need to be able to allow users to access network resources from them. This is how Workplace Join came about. Workplace Join enables users to have a single-sign-on experience and enables them to get to the resources they need. You also can manage and secure the devices. In Windows Server 2012 R2, you can use Workplace Join with Windows 8.1 and iOS devices.

Workplace Join uses the Device Registration Service (DRS), part of the Active Directory Federation Services role in Windows Server 2012 R2, to create a device object in AD DS and use a certificate to identify the device in the future. If you add Web Application Proxy, users can join your enterprise from any Internet-enabled location.

Various walkthrough guides are available on TechNet to help you use this technology to join devices. Here are two of those:

- "Walkthrough Guide: Workplace Join with a Windows Device": *http://technet.microsoft. com/en-us/library/dn280938.aspx*

- "Walkthrough Guide: Workplace Join with an iOS Device": *http://technet.microsoft.com/ en-us/library/dn280933.aspx*

Thought experiment
Creating and configuring authentication solutions

In this thought experiment, apply what you've learned about this objective. You can find answers to these questions in the "Answers" section at the end of this chapter.

You've been asked to create and configure a multifactor authentication solution that can be used to validate users in an enterprise domain. You've also been instructed to include digital certificates in that solution. Your client doesn't want to rely on a third-party CA, and instead wants to use the Active Directory Certificate Services (AD CS) in Windows Server 2012 R2. Answer the following questions regarding this task.

1. The network currently doesn't include a PKI infrastructure. Will you need to add it?

2. Where will the client certificates you create be stored?

3. Where will the trusted root certificates you create be stored?

4. What command can you run on a client computer in a Run dialog box to view the certificates stored on that machine?

Objective summary

- Multifactor authentication lets you further secure the authentication process with certificates, virtual smart cards, picture passwords, and biometrics by requiring more than one method of authentication before access is granted.

- Different networks exist for different needs. Homegroups enable simple sharing for home networks; workgroups let you share and manage shared data in a nondomain setting; and domains are used by larger enterprises and include Active Directory Domain Services (AD DS) to secure and manage authentication.

- You can further secure authentication by including Secure Channel, account policies, credential caching, and Credential Manager to help control access and manage logon credentials.

- Local accounts are good for homegroups and workgroups, but now even those networks rely on Microsoft accounts for authorization management. Microsoft accounts can also be incorporated into domains to sync settings such as desktop backgrounds.

- Workplace Join lets you enroll and control mobile devices on your domain for the purpose of letting your users bring their own devices to work.

Objective review

Answer the following questions to test your knowledge of the information in this objective. You can find the answers to these questions and explanations of why each answer choice is correct or incorrect in the "Answers" section at the end of this chapter.

1. Which two of the following Windows PowerShell commands can you use to manage a CA database?

   A. *Backup-CARoleService*

   B. *Restore-CARoleService*

   C. *Backup-CACertStore*

   D. *Restore-CACertStore*

2. Which two of the following technologies offers authentication protection, confidentiality of the machine and its contents, private keys for security, and encrypted card information that can't be mined or removed?

   A. Physical smart card

   B. A compatible TPM chip

   C. Virtual smart card

   D. A biometric fingerprint reader

   E. BitLocker Drive Encryption

3. You create a homegroup on one computer and join it from another. This process goes smoothly. However, when you try to access data shared with the homegroup from the second computer, you can't. What's most likely the problem?

   A. You aren't connected to the network.

   B. You aren't using BitLocker Drive Encryption.

   C. The time is configured incorrectly on the second computer.

   D. You aren't running a compatible version of Windows.

4. Which of the following network types is a distributed concept, in which users manage their own data sharing?

   A. Workgroup

   B. Homegroup

   C. Domain

   D. Workgroup or domain

5. You want to secure communications over an untrusted network for applications that need Internet access. You want to use TLS and SSL to achieve this. Which of the following technologies offers this? Must the solution include a PKI infrastructure?

   A. VPN; no

   B. Remote Desktop Services; yes

   C. App-V; no

   D. Secure Channel; yes.

6. You are trying to configure Group Policy to set an account lockout duration when users try and fail to authenticate at their computers after a specific number of events. The options are grayed out. Why?

   A. You must first configure the policy Account Lockout Threshold.

   B. You must first configure the policy Reset Account Counter After.

   C. You are trying to configure the policy for a workgroup computer, but these policies are available only in domains.

   D. You are in the Group Security Policy console and need to be in the Group Policy Editor.

7. Your users sometimes have problems when trying to authenticate from a branch office because they can't access the domain controller in the main office that's used to perform authentication tasks. Which of the following items should you configure?

   A. Account Policies

   B. Credential caching

   C. Password Replication Policies

   D. An RODC server

   E. Secure Channel

8. Can Credential Manager and Credential Locker be used to store passwords for Windows Store apps? What about for passwords saved for local network resources?

   A. Yes; no

   B. No; yes

   C. Yes; yes

   D. No; no

9. You want to allow your domain users to access the same desktop background, app settings, browser history, and so on that they see on their main computers at home (or in another office). What should you do?

   A. A Microsoft account would be optimal, but can't be used in a domain.

   B. Let the users associate their Microsoft accounts with their domain accounts.

   C. Use Workplace Join.

   D. Incorporate a Web Application Proxy server onto your network.

Objective 2.4: Support data storage

When users store their data, it must be secure and available. You can achieve this goal in many ways, from local to server storage, to storage in the cloud, to storage created from multiple places in the form of a pool or group. In this objective you'll learn about a few of these, including storage spaces, BranchCache, and OneDrive. But first, look at Distributed File System (DFS).

This objective covers how to:

- Support Distributed File System (DFS) clients, including caching settings
- Understand storage spaces, including capacity and fault tolerance
- Optimize data access by using BranchCache
- Support OneDrive

Supporting Distributed File System (DFS)

When you require your clients to save data on multiple drives, the process involved in saving and accessing that data can become quite cumbersome for them. If this is the case and if you want to simplify things, and you also want to maintain multiple copies of the data easily, you can use Distributed File System (DFS). DFS enables you to share folders that you want to use for client data storage from the various servers in your enterprise, and then group those folders into a single logical unit. When users save to this group of folders, it appears to them as though they are accessing only one folder (with subfolders as applicable). This enables you to make use of free data storage space available anywhere in your enterprise (and elsewhere) and doesn't confuse users or require them to know where you want them to store their data if multiple options are available to them.

REAL WORLD **USING DFS**

Suppose you work in a company that has three file servers, and each of those servers has shared folders that users access to save and retrieve data. Normally accessing the three servers means going to \\server1 or \\server2 or \\server3, which can be difficult for those users who are not tech-savvy. In another scenario, perhaps you have three mapped drives such as S:\ and T:\ and U:\, again, places where your users can save data. Whatever the case, you need to simplify this configuration for users.

You can with DFS. Instead of requiring users to know the paths to these folders or drives, you can provide users a single Universal Naming Convention (UNC) path such as \\corp that they can use to access all of the folders or mapped drives from a single place. This allows you to simplify things and to also maintain multiple copies of the data easily.

Don't confuse DFS with folder redirection, offline files, Storage Spaces, or roaming user profiles though; DFS is different from those in many ways.

You should be familiar with a few terms regarding DFS:

- **DFS Namespaces (DFSN or DFS-N)** Users see this folder namespace when they need to access the location they use to store files. It's a virtual view of the folders you've grouped. The file shares can be on different servers and in different sites. Each namespace you create appears to users as a single shared folder with subfolders.

- **DFS Replication (DFSR or DFS-R)** This is what enables you to synchronize folder contents between servers. This replication can occur across LAN or WAN network connections. DFS Replication uses a compression algorithm known as *remote differential compression (RDC)*, which detects changes to a file's data and replicates only the changed file blocks, rather than the entire file.

- **Link Target** This is the mapping destination of a link, which can be a UNC path, and is a link to a shared folder or another DFS path.

- **Referral** This is a list of targets (which users can't see) sent to a DFS client from DFS when users access a root or a link in the DFS namespace (see the next two bullets for more on this). The referral information is cached on the client for a specific amount of time that you can specify in the DFS configuration.

- **Link Referral** This referral contains a list of link targets for a specific link.

- **Root Referral** This referral contains a list of root targets for a particular root.

- **Referral cache** After a target is found, the referral is cached to the user's computer for subsequent requests. The entries here have a specified Time To Live, and clients won't ask for a new referral until this period has passed.

> **NOTE DFS NAMESPACES AND DFS REPLICATION**
>
> DFS Namespaces and DFS Replication are services in the File And Storage Services role for Windows Server 2012. No additional hardware or software is required for running DFS Management or using DFS Namespaces.

The objective for this exam includes a note about "client caching" and DFS, so take a look at that. You already know that referral information is cached on the client for a specific amount of time that you can set in the DFS configuration. You can make that specification in many ways including through the DFS Management MMC (part of the DFS Management Tools in RSAT). You can also use the command-line tool Dfsutil.exe. Here are some of the parameters you should be familiar with:

- */Cache* Use this to view or flush the Referral cache.

- */Target* Use this to display, create, or modify the link target.

- */diag* Use this to perform diagnostics.

- */pktflush* Use this to clear the DFS cache.

Understanding Storage Spaces

New to Windows 8-based computers, Storage Spaces lets you combine free space from multiple disks to create a new type of virtual disk for storing data. It does this by using the unallocated space on those disks to create a storage pool. This makes expanding the storage space easy simply by adding disks.

When you create a new storage pool, you create a new virtual disk. When you create that disk, you specify the size. With thin provisioning, the specified size can be greater than the size of the storage pool and you'll be prompted when additional space is needed. However, when you use fixed provisioning, the specified size cannot exceed the size of the storage pool.

Here are a few things to know before you get started:

- You can't use the disk that contains the operating system as part of the storage pool.
- Serial Advanced Technology Attachment (Serial ATA or SATA) or Serial Attached SCSI (SAS) connected disks are acceptable.
- RAID adapters, if used, must have all RAID functionality disabled.
- You can use USB drives, but USB 3.0 drives are recommended for best performance.
- USB 2.0 drives should be plugged directly into different USB controllers on your computer; don't use USB hubs.
- Various kinds of storage layouts for storage pools are available, including simple (no fault tolerance), mirror, and parity. A two-way mirror mirrors data on two drives; a three-way mirrors on three. Parity enables two drives to hold data and a third to hold parity information for fault tolerance. You can create a storage space from one disk, but you lose fault tolerance when you do.
- You can use Windows PowerShell to manage storage pools and disks. Review common PowerShell commands including *Set-PhysicalDisk*, *Repair-VirtualDisk*, and *Remove-PhysicalDisk*.
- You can use Storage Spaces in place of more expensive Storage Area Network (SAN) devices under the right circumstances.
- If you move a storage pool, you must keep the pool together.
- If you remove and then try to reuse a disk used in a storage pool, you must format it first.

> **MORE INFO** **LEARNING ABOUT STORAGE SPACES**
>
> Refer to this TechNet article to learn more about Storage Spaces: *http://technet.microsoft.com/en-us/library/hh831739*. To learn more about Storage Spaces in Windows 8.1, go to *http://windows.microsoft.com/en-us/windows-8/storage-spaces-pools*.

To use Storage Spaces, you must first create a storage pool:

1. Connect the disks to use. Format them before setup. (Or, make sure you're willing to let Windows do it during setup.)

2. Open Control Panel, click System And Security, and click Storage Spaces.

3. Click Create A New Pool And Storage Space (see Figure 2-28).

FIGURE 2-28   Creating a storage pool.

4. Select the drives to use and click Create Pool.

5. In the Create A Storage Space window, make additional configurations, such as the name of the pool, resilience type, capacity, and so on. Click Create Storage Space.

> **NOTE   CREATING A STORAGE SPACE**
>
> When creating a storage space, create a capacity larger than the installed drives to use a feature known as *thin provisioning*. When you do, you'll be prompted when more space is required.

For the types of storage spaces and pools you can create, make sure that you understand the differences among them and know when to use them to meet specific requirements (such as providing fault tolerance or limiting the amount of unused space) before taking the exam:

■ *Simple spaces* increase performance, but provide no fault tolerance. They're best for storing and managing temporary data and require at least one drive. (Two drives are required to increase performance.)

■ *Mirror spaces* increase performance and provide fault tolerance by replicating your data to more than one drive. Two-way mirrors protect you if one drive fails; three-way mirrors protect you if two of the three drives fail. Two-way mirror spaces require at least two drives, and three-way mirror spaces require at least five. This is because the file in its entirety is stored on three drives, and you'll need two more to provide fault tolerance.

■ *Parity spaces* are designed for efficiency. If you're asked about efficiency on the exam, check to see whether parity meets the other requirements. You'll need at least three drives. If you opt for a parity drive and one fails, make sure that the new drive is added before you remove the failed one.

Optimizing data access by using BranchCache

BranchCache is employed only when you have a main office and at least one branch office and when you also want to optimize how data passes between/among them. Using this technology to optimize involves transmitting data (think about very large files) from the main office to a branch office, and then caching the data somewhere at the branch office for others to access should they need it. This reduces traffic but also makes for a better end-user experience because cached data can be acquired more quickly than data traveling over a slow WAN link or a VPN. A system in place checks to see whether the data has changed since being cached to keep the cache current. This system involves the client authenticating at the BranchCache server in the main office and using metadata and hashes to determine whether the data is available and current and/or needs to be sent/resent. BranchCache also stores the data in the cache with encryption to secure it.

To configure BranchCache, you need to put a few things in place. For one, you need a server enabled for BranchCache at the main office. This is often referred to as a *content server*. You can use various servers for this, including various web servers, application servers, and even file servers. With that server in place, you need some way to cache the data at the branch office. You could do so by configuring a Windows Server 2012 server at the branch office (which you generally do for 50 or more clients), or you could allow your client computers to cache the information locally on their own systems (which you generally do for 50 or less). For the latter, the system that holds the cache for the branch office is the first client to download it. Creating a BranchCache server is called *hosted mode*. Enabling clients to cache the data is called *distributed mode*. You must configure Group Policy as applicable so that clients can use BranchCache and know where to get the cached data. (You can use a mix of hosted and distributed, choosing the desired option at each of your branch offices.)

You can enable BranchCache on a Windows Server 2012 server. You can also enable it by using this Windows PowerShell command:

```
Install-WindowsFeature BranchCache
```

Using Windows Server 2012, Windows 8, and Windows 8.1 clients here is important for many reasons, of which the following are just a few:

- Client configuration is automatic with this configuration.
- You can remotely manage BranchCache servers.
- Because Windows 7 clients require a special certificate that's compatible with TLS, they require more management and setup.

You'll likely opt for Windows PowerShell when managing BranchCache. You should be
familiar with a few commands listed in Table 2-5.

TABLE 2-5 Commands for managing BranchCache

Command	Purpose
Disable-BC	Disables BranchCache
Enable-BCDistributed *Enable-BCHostedServer* *Enable-BCLocal*	Enable BranchCache
Get-BCDataCache	Retrieves the BranchCache data cache
Get-BCStatus	Retrieves status information
Set-BCCache	Modifies a cache file configuration
Enable-BCHostedClient	Enables BranchCache on a Windows 8 client

You can view other commands at *http://technet.microsoft.com/library/hh848392.aspx*.

The BranchCache Group Policy settings are available from Computer Configuration,
Policies, Administrative Templates, Network, BranchCache. Figure 2-29 shows the setting Turn
On BranchCache. Note the others.

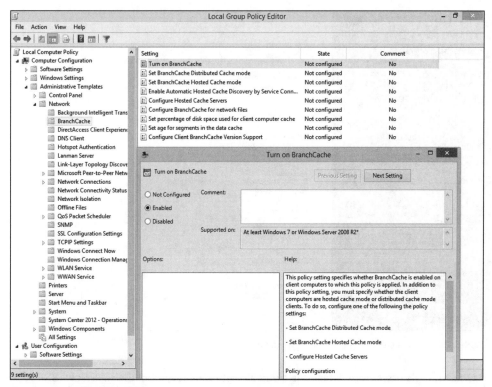

FIGURE 2-29 Use Group Policy to enable BranchCache clients.

> **NOTE UNDERSTANDING BRANCHCACHE**
>
> Spend some time reviewing BranchCache. You can find a good TechNet article that covers just about everything you'll need to know at *http://technet.microsoft.com/en-us/library/ hh831696.aspx*.

Supporting OneDrive

When you create and sign in with a Microsoft account, you can sync settings related to your Start screen, desktop, web browser, some passwords, language preferences, and so on to servers in the cloud. Whatever you opt to sync is applied to any computer you log on to later by using that account (although in a domain setting you'll have to connect the account first, with the blessing of your network administrator). You configure what to sync in PC Settings, OneDrive, Sync Settings (see Figure 2-30). Make sure that you are familiar with what can be synced here; you might be tested on it. (OneDrive is the new name for SkyDrive.)

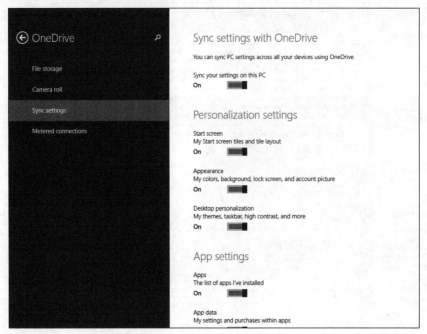

FIGURE 2-30 Clients can choose what to sync to OneDrive.

OneDrive lets users store data in the cloud almost seamlessly from their Windows 8.1 computers. OneDrive is an app on the Start screen and an option in the Navigation tab of File Explorer. Users can access data stored in OneDrive from virtually any device that has an Internet connection. Users can also share any part of what they've stored there with others, allowing them to read or read/edit the data. They need a Microsoft account and the applicable app or browser to access the data. Users can also access the files locally, when a connection isn't available.

Users can access OneDrive in a number of ways:

- **Via a web browser**   Browse to *http://onedrive.com* and log on to access, upload, share, and otherwise manage files and folders. You can also create and edit documents, presentations, notebooks, and so on here.

- **By using the OneDrive app in Windows**   Open the OneDrive app from the Start screen to access, upload, open, and manage files, and to create new folders.

- **By using the OneDrive app on smartphones**   You can view and open files, view recently accessed files, view and access shared files, and upload files. You can also create new folders and configure a few settings for uploading photos.

- **Via a desktop application**   You can access OneDrive from an application such as Microsoft Office 2013.

Setting up OneDrive involves simply logging on to the Windows 8-based computer with a Microsoft account; Windows does the rest. You should look at some configuration options right away, though. You can configure the option to access all files offline from the Settings charm (click Options) from inside the OneDrive app. This might be the first thing you'll want to configure if you have the available OneDrive space. (By default, users get 7 gigabytes (GB) of storage space, but you can buy more if you need it.)

EXAM TIP

For the exam, you need to know what can and can't be saved to OneDrive. You can save Windows settings, application settings, and some credentials, but you can't save your Xbox music purchases, apps, or even entire folders (such as your Documents or Pictures folder). You must upload files one at a time, although you can upload compressed folders.

Finally, you can configure OneDrive settings from the OneDrive website. Log on at *http://OneDrive.com,* click the Tools icon (see Figure 2-31) in the top-right corner, and then click Options (see Figure 2-31). Note the options that appear on the left side:

- **Storage**   Use this to view available storage space and buy more.
- **Plans**   Use this to view storage plans and select one.
- **Office File Formats**   Use this to choose a default format for Office documents: Microsoft Office Open XML Format (.docx, .pptx, .xlsx) or OpenDocumentFormat (.odt, .odp,. ods).
- **People Tagging**   This option lets you specify how people can tag you on OneDrive (Your Friends or Just You) and configure who can add people tags (Your Friends Who Can View Your Photo Albums or Don't Allow Anyone To Add People Tags).
- **Device Backups**   Use this to see all your devices and the date those devices where last backed up.

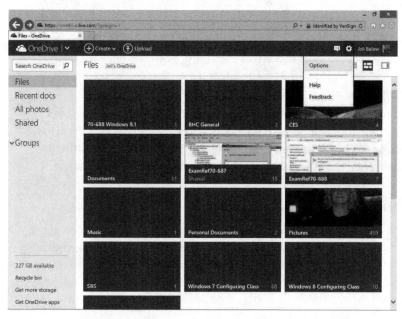

FIGURE 2-31   Users might prefer to access OneDrive from Internet Explorer.

Objective summary

- You can use DFS to group shared folders on domain servers for the purpose of combining free space while minimizing the work users must do to save their files there. You configure DFS on servers.

- Storage Spaces lets you combine free space from multiple disks to create a virtual disk for storing data. It's used on Windows 8.1 clients. This makes expanding the storage space easy, simply by adding disks.

- You can use BranchCache when you have a main office and at least one branch office and you often send large files across the VPN or WAN link between them. BranchCache enables you to cache files on either a branch server or branch clients to minimize transmissions.

- A Microsoft account lets a user sync settings related to the Start screen, desktop, web browser, some passwords, language preferences, and so on to servers in the cloud. Whatever you opt to sync is applied to any computer you log on to later with that account. This must be made available to clients by administrators in a domain.

Objective review

Answer the following questions to test your knowledge of the information in this objective. You can find the answers to these questions and explanations of why each answer choice is correct or incorrect in the "Answers" section at the end of this chapter.

1. What command would you use with fsutil.exe to clear the DFS cache on a client computer?

   A. */cacheflush*

   B. */cache*

   C. */pktflush*

   D. */clearcache*

2. Which of the following are suitable disk types that you can use with Storage Spaces?

   A. USB 2.0

   B. USB 3.0

   C. Serial ATA

   D. Serial Attached SCSI

   E. All of the above

3. You are configuring BranchCache and have about 30 computers in one of your branch offices. The computers in that office are running Windows 8.1, are equipped with large hard drives, and have lots of RAM. How should you configure BranchCache?

   A. In hosted mode

   B. In distributed mode

   C. In ad hoc mode

   D. None of the above

4. Which command-line tool (command) would you use to configure BranchCache in distributed mode?

   A. *netsh branchcache set service mode=DISTRIBUTED*

   B. *netsh branchcache mode=DISTRIBUTED*

   C. *Enable-BCDistributed*

   D. *Enable-BCLocal*

5. Your clients want to use their smartphones and tablets to access OneDrive. Which of the following would you suggest they use to access documents and other files?

   A. The OneDrive app for Windows and a web browser

   B. The OneDrive app for smartphones and a web browser

   C. A web browser and a desktop application

   D. The OneDrive app for smartphones and a desktop application

Objective 2.5: Support data security

This last objective focuses on data security. Here you'll learn about securing data through share permissions, NTFS, and Dynamic Access Control, as well as using EFS, controlling access to removable media, and using technologies such as BitLocker and BitLocker To Go.

> **This objective covers how to:**
> - Manage permissions, including Share, NTFS, and Dynamic Access Control (DAC)
> - Support Encrypting File System (EFS), including Data Recovery Agent
> - Control access to removable media
> - Support BitLocker and BitLocker To Go, including Data Recovery Agent and Microsoft BitLocker Administration and Monitoring (MBAM)

Managing permissions

In this section you'll learn about three kinds of permissions: Share, NTFS, and Dynamic Access Control (DAC). Share and NTFS were also covered in *Exam Ref 70-687: Configuring Windows 8.1* under the "Configure file and folder access" objective; here, they are listed under the "Support data security" objective, so I'm not sure how much the objectives vary. That said, what you'll see here regarding Share and NTFS is the same thing discussed in the other book, but condensed. DAC is new to this exam.

If any of this isn't familiar to you, make sure you review the concepts on TechNet before taking the exam.

Applying Share permissions

You apply Share permissions when the operating system is configured with FAT or FAT32, or anytime you share a folder on a computer. Only three shared permissions—Read, Change, and Full Control—are available from the Sharing tab of the resource's Properties dialog box. These sharing options don't offer a lot of control, but they do offer some. Share permissions help you manage user access to network resources but offer no security when a user logs on locally.

Share permissions have the following characteristics:

- They apply only to users who gain access to the resource over the network; they don't apply to users who log on locally. To protect a resource in these cases, you must use NTFS to set permissions.
- Share permissions are the only way to secure network resources on FAT and FAT32 volumes, because NTFS permissions aren't available on those volumes.
- They specify the maximum number of users who are allowed to access the shared resource or folder over the network.

- When both Share and NTFS permissions are applied, the cumulative permissions for both sets are compared, and the most restrictive permission is applied.

Table 2-6 shows the Share permissions and their descriptions.

TABLE 2-6 Share permissions and their descriptions

Share permission	Description
Read	Display folder names, file names, and attributes; process program files; access other folders inside the shared folder
Change	Perform all read actions; create and add files to folders; change and append data to files; change file attributes; delete folders and files
Full Control	Perform all change permissions; change file permissions; take ownership of files

Here are a few more things to know about share permissions:

- Share permissions are completely separate from NTFS permissions.

- Share permissions are the simplest permissions you can configure.

- On networks that employ NTFS, most often you simply grant the Share permission Full Control to Everyone, and then configure the desired NTFS permissions as desired. When both Share and NTFS are applied, the most restrictive wins—in this case, the NTFS permission.

- NTFS permissions on a subfolder inherit the permissions assigned to the parent folder. Share permissions don't combine in the same way. Succinctly, Share permissions applied to a folder that sits inside another folder don't inherit the parent folder's permissions. They use the permissions explicitly assigned to the folder in question.

Applying NTFS permissions

Because NTFS permissions are so much more robust than Share permissions, when the file system is NTFS, administrators make the most of it. They generally set the Share permissions for Everyone to Full Control and configure the NTFS permissions as desired. You configure NTFS from the Security tab of the resource's Properties dialog box. Remember, the more restrictive of the two types of permissions is applied to the resource when both exist, so it doesn't matter that the Share permissions gives everyone unlimited access as long as NTFS is configured not to. NTFS also offers the ability to assign disk quotas, encrypt files and folders, and audit object access. These features aren't available on FAT or FAT32 drives. Note that if Deny permission is applied, it overrides other permissions for a resource.

UNDERSTANDING PERMISSION TERMINOLOGY AND RULES

Any protected element or resource has an access control list (ACL). This is basically just a list of permissions that have been applied to the element or resource. The individual permissions applied are access control entries (ACEs). Every ACE has at least one security principal, which is the user, group, or computer given permissions, along with the permissions that have been configured for it or them. This means that permissions are stored with the protected resource; they aren't stored with the user, group, or computer that's granted access.

You can use the basic permissions to create very specific access options to a shared resource. You can grant a single user full control to a resource and at the same time grant all users in the Users group only Read access. You can configure it so that a specific person or group of persons can't access the resource at all, or that an entire group, such as HomeUsers, can read, write, list folder contents, and read and process while using the resource but can't modify or take ownership of it. The scenarios are almost endless.

If a user is configured permissions to a resource from more than one place, the permissions granted are cumulative. For example, if Bob is a member of the Users group, which has only the NTFS permission Read, but he's also a member of the Sales group, which has the NTFS permission Modify, Bob can both read and modify. Remember, Share permissions are cumulative and NTFS permissions are cumulative, and if both exist, the more restrictive of the results of these are applied. If Deny is assigned to user from anywhere though, they can't access the resource.

EXAM TIP

Allow permissions are cumulative. Deny permissions override Allow permissions. Explicit permissions take precedence over inherited permissions. You will likely see a question on the exam that outlines a scenario that includes all of these factors, so make sure you know how to calculate the effective permissions when multiple permissions exist.

UNDERSTANDING BASIC AND ADVANCED PERMISSIONS

Basic permissions are combinations of advanced permissions. Table 2-7 shows the six basic permissions from the Security tab of any NTFS resource's Properties dialog box, shown in Figure 2-32.

TABLE 2-7 Basic permissions

Permission	Description
Full Control	Modify, take ownership, delete items, and perform all other actions listed for the permissions listed next
Modify	Delete the folder, modify the file, delete the file, and perform other actions for Write and Read & Execute
Read & Execute	Navigate through folders, run applications, and perform actions for Read and List Folder Contents
List Folder Contents	View the names of the files and subfolders in a folder

Permission	Description
Read	See files and subfolders, read the contents of a file, view ownership, permissions and attributes for a file or folder
Write	Create new files and subfolders inside a folder, modify folder attributes, view the ownership and permission for a folder or file, modify file attributes, and write over a file

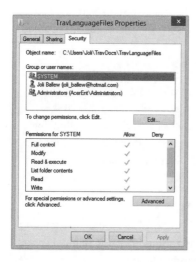

FIGURE 2-32 The Security tab of a resource offers options to personalize security options.

You can view all 14 advanced permissions by navigating to the Advanced Security Settings For window for any NTFS resource. You should know the names of these advanced permissions, how to find them, and how they protect the element. From this window you can also view the assigned permissions, including Share permissions, and you can view the calculated "effective access" from the same-named tab. To get to this window and view these settings and options, follow these steps:

1. Right-click any shared folder and click Properties.

2. Click the Security tab.

3. Click Advanced.

4. Click any permission entry and click View. (Notice the option to disable inheritance. Keep this location in mind when you read the next section.)

5. From the resulting Permissions Entry For window you can view the basic permissions assigned to this group.

6. Click Show Advanced Properties. A list of assigned advanced permissions appears.

UNDERSTANDING INHERITANCE

Permissions generally run from top to bottom of any folder hierarchy. So if you grant the NTFS Read access to a folder for a user group and then create a subfolder there, the same permissions are applied to it for the same user group. If it didn't work this way, assigning permissions would be nearly impossible.

Sometimes you might need to turn off inheritance for a folder or other element. Disable Inheritance is an option. If you would prefer not to disable inheritance but instead need to deny access to a specific person or group, you can assign the Deny permission as applicable.

> **NOTE ASSIGNING CONTRADICTING EXPLICIT PERMISSIONS**
>
> You can assign contradicting explicit permissions when inheritance causes a problem. For example, if the entire Sales group is denied access to a folder but a single member of the group should have access to it (perhaps the CFO of Sales), you can explicitly assign that one user account the Allow permission for Full Control on the resource. Explicit permissions like these override inherited permissions and thus resolve the problem quite easily.

UNDERSTANDING MOVE, COPY, AND PERMISSION INHERITANCE

Sometimes you need to copy or move an NTFS-protected element. When you do, depending on the circumstances, permissions are sometimes retained and sometimes not. In most cases, the resource inherits the NTFS permission assigned to the parent folder.

Table 2-8 explains how inheritance and move and copy work.

TABLE 2-8 How inheritance works with move and copy

If you...	Result
Copy NTFS files or folders from one location to another on the same NTFS volume...	The resource inherits its new parent folder's permissions.
Copy NTFS files or folders from one location to another on a different NTFS volume...	The resource inherits its new parent folder's permissions.
Move NTFS files or folders from one location to another on the same NTFS volume...	The existing permissions move with them.
Move NTFS files or folders from one location to another on a different NTFS volume...	They inherit permissions from the new parent folder on the new volume.
Copy or move NTFS files or folders to a FAT or FAT32 drive...	They lose all NTFS permissions because those aren't supported on those file systems.

USING ICACLS.EXE

The Icacls.exe command lets you configure basic and advanced permissions from an elevated command prompt. You can view all Icalcs.exe parameters on TechNet at *http://technet.micro-soft.com/en-us/library/cc753525.aspx*. You should be ready for exam questions based on this, so it's a good idea to review this article.

Generally, the Icacls.exe command is used as follows:

```
icacls.exe <file name> /grant
```

or

```
Icalcs.exe <file name> /deny
```

This command uses various parameters, including but not limited to the following:

- *F* for full access
- *M* for modify
- *RX* for read and execute
- *R* for read only
- *W* for write
- *MA* for maximum allowed
- *T* to process the command on all files and subfolders inside the *<file name>*
- *C* to continue, even if errors occur

UNDERSTANDING RESOURCE OWNERSHIP

Locking everyone out of a resource is possible. When that happens, the resource is said to be *orphaned*. A resource might also be orphaned if the user who originally created it is no longer available to provide access (perhaps to a confidential file or folder). To access the resource, you need to take ownership of it as an administrator. To do so, click Change in the Advanced Security Settings For window.

EXAM TIP

You might be asked on the exam what you should do if you lock yourself out of an element, and the answers might only include doing so with *icacls*. First you must open an elevated command prompt, then you can use the command *icacls <file name> /reset* along with additional parameters as desired (perhaps */C* to ignore errors).

Using Dynamic Access Control (DAC)

Windows Server 2012 and Windows 8 introduced Dynamic Access Control (DAC) and its associated elements. DAC lets administrators apply permissions and restrictions in new ways, which can vary for each device from which they access a resource. For example, it might be okay with you if a user who's sitting at her desk and using her desktop computer has access to sensitive corporate data. However, it might not be okay if that same user wants to access the data from a tablet over a VPN, the Internet, or even DirectAccess. You might not want users to access a sensitive resource if they are using devices that don't meet your security requirements either. Thus, DAC lets you dynamically control user access based on various factors, including what kind of device a person is using.

Features and concepts of Dynamic Access Control include the following:

- **Central access rules**   These rules can be created for groups, user claims, device claims, and resource properties. Rules protect resources.
- **Central access policies**   These policies contain conditional expressions (as discussed shortly in "Expressions" just below). Expressions can be almost anything from the current security state of the device, group membership, location, and more, and you can create polices based on these to protect resources.
- **Claims**   A claim is simply a single bit of information about a user, such as an AD DS attribute associated with a user, a computer, a device, or a resource. Multiple claims can be used to protect resources.
- **Expressions**   You set these conditions to control access management. They can include the state of the device, its location, and the groups the user belongs to.
- **Proposed permissions**   These let you propose permissions before actually applying them so that you can more accurately determine the effect of those changes before you apply them.

Learn more about DAC at *http://technet.microsoft.com/en-us/library/dn408191.aspx*.

Supporting Encrypting File System (EFS)

You can use both Encrypting File System (EFS) and Data Recovery Agents to protect sensitive data. EFS can protect data, and a Data Recovery Agent (DRA) can help you recover it if the encryption key is lost or the machine compromised.

> **MORE INFO   PLANNING FOR THE DRA**
>
> A DRA has its own certificate and that certificate is added to all encrypted content when the DRA is created. It is important to plan ahead when using a DRA and understand what happens in specific scenarios. For instance, problems ensue when a scenario like this occurs: You deploy EFS and users begin encrypting data. You later realize that you forgot to add a DRA and you add the DRA after the fact. A week later, a user leaves the company and you try to recover the user's EFS data but you can't. This is because the DRA was created after the data was encrypted. To resolve this, you'd need to go out and touch every single encrypted file with the command *cipher.exe /u*. There's more on the Cipher.exe command later in this chapter.

Using encryption

Encryption protects data from unauthorized access when other security measures fail. Often, failure has to do with someone gaining physical access to a machine and having the knowledge and time to figure out how to access its data. This type of breach can occur in many ways; however, with Encrypting File System (EFS), the public and private keys generated during encryption ensure that only the user who encrypted the file can decrypt it. Technically, encrypted data can be decrypted only if the user's *personal encryption certificate* is available, which is generated through the private key. Another user can't access this key, nor can anyone who tries to access data to copy or move it who doesn't have the proper credentials.

> **NOTE PKI AND AES**
>
> The public and private keys generated when data is encrypted are the basis of Windows Public Key Infrastructure (PKI). For more information about PKI, search for PKI on TechNet. Also, EFS uses the Advanced Encryption Standard (AES), which uses a 256-bit key algorithm, an industry standard, and can be used to encrypt non-system volumes or only selected files and folders.

Here's a little more about EFS:

- The process of encryption and decryption happens on the fly and is invisible to users. Encryption occurs when you close files; decryption occurs when you open them.

- EFS can be used only on NTFS volumes and isn't available on any form of FAT.

- EFS keys aren't assigned to a computer; instead, they are assigned to a specific user. This means another user logging on to the computer using his or her own user account has no access to the other user's private key and can't access the other user's data.

- Even a hacker who can sit down at a computer and access an option to copy protected files will receive an Access Denied message.

- You can't use EFS and compression together. It's one or the other.

- After a file or folder is encrypted, File Explorer displays it in green.

Configuring EFS is an objective on Exam 70-687, Configuring Windows 8.1, so I'll discuss it only briefly here. To encrypt a shared folder, right-click it, click Properties, and click Advanced on the General tab of the Properties dialog box. Select the option to encrypt the folder. You can use this same dialog box to remove encryption if you want to later. Be sure to back up your encryption key when prompted.

Performing backup and recovery

You can use CertMgr to recover your EFS-encrypted files by importing your EFS certificate backup. Like with exporting certificates, you use a wizard to do so. To get started from the CertMgr window, select the Personal folder, click Action, and then click All Tasks. From there, select Import. Work through the prompts to import the required data.

You also can use the command line to manage encryption. Use Cipher.exe to perform encryption and decryption tasks (you might see this command on the exam). For more information about Cipher.exe, refer to *http://technet.microsoft.com/en-us/library/cc771346.aspx*. Here are a few of the most common parameters used with the command:

- */d* to decrypt specified files and directories.

- */s:<directory>* to perform the specified operation on all subdirectories in the specified directory.
- */c* to display information about an encrypted file.
- */u* to touch all encrypted files on the local drives.
- */u /n* to find encrypted files.
- */?* to display help.
- */x* to back up your encryption keys (see Figure 2-33). Click OK here to type the name to give the new file and a password. The file has a .pfx extension. (To restore your EFS key, double-click the .pfx file and run the resulting wizard.)
- */r:<nameof recoveryagent>* to create a new recovery data agent. This creates two files ending in .CER and .PFX.

FIGURE 2-33 Use the Cipher.exe command to back up encryption keys.

To create a recovery agent using the Cipher.exe command on a non-domain joined Windows 8 Enterprise computer, follow these steps:

1. Open an elevated command prompt.
2. Type **cipher.exe /x** and press Enter.
3. Follow the prompts to name the file and apply a password.
4. Type **cipher.exe /r:IamARecoveryAgent** (or something similar) and press Enter.
5. Follow the prompts to complete the process by creating a password.
6. Locate the file that contains your recovery keys. Look in C:\Windows\System32 if a search doesn't provide results quickly.
7. Double-click the file and follow the prompts to complete the certificate import process. Click Finish when complete, taking note of what's listed (see Figure 2-34).

FIGURE 2-34 Work through the wizard to complete the import process.

8. Using an Administrator account, open the Local Group Policy Editor.

9. Navigate to Local Computer Policy, Windows Settings, Security Settings, Public Key Policies, Encrypting File System.

10. Right-click Encrypting File System and click Add Data Recovery Agent.

11. Work through the wizard and click Browse Folders when prompted to locate the .cer file you created earlier.

12. Click Open and Yes, click Next, and click Finish. You'll see the new certificate, as shown in Figure 2-35.

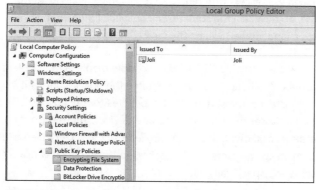

FIGURE 2-35 A new data recovery agent has been added.

Controlling access to removable media

Users commonly carry USB flash drives with them everywhere they go. Having access to a portable drive means users can easily take data with them without having to carry a laptop, connect to a network or domain, transfer data to a tablet, or access a cloud drive. Unfortunately, this is also a common way for viruses to spread and for sensitive data to be taken off premises (and potentially lost or stolen). In an even worse scenario, a malicious user could access another's computer and copy data without anyone knowing, if the opportunity arises because a workstation was left unattended or unlocked. Beyond USB drives, users can also copy data to CDs, DVDs, and even memory cards.

Deciding who can use these kinds of drives to transfer data is difficult. Some employees will need this ability; some won't. You'll have to take careful inventory and decide which employees fit into these two groups and configure your GPOs accordingly. Whatever you decide, the option to configure settings for removable storage access, whether on a local machine or on a domain server, is available in the Group Policy Management Editor.

To access removable access policies, follow these steps:

1. Open the Group Policy Management Editor (gpedit.msc).

2. Navigate to Computer Configuration, Policies, Administrative Templates, System, Removable Storage Access. Notice the options.

   Alternatively, to configure this for an individual user, navigate to User Configuration, Policies, Administrative Templates, System, Removable Storage Access.

3. Double-click the setting to configure. To enable the setting, click Enable.

4. Click OK.

EXAM TIP

What can a remotely logged on user access with regard to removable media? Read from USB and DVD only. Of course, on the exam the scenario will be much longer and more complex, but the end question (and answer) will be the same.

Take some time now to review the available GPOs for removable media, and double-click each entry to see what each offers. You need to be able to name the policies and know what they do if you enable them. For instance, the setting All Removable Storage Classes: Deny All Access lets you block access to all classes of removable storage devices, and this policy takes precedence over all policy settings for individual classes. Similarly, CD And DVD: Deny Read/Write/Execute Access, if enabled, prevents users from all access to the CD or DVD drivers in the computer, or, only the access you specifically allow or deny.

Supporting BitLocker and BitLocker To Go

BitLocker Drive Encryption lets you encrypt entire hard disks and disk volumes, which includes the Windows operating system drive, user files, and system files. You can use BitLocker to protect 32-bit and 64-bit computers running Windows 7 or later client operating systems (Professional and higher) and Windows server-based operating systems (Windows Server 2008 R2 and later). On computers with Trusted Platform Module (TPM) version 1.2 or 2.0, BitLocker can also ensure that data is accessible only if the computer's startup features and settings haven't been compromised (altered) and if the disk is still installed in the original computer.

BitLocker To Go lets you protect removable USB devices with BitLocker Drive Encryption. These devices can be flash drives; Secure Digital (SD) cards; removable hard disks formatted with NTFS; or Fat16, FAT32, or exFat file systems. Just like BitLocker, users must input a password or a smart card with a PIN to unlock the drive. It also can be unlocked automatically, with administrator approval. TPM isn't required for these kinds of drives because there's no such thing as a "startup" device like there is on a laptop, tablet, or desktop computer.

After you incorporate BitLocker or BitLocker To Go into your enterprise, you need to be able to recover protected disks and devices when the need arises, and you need to have something in place to administer and manage those disks and devices. This is where recovery agents and Microsoft BitLocker Administration and Monitoring (MBAM) come into play.

Using BitLocker

BitLocker provides one more level of protection for your users and their devices. When using BitLocker, you can require users to enter a password to unlock the drive when they want to use it. However, you also can require multifactor authentication, perhaps by adding a smart card or a USB drive with a startup key on it, on computers with a compatible TPM. You can manage BitLocker through Group Policy. For instance, you can require that BitLocker be enabled before the computer can be used to store data.

> **NOTE ENABLING BITLOCKER BEFORE DEPLOYING THE OPERATING SYSTEM**
>
> You can enable BitLocker before you deploy the operating system. When you do, you can opt to encrypt used disk space only or encrypt the entire drive.
>
> Two partitions are required to run BitLocker because pre-startup authentication and system integrity confirmation must occur on a separate partition from the drive that is encrypted.

You need to read all you can about BitLocker on TechNet, because this chapter doesn't have enough room to discuss everything. You can start with an overview at *http://technet. microsoft.com/en-us/library/hh831507.aspx#BKMK_Overview*. Concentrate on the following:

- **The requirements for hardware and software**   These include TPM versions, BIOS configuration, firmware requirements, drive size, and so on.

- **How to tell whether your computer has a TPM**   As administrator, you can enter **TPM.msc** in a Run dialog box. End users can access Control Panel and click All Items, open BitLocker Drive Encryption, and see if they can turn on BitLocker. If a TPM isn't found, you have to set the required Group Policy setting (Require Additional Authentication At Setup), which is located in Computer Configuration, Policies, Administrative Templates, Windows Components, BitLocker Drive Encryption, Operating System Drives. You must enable this, and then select the Allow BitLocker Without A Compatible TPM check box (see Figure 2-36).

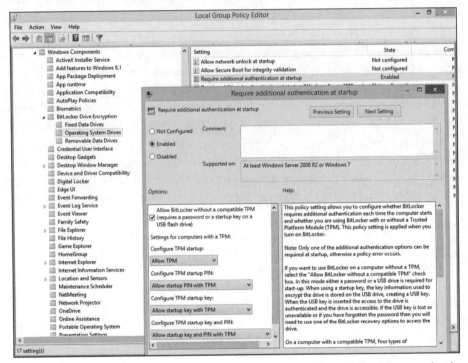

FIGURE 2-36   You can configure BitLocker settings from the Local Group Policy Editor on a local machine.

NOTE **ENABLING BITLOCKER ON AN OPERATING SYSTEM DRIVE WITHOUT A COMPATIBLE TPM**

You can enable BitLocker on an operating system drive without a compatible TPM only if the BIOS or Unified Extensible Firmware Interface (UEFI) can read from a USB flash drive in the startup environment. This is because BitLocker requires a startup key. If you do this, though, you can't take advantage of the pre-startup system integrity verification or multi-factor authentication.

- **The credentials required to configure BitLocker**   Only administrators can manage fixed data drives, but standard users can manage removable data drives (the latter can be disabled in Group Policy). Standard users can also change the PIN or password on operating system drives they have access to via BitLocker.

- **How to automate BitLocker deployment in an enterprise**   One way is to use the command-line tool Manage-bde.exe. Using this tool in your own work is detailed later in this section. Other ways include using WMI and Windows PowerShell scripts.

- **The reasons BitLocker might start in recovery mode**   Reasons include disabling the TPM, making changes to the TPM firmware, making changes to the master boot record, not setting the PIN after enabling on a drive and PC with a TPM, and so on.

- **How to manage recovery keys**   Recovery keys let you access a computer if BitLocker won't allow access. You can store these keys for fixed drives in many ways, including saving them to a folder, saving them to your Microsoft account online, printing them, and storing the keys on multiple USB drives. Active Directory can be used too and is the most important storage location.

CONFIGURING BITLOCKER FROM CONTROL PANEL

You need to know a few more things before you configure BitLocker. The first time you enable BitLocker, you'll be prompted to create a startup key, which is used to encrypt and decrypt the drive. This key can be stored on a USB drive or the TPM chip. If you opt for USB, every time you want to access the computer you'll have to insert that USB drive and enter the key. If a compatible TPM chip is used, the key retrieval is automatic. You can also opt for a PIN, which can be created only after BitLocker is enabled. If you lose the startup key, you'll have to use a recovery key to unlock the drive. This is a 48-digit number that can be stored in numerous ways, including on a USB drive.

Protecting encrypted data via BitLocker involves five authentication methods, which consist of various combinations of TPM, startup PIN, and startup keys, or just a TPM or just a startup key:

- **TPM + startup PIN + startup key**   This is the most secure combination but requires three authentication tasks. The encryption key is stored on the TPM chip, but an administrator must type a PIN and insert the startup key (available on a USB drive).

- **TPM + startup key**   The encryption key is stored on the TPM chip. An administrator must insert a USB flash drive that contains a startup key.

- **TPM + startup PIN**   The encryption key is stored on the TPM chip. An administrator must enter a PIN.

- **Startup key only**   An administrator must insert a USB flash drive with the startup key on it. The computer doesn't have to have a TPM chip. The BIOS must support access to the USB flash drive before the operating system loads.

- **TPM only**   The encryption key is stored on the TPM chip, and no administrator logon is required. TPM requires that the startup environment hasn't been modified or compromised.

Also, the drive that contains the operating system must have two partitions, the system partition and the operating system partition, both of which must be formatted with NTFS.

To configure BitLocker and encrypt the operating system drive on a Windows 8.1 computer, follow these steps:

1. Open Control Panel, change the view to Small Icons or Large Icons, and click BitLocker Drive Encryption.

2. Click Turn On BitLocker. (If you receive an error that no TPM chip is available, enable the required Group Policy setting, as shown earlier in Figure 2-35.)

3. Choose how to unlock your drive at startup. For this example, choose Enter A Password (see Figure 2-37).

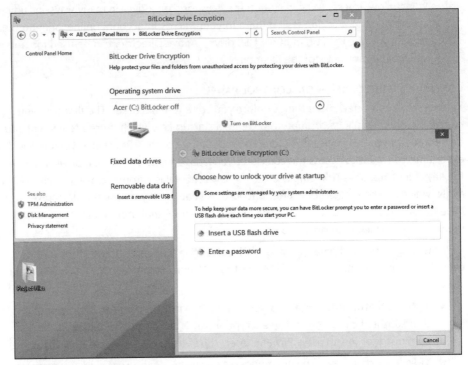

FIGURE 2-37 Enabling BitLocker on a fixed drive.

4. Enter the password and reenter to confirm, and then click Next.

5. Choose to save the password. For this example, choose Save To Your Microsoft Account. Click Next. (In this instance, you can perform this step again to perform a secondary backup before moving on.)

6. Choose to either encrypt the used disk space or the entire drive. Click Next.

7. Leave Run BitLocker System Check selected, and click Continue.

8. Restart your computer if prompted; otherwise click Start Encrypting.

Once encryption has started (or completed), return to the Control Panel and review the BitLocker window. From there you can perform additional tasks, including backing up your recovery key, changing your password, removing the passwords, and turning off BitLocker. The icon next to the options indicate which require administrator approval.

EXAM TIP

I'm not sure how many, if any, questions you'll see on the exam about the available Group Policy settings for BitLocker and BitLocker To Go. However, being prepared is wise. Be sure at least to scan the available options from a Local Group Policy Editor console: Computer Configuration, Administrative Templates, Windows Components, BitLocker Drive Encryption. You'll find three folders—Fixed Data Drives, Operating System Drives, and Removable Data Drives—as well as a few stand-alone options when the BitLocker Drive Encryption container is selected.

CONFIGURING BITLOCKER USING COMMAND-LINE TOOLS

You don't have to use Control Panel to manage BitLocker Drive Encryption: you can work from a command line. A few commands you can use turn BitLocker on or off, specify unlock mechanisms, update recovery methods, and unlock BitLocker-protected data drives. Many of these commands are used in large enterprises and not applicable to this objective; however, you might use several parameters with the *manage-BDE* command, including but not limited to the following:

- ***-status***   Use this for information about the attached drives, including their BitLocker status, size, BitLocker version, key protector, and lock status.

- ***-on***   This parameter encrypts the drive and turns on BitLocker. It's used with a drive letter such as C: that follows the *-on* parameter.

- ***-off***   This parameter decrypts and then turns off BitLocker. It's used with a drive letter such as C: that follows the *-off* parameter.

- ***-pause* and *-resume***   Use *-pause* with a drive letter to pause encryption; use *-resume* with a drive letter to resume encryption.

- ***-lock* and *-unlock***   Use these parameters with a drive letter to lock and unlock.

- ***-changepin***   Use this to change the PIN for the BitLocker-protected drive.

- ***-recoverypassword***   Use this to add a numerical password protector.

- ***-recoverykey***   Use this to add an external key protector for recovery.

- ***-password***   Use this to add a password key protector.

You can also use Windows PowerShell to manage BitLocker. There is a BitLocker PowerShell module with 13 cmdlets available. For more information refer to this article on TechNet: *http://technet.microsoft.com/en-us/library/jj649829.aspx*.

Configuring BitLocker To Go

BitLocker To Go lets you protect removable USB devices with BitLocker Drive Encryption. These devices can be flash drives, Secure Digital (SD) cards, or removable hard disks formatted with NTFS, Fat16, FAT32, or exFat file systems. The process to create a BitLocker To Go drive is similar to the process used to encrypt a fixed disk using BitLocker. Just insert the USB drive, open Control Panel, access the BitLocker window, and then under Removable Data Drives – BitLocker To Go, work through the setup process.

As noted in an Exam Tip earlier, you should familiarize yourself with the available BitLocker and BitLocker To Go Group Policy settings. You can locate them in the Group Policy Management Editor in Computer Configuration, Policies, Administrative Templates, Windows Components, BitLocker Drive Encryption. The BitLocker To Go options are available in the Removable Data Drives container. The eight items listed are summarized in Table 2-9.

TABLE 2-9 BitLocker To Go options

Option	Description
Control Use Of BitLocker On Removable Drives	Defines whether users can add or remove BitLocker encryption to removable drives.
Configure Use Of Smart Cards On Removable Drives	Defines whether users must use a smart card to access an encrypted drive.
Deny Write Access To Removable Drives Not Protected By BitLocker	Prevents users from writing to unencrypted removable drives.
Configure Use Of Hardware-Based Encryption For Removable Data Drives	Defines whether BitLocker software encryption can be used instead of hardware encryption on computers that don't support the latter.
Enforce Drive Encryption Type Of Removable Data Drives	Defines a specific encryption type that must be used with removable drives: Full encryption or Used Space Only encryption. (This option was added in Windows 8.1, so look for it on the exam.)
Allow Access To BitLocker-Protected Removable Data Drives From Earlier Versions Of Windows	Defines whether FAT-formatted removable BitLocker drives are accessible from earlier Windows versions.
Configure Use Of Passwords For Removable Data Drives	Defines whether removable drives must be password protected.

Option	Description
Choose How BitLocker-Protected Removable Drives Can Be Recovered	Defines whether Data Recovery Agents (DRAs) can be used to access the data on removable BitLocker Drives. The DRA is a user account that an administrator has authorized to recover BitLocker drives in an organization. By default, domain administrators are DRAs.

Exploring startup key storage and recovery options

One aspect of the BitLocker technology is to apply the startup key storage options. However, to understand what a startup key is, you must first understand what it isn't. You need to contend with several key management terms:

- **TPM owner password** You must initialize the TPM before you can use it with BitLocker Drive Encryption. When you do, you create a TPM owner password that's associated only with the TPM. You supply the TPM owner password when you need to enable or disable the TPM or reset the TPM lockout.

- **Recovery password and recovery key** The first time you set up BitLocker, you are prompted to configure how to access BitLocker-protected drives if access is denied. This involves creating a recovery key. You need the recovery key if the TPM can't validate the startup features and settings, but most of the time a failure to access a BitLocker drive occurs because an end user has forgotten the PIN or password.

- **Password** You can use a password to protect fixed, removable, and operating system drives. You can also use a password with operating system drives that don't have a TPM. The password can consist of 8 to 255 characters as specified by the following Group Policy settings: Configure Use Of Passwords For Operating System Drives, Configure Use Of Passwords For Removable Data Drives, and Configure Use Of Passwords For Fixed Data Drives.

- **PIN and enhanced PIN** If you use a TPM, you can configure BitLocker with a PIN that the user must type to gain access to the computer. The PIN can consist of 4 to 20 digits as specified by the Configure Minimum PIN Length For Startup Group Policy setting. Enhanced PINs use the full keyboard character set in addition to the numeric set to allow for more possible PIN combinations. You must enable the Allow Enhanced PINs For Startup Group Policy setting before adding the PIN to the drive.

- **Startup key** You use a startup key that's stored on a USB flash drive, with or without a TPM. The USB flash drive must be inserted every time the computer starts. The USB flash drive must be formatted by using the NTFS, FAT, or FAT32 file system.

Now that you know what a startup key is, you can better understand your storage options. To save a computer's startup key on a USB flash drive, follow these steps:

1. Right-click a BitLocker-protected drive.

2. Select Manage BitLocker.

3. Select Back Up Your Recovery Key.

4. Insert a removable drive, choose it from the list as applicable, and click Save.

EXAM TIP

BitLocker Network Unlock simplifies management of BitLocker-enabled TPM + PIN workstations and servers in a domain. Network Unlock allows the PIN entry prompt to be bypassed when a domain-connected computer restarts. The computer is automatically unlocked by using a trusted key that's provided by the Windows Deployment Services server as its secondary authentication method. For more information and to review the requirements, refer to this TechNet article: *http://technet.microsoft.com/en-us/library/jj574173.aspx.*

Understanding BitLocker and BitLocker To Go data recovery

BitLocker or BitLocker To Go might enter recovery mode for many reasons after it's applied to a device. Some reasons include meeting a threshold set in Group Policy (such as MaxFailedLogonAttempts), changing the startup order of the device, changing the NTFS partition table, entering the PIN incorrectly too many times, and turning off or disabling the TPM; changes found in the Master Boot Record. You can see the entire list at *http://technet.microsoft.com/en-us/library/dn383583.aspx#BKMK_WhatIsRecovery.* When BitLocker recovery mode is engaged, something or someone must be ready to restore access to the drive.

You can recover drives in various ways, including the following:

- Let the user supply the 48-digit recovery password.
- Use a data recovery agent to unlock the drive.
- Let a domain administrator obtain the recovery password from AD DS.
- Use another method, such as Windows PowerShell.

Self-recovery is an option if the user has saved the password or recovery key to a USB flash drive. This isn't considered the best method for many reasons, one of which is that many users forget to perform the backup, lose the USB flash drive, or keep the drive with their computer (compromising the security of the computer as well as the BitLocker key). Non-domain users can store their passwords on OneDrive if they want.

Beyond self-recovery, you can consider a few other ways to recover a locked drive. One way to force recovery for a local or remote computer involves a command prompt:

1. Right-click Start and click Command Prompt (Admin).

2. To recover a local computer, at the command prompt, enter the following command:

   ```
   manage-bde -forcerecovery <Volume>
   ```

3. To recover a remote computer, at the command prompt enter the following command:

   ```
   manage-bde. -ComputerName <ComputerName> -forcerecovery <Volume>
   ```

If a user has forgotten the PIN and you want to reset it, follow these steps:

1. Use the recovery password to unlock the computer.

2. Right-click the drive and click Change PIN.

3. Click Reset A Forgotten PIN.

4. Type and confirm the new PIN and click Finish.

Use the following Windows PowerShell commands:

1. Remove the previous recovery password:

    ```
    Manage-bde –protectors –delete C: –type RecoveryPassword
    ```

2. Add a new recovery password:

    ```
    Manage-bde –protectors –add C: –RecoveryPassword
    ```

3. Get the ID of the new recovery password:

    ```
    Manage-bde –protectors –get C: –Type RecoveryPassword
    ```

4. Back up the new recovery password to AD CS:

    ```
    Manage-bde –protectors –adbackup C: –id {EXAMPLE6-5507-4924-AA9E-AFB2EB003692}
    ```

Finally, if you've decided to back up passwords to an AD DS, you must also configure the appropriate Group Policy settings in the Local Group Policy Editor or the Group Policy Management Console under Computer Configuration, Policies, Administrative Templates, Windows Components, BitLocker Drive Encryption. You'll need to make decisions about and configure the following:

- Choose how BitLocker-Protected Operating System Drives Can Be Recovered
- Choose how BitLocker-Protected Fixed Drives Can Be Recovered
- Choose how BitLocker-Protected Removable Drives Can Be Recovered

You can also select the Do Not Enable BitLocker Until Recovery Information Is Stored In AD DS check box to keep users from enabling BitLocker unless the computer is connected to the domain and until the backup of BitLocker recovery information is successful.

All these options have their place in various types of businesses and enterprises. However, large enterprises should consider managing BitLocker and BitLocker To Go with the Microsoft BitLocker Administration and Monitoring (MBAM) Tool version 2.0, which is included in the Microsoft Desktop Optimization Pack (MDOP) for Microsoft Software Assurance. With it, network administrators can protect computers and removable drives running Windows 7, Windows 8, and Windows To Go.

Understanding Microsoft BitLocker Administration and Monitoring

As your enterprise grows, you'll find that you spend more and more time managing BitLocker and BitLocker To Go clients and devices. You have to recover lost PINs, ensure that users and computers are in compliance with network policies, and so on. Microsoft BitLocker Administration and Monitoring (MBAM) enables end users to recover their own PINs and recover their devices when they go into recovery mode, perhaps due to a change in the BIOS or the boot record. MBAM offers a self-service portal they can use as well. MBAM can also help you manage compliance by simplifying how to review the status of your inventory, provision BitLocker, integrate with System Center, and prohibit certain types of devices, among other things. Note that MBAM comes with MDOP which requires Software Assurance (SA) licensing.

Here are a few more things the latest edition of MBAM offers:

- Support is available for managing Windows To Go devices.
- BitLocker pre-provisioning with Windows PE includes the use of Used Disk Space Only Encryption on Windows 8 devices.
- MBAM can take ownership of the TPM without requiring a restart (if TPM is turned on in BIOS).
- Devices left in "protection suspended" mode automatically resume protection after restart.
- Windows 8 Operating System Drives can be protected with the Password protector.
- You can deploy MBAM with less infrastructure.

To deploy MBAM, you'll need to plan for the following:

- Administration and Monitoring Server
- Self-Service Server
- Recovery Database
- Compliance and Audit Database
- Compliance and Audit Reports
- Policy Template

MORE INFO **USING MBAM**

This great article on MBAM offers links for learning more: *http://blogs.windows.com/windows/b/springboard/archive/2013/04/10/get-ready-to-deploy-mbam-2-0.aspx.*

Thought experiment

Protecting data conditionally

In this thought experiment, apply what you've learned about this objective. You can find answers to these questions in the "Answers" section at the end of this chapter.

You need to support users that access data in your enterprise from various devices and locations. You want them to be able to access the data from their laptops and desktop computers, but you don't want them to access the data from their phones or tablet computers. Answer the following questions regarding how you would set this up.

1. What kind of the technology can you use to dynamically control user access based on various factors, including the kind of device being used?

2. What types of policies should you create to protect a resource based on the current security state of the device, group membership, or location?

3. How can you test these rules and policies before deploying them in your enterprise?

Objective summary

- You can apply Share permissions when the operating system is configured with FAT or FAT32 or anytime you share a folder on a computer. The three Share permissions offer minimal protection: Read, Change, and Full Control.

- NTFS permissions are much more robust than Share permissions and are used in enterprises to protect resources.

- DAC lets administrators apply permissions and restrictions conditionally based on various factors, including what type of device the user is working from, what group the user is part of, and where the user is located.

- Encryption protects data from unauthorized access when the machine has been compromised, including if the hard drive has been removed and attached elsewhere.

- You use CertMgr to back up and recover your EFS-encrypted files. You can also use the command-line tool cipher.exe to manage encryption at an elevated command prompt.

- Use Group Policy to configure settings for removable storage access.

- BitLocker Drive Encryption lets you encrypt entire hard disks and disk volumes. On computers with TPM, BitLocker can also ensure that data is accessible only if the computer's startup features and settings haven't been compromised.

- BitLocker To Go lets you protect removable USB devices with BitLocker Drive Encryption.

- You can recover protected disks and devices in many ways when BitLocker recovery is engaged, including self-service, pulling the password from AD DS, using MBAM, and using Windows PowerShell.

Objective review

Answer the following questions to test your knowledge of the information in this objective. You can find the answers to these questions and explanations of why each answer choice is correct or incorrect in the "Answers" section at the end of this chapter.

1. Which of the following are true of Share permissions?

   A. They apply to users who gain access to the resource over the network and to users who log on locally.

   B. They are the only way to secure network resources on FAT and FAT32 volumes.

   C. Three permissions are available: Read, Write, and Full Control.

   D. All of the above.

2. If a user is a member of a group with the Share permission Full Control to a folder named Resources, and if that same user is a member of a group with the NTFS permission Read, as well as a member of a third group with the NTFS permission Modify, what is the user's effective permission to the folder?

   A. Read

   B. Modify

   C. Full Control

   D. None of the above

3. What command can you use at an elevated command prompt to find all encrypted files on a local drive?

   A. *Cipher.exe /c*

   B. *Cipher.exe /x*

   C. *Cipher.exe /r*

   D. *Cipher.exe /u /n*

4. You need to block access to all classes of removable storage devices, and the policy should take precedence over all policy settings for those classes of devices. What Group Policy should you enable?

   A. CD And DVD: Deny Read/Write/Execute Access

   B. Prevent Installation Of Devices That Match Any Of These Device IDs

   C. Set All Removable Storage Classes: Deny

   D. Prevent Installation Of Devices Using Drivers That Match These Device Setup Classes

5. Which of the following is true with regard to BitLocker? (Choose all that apply.)

   A. You can use BitLocker to protect 32-bit and 64-bit computers running Windows 8.1 Pro, Windows 8.1 Enterprise, and Windows Server 2012.

   B. On computers that have a TPM version 1.2 or 2.0, BitLocker can ensure that data is accessible only if the computer's startup features and settings haven't been compromised (altered) and if the disk is still installed in the original computer.

   C. You can enable BitLocker before you deploy the operating system. When you do, you can opt to encrypt used disk space only or encrypt the entire drive.

   D. You can automate deployment of BitLocker in an enterprise with the command-line tool Manage-bde.exe.

   E. All of the above.

6. You want to encrypt data by using BitLocker on a computer that has a TPM. You also want to store the encryption key on the TPM chip. Which of the following options are available to you?

   A. TPM + startup PIN + startup key

   B. TPM + startup key

   C. TPM + startup PIN

   D. Startup key only

   E. TPM only

   F. Any option above can store the encryption key on the TPM chip.

7. A user has forgotten his PIN that he uses to unlock his BitLocker-enabled computer. He can't find his 48-digit recovery password. Which of the following can you use to unlock the drive without physically visiting his office?

   A. At a command prompt, enter the following command:

   ```
   manage-bde -ComputerName <ComputerName> -forcerecovery <Volume>
   ```

   B. From the Start screen, type and then click Manage BitLocker, click Duplicate Start Up Key, insert the clean USB drive on which you will write the key, and then click Save.

   C. Inform the user how to access the MBAM Self-Service Center (assuming you have that set up in your enterprise).

   D. Use the following PowerShell cmdlet:

   ```
   Manage-bde -protectors -ComputerName -delete C: -type RecoveryPassword
   ```

Answers

This section contains the solutions to the thought experiments and answers to the lesson review questions in this chapter.

Objective 2.1: Thought experiment

1. WPA v2 offers AES and eliminates TKIP.

2. The best thing to do is to retire the netbook. You don't want to downgrade the entire network's security to support this one device.

3. No. A RADIUS server is best incorporated into larger enterprises and isn't recommended for small networks.

Objective 2.1: Review

1. **Correct answer:** A

   A. **Correct:** An IPv4 address is a 32-bit number that consists of four octets that are 8 bits each. It looks like this when written in the base 10 numbering system: 124.205.15.2, with the highest number in any octet 255 or less.

   B. **Incorrect:** An IPv4 address is a 32-bit number, not a 64-bit number.

   C. **Incorrect:** Although an IPv4 address is a 32-bit number, it consists of four octets that are 8 bits each.

   D. **Incorrect:** An IPv6 address is a 128-bit number separated into eight blocks that are 16 bits each.

2. **Correct answer:** B

   A. **Incorrect:** If the first octet defined the network ID, it would be a Class A address.

   B. **Correct:** The first two octets define the network ID in a Class B address.

   C. **Incorrect:** If the first three octets defined the network ID, it would be a Class C address.

   D. **Incorrect:** A subnet mask (perhaps 255.255.0.0) can be converted to binary (11111111 11111111 00000000 00000000), and this particular subnet mask does coincide with a Class B network but doesn't define the network ID for a resource.

3. **Correct answers:** A, B

   A. Correct: DHCP servers can assign both IPv4 and IPv6 addresses to hosts on a network.

   B. Correct: DHCP servers can provide clients the necessary IP addresses of the applicable DNS server and gateway.

   C. Incorrect: DHCP doesn't have to be used for all network resources in any instance. Although not using DHCP in large enterprises would be nearly impossible, static addresses are still needed for specific hosts, including network printers, gateways, and DNS servers.

   D. Incorrect: Because C is incorrect, all of the above can't be the correct answer.

4. **Correct answer:** A

   A. Correct: 6to4 is used with clients that are sending data from a public IP address.

   B. Incorrect: ISATAP is used to connect to other ISATAP clients.

   C. Incorrect: Teredo is used when the DirectAccess client is sitting behind a NAT device and has been assigned a private IP address.

   D. Incorrect: IP-HTTPS is used when the client is sitting behind a limiting firewall.

   E. Incorrect: 6to4 is used when a client is sending from a public IP address.

5. **Correct answer:** D

   A. Incorrect: DNS zones represent groups of computers that can use DNS to perform name-resolution tasks.

   B. Incorrect: A trust anchor is a public cryptographic key. This key is what enables a DNS server to validate DNS responses.

   C. Incorrect: NRPT is the Name Resolution Policy Table, which contains namespaces and other settings that are stored in the Windows Registry. This information is used to determine how the DNS client will behave when it asks for responses and receives them.

   D. Correct: PNRP is defined as suggested here. PNRP uses "clouds" of computers that can locate one another.

   E. Incorrect: DNSSEC allows for a DNS zone and all the records in it to be cryptographically signed. Thus, when a DNS server that hosts a signed zone receives a name-resolution inquiry, that server returns digital signatures along with the requested records. A name resolver or another server can validate that the responses are accurate and haven't been altered using these signatures.

6. **Correct answer:** C

   A. **Incorrect:** 802.11a runs on the 5 GHz frequency, for one.

   B. **Incorrect:** 802.11b has transmission rates of 11 Mbps, for one.

   C. **Correct:** 802.11n will replace 802.11a, b, and g, and supports Wi-Fi Protected Access version 2 (WPA v2). It can be used on two frequencies: 2.5 GHz and 5 GHz. It supports transmission rates of up to 200 Mbps.

   D. **Incorrect:** 802.11i provides enhanced encryption but doesn't meet the requirements listed here.

   E. **Incorrect:** 802.1x must be used with a RADIUS server and is compatible with all other listed standards.

7. **Correct answer:** D

   A. **Incorrect:** You type this command after you type what's listed in answer D.

   B. **Incorrect:** The shared connection isn't ready yet. You must create the network and start it first.

   C. **Incorrect:** You don't need to create an inbound rule in Windows Firewall with Advanced Security to allow the second device access.

   D. **Correct:** You must open an administrator command prompt and enter the following:

   ```
   netsh wlan set hosted network mode=allow ssid=<networkname> key=<password>
   ```

8. **Correct answer:** E

   A. **Incorrect:** Program is correct, but the other answers are too.

   B. **Incorrect:** Port is correct, but so are the other answers.

   C. **Incorrect:** Predefined is correct, but the other answers are too.

   D. **Incorrect:** Custom is correct, but so are the other answers.

   E. **Correct:** All of the above is correct.

9. **Correct answer:** A

   A. **Correct:** SHA-1 AES-CBC 128 Diffie-Hellmann Group 2 and SHA-1 3DES Diffie-Hellmann Group 2 are the proper options.

   B. **Incorrect:** Data Integrity Algorithms and Data Integrity And Encryption Algorithms are used with Data Protection (Quick Mode).

   C. **Incorrect:** Kerberos V5 is used for authentication.

   D. **Incorrect:** None of the above is incorrect because A is correct.

Objective 2.2: Thought experiment

1. DirectAccess offers the features you require.

2. You don't need any public IP addresses if the DirectAccess server sits behind a NAT device.

3. A Network Location Server determines this.

4. RRAS.

Objective 2.2: Review

1. **Correct answer:** C.

   A. **Incorrect:** This protocol doesn't support the use of a preshared key.

   B. **Incorrect:** This protocol doesn't support the use of a preshared key.

   C. **Correct:** This is the only protocol listed that supports a preshared key.

   D. **Incorrect:** This protocol doesn't support the use of a preshared key.

   E. **Incorrect:** This is Remote Desktop Protocol and isn't correct.

2. **Correct answer:** B

   A. **Incorrect:** Administrators use CMAK to create VPN profiles, among other things.

   B. **Correct:** Connection Manager is a feature that lets a user connect to a VPN.

   C. **Incorrect:** This command retrieves only the specified VPN connection profile information.

   D. **Incorrect:** RSAT is used to manage servers and clients from your own laptop or personal desktop computer.

3. **Correct answer:** D

   A. **Incorrect:** Internet Key Exchange, Version 2 (IKEv2) protocol supports IPv6 and VPN Reconnect, authentication with EAP, PEAP, EAP-MSCHAPv2, and smart cards and isn't used with RD Gateway.

   B. **Incorrect:** Secure Socket Tunneling Protocol (SSTP) encapsulates PPP traffic through the Secure Sockets Layer (SSL) protocol, uses certificates for authentication, and isn't used with RD Gateway.

   C. **Incorrect:** Applicable and compatible transition protocols are used with DirectAccess clients who need to communicate IPv6 data over IPv4 networks but aren't applicable here.

   D. **Correct:** Remote Desktop Protocol (RDP) over HTTPS is the proper protocol.

4. **Correct answers:** A, B, C, D

   A. **Correct:** Windows 7 Enterprise can be used.

   B. **Correct:** Windows 7 Ultimate can be used.

   C. **Correct:** Windows 8 Enterprise can be used.

   D. **Correct:** Windows 8.1 Enterprise can be used.

   E. **Incorrect:** Windows XP with SP3 can't be used.

   F. **Incorrect:** Windows Vista Business can't be used.

5. **Correct answers:** B, C

   A. **Incorrect:** Clients must be joined to the domain; a workgroup won't do.

   B. **Correct:** Windows Firewall must be enabled on all profiles.

   C. **Correct:** You must install and configure a DNS server.

   D. **Incorrect:** All of the above isn't correct because answer A isn't correct.

6. **Correct answer:** A

   A. **Correct:** *enter -pssession* is the proper command.

   B. **Incorrect:** *enable-psremoting* configures the computer to receive remote commands.

   C. **Incorrect:** *start-job* starts a Windows PowerShell background job.

   D. **Incorrect:** *set-pssessionconfiguration* changes the properties of a registered session configuration.

7. **Correct answers:** A, B, C

   A. **Correct:** An AD DS domain controller is required on the domain for clients to be authenticated, authorized, and so on.

   B. **Correct:** A Network Policy Server evaluates the health of each client.

   C. **Correct:** A Certification Authority is required to manage IPsec certificates.

   D. **Incorrect:** RRAS is used with NAP and VPN enforcement.

8. **Correct answer:** C

   A. **Incorrect:** *Netsh nap client reset* resets a configuration.

   B. **Incorrect:** *Netsh nap client set* sets a configuration.

   C. **Correct:** *Netsh nap client dump* lets you display a configuration script.

   D. **Incorrect:** *Netsh nap client show* shows configuration and state information.

Objective 2.3: Thought experiment

1. Yes. AC CS in Windows Server 2012 requires an existing PKI infrastructure.

2. Client certificates are stored in the personal certificate store for the applicable user account on the client's computer.

3. Trusted root certificates are stored in the Trusted Root Certification Authorities store on the client's computer.

4. CertMgr.msc can be used to open the CertMgr window.

Objective 2.3: Review

1. **Correct answers:** A, B

   A. **Correct:** *Backup-CARoleService* is the correct command for backing up the CA database.

   B. **Correct:** *Restore-CARoleService* is the correct command for restoring the CA database.

   C. **Incorrect:** This isn't a valid Windows PowerShell command.

   D. **Incorrect:** This isn't a valid Windows PowerShell command.

2. **Correct answers:** B, C

   A. **Incorrect:** A physical smart card can be removed.

   B. **Correct:** The solution here requires a compatible TPM chip and a virtual smart card.

   C. **Correct:** The solution here requires a compatible TPM chip and a virtual smart card.

   D. **Incorrect:** A biometric fingerprint reader doesn't offer private keys for security.

   E. **Incorrect:** BitLocker Drive Encryption is used to protect data on the drive and isn't for authentication purposes.

3. **Correct answer:** C

   A. **Incorrect:** If you've joined the homegroup, you are connected to the network.

   B. **Incorrect:** BitLocker Drive Encryption isn't required to join a homegroup.

   C. **Correct:** The time is configured incorrectly on the second computer.

   D. **Incorrect:** If you have joined the homegroup, you are running a compatible version of Windows.

4. **Correct answers:** A, B

   A. Correct: A workgroup uses a distributed method for sharing data.

   B. Correct: A homegroup uses a distributed method for sharing data.

   C. Incorrect: A domain uses a centralized method of sharing and managing data and uses AD DS for authentication and user access.

   D. Incorrect: Although a workgroup is a distributed sharing method, a domain isn't.

5. **Correct answer:** D

   A. Incorrect: A VPN enables users to access your local network when they are away from the office. VPNs might use PPTP or L2TP to secure the connection.

   B. Incorrect: Remote Desktop Services enables users to access session-based desktops, virtual machine-based desktops, or applications from both within a network and from the Internet.

   C. Incorrect: App-V enables the application to run in a virtualized environment without having to install or configure it on the local machine.

   D. Correct: Secure Channel is a Security Support Provider (SSP), and the TLS/SSL protocol uses a client/server model that's based on certificate authentication. It does require a PKI infrastructure.

6. **Correct answer:** A

   A. Correct: You must first configure the policy Account Lockout Threshold to state how many times a user can try to authenticate before additional measures are taken.

   B. Incorrect: The policy Reset Account Counter After is optional.

   C. Incorrect: These policies are available in both workgroups and domains.

   D. Incorrect: The Group Security Policy console is the appropriate place to create these policies.

7. **Correct answers:** B, C, D

   A. Incorrect: Account Policies don't provide the desired results; these are Group Policy settings and aren't used to address issues with authentication over a WAN.

   B. Correct: Credential caching can be used to store credentials on a local RODC server.

   C. Correct: Password Replication Policies are used to determine that credential caching can be used (and how to use it).

   D. Correct: An RODC server is required to manage credential caching in the branch office.

   E. Incorrect: Secure Channel is a technology used to secure connections used by applications over untrusted networks.

8. **Correct answer:** C

   A. **Incorrect:** Credential Manager can store Windows Store passwords as well as local ones.

   B. **Incorrect:** Credential Manager can store Windows Store passwords as well as those input for local resources.

   C. **Correct:** Credential Manager can store Windows Store passwords and passwords for local resources.

   D. **Incorrect:** Credential Manager can store both Windows Store passwords and local use passwords.

9. **Correct answer:** B

   A. **Incorrect:** A Microsoft account can be used in a domain if it isn't restricted through Group Policy.

   B. **Correct:** Allow the user to associate their own Microsoft account to achieve this.

   C. **Incorrect:** Workplace Join allows users to connect to your domain with their own personal devices.

   D. **Incorrect:** If you add Web Application Proxy, users can join your enterprise from any Internet-enabled location by using a device you've allowed using Workplace Join.

Objective 2.4: Thought experiment

1. You should choose a parity option. This offers fault tolerance and makes efficient use of the disk space.

2. To create a three-way parity solution, you should use five.

3. You shouldn't use a USB hub with USB 2.0 ports. You can use a hub with USB 3.0 ports, though.

Objective 2.4: Review

1. **Correct answer:** C

   A. **Incorrect:** */cacheflush* isn't a valid command.

   B. **Incorrect:** */cache* is used to flush the cache, not clear it.

   C. **Correct:** */pktflush* is used to clear the DFS cache.

   D. **Incorrect:** */clearcache* isn't a valid command.

2. **Correct answer:** E

   A. **Incorrect:** USB 2.0 is a valid option, but so are all the others listed.

   B. **Incorrect:** USB 3.0 is a valid option, but so are all the others listed.

   C. **Incorrect:** Serial ATA is a valid option, but so are all the others listed.

   D. **Incorrect:** Serial Attached SCSI is a valid option, but so are all the others listed.

   E. **Correct:** All of the above is correct.

3. **Correct answer:** B

   A. **Incorrect:** Hosted mode is best used when the branch office has 50 or more computers.

   B. **Correct:** Distributed mode is best here because the branch office has fewer than 50 computers and they all can cache the applicable files.

   C. **Incorrect:** Ad Hoc mode isn't a valid mode.

   D. **Incorrect:** Distributed mode is the best choice.

4. **Correct answer:** A

   A. **Correct:** *netsh branchcache set service mode=DISTRIBUTED* is the applicable command.

   B. **Incorrect:** The *netsh branchcache* command must include *set service*.

   C. **Incorrect:** *Enable-BCDistributed* is a Windows PowerShell command.

   D. **Incorrect:** *Enable-BCLocal* is a Windows PowerShell command.

5. **Correct answer:** B

   A. **Incorrect:** The OneDrive app for Windows is for tablets, laptops, and desktops not for smartphones. A web browser would be fine for a tablet.

   B. **Correct:** The OneDrive app for smartphones is a good choice. A web browser on a tablet is a good choice (as is the Windows app).

   C. **Incorrect:** A Web browser on a smartphone would be too difficult to see. A desktop application on a tablet would allow you to open documents and other files but might or might not be the best option for your clients.

   D. **Incorrect:** The OneDrive app for smartphones is a desirable option. A desktop application isn't the best option for a tablet; a Web browser or the Windows app most likely is.

Objective 2.5: Thought experiment

1. DAC enables you to support users that access data in your enterprise from various devices and from various places.

2. Central Access Policies contain conditional expressions that you can use to protect resources as determined by their current state, group, or location.

3. Proposed permissions let you more accurately determine the effect of the changes before you apply them.

Objective 2.5: Review

1. **Correct answer:** B

   A. **Incorrect:** They apply to users who gain access to the resource over the network but don't apply to users who log on locally.

   B. **Correct:** They are the only way to secure network resources on FAT and FAT32 volumes.

   C. **Incorrect:** Three permissions are available, but they are Read, Change, and Full Control.

   D. **Incorrect:** Only B is correct.

2. **Correct answer:** B

   A. **Incorrect:** The Share permission applied to the folder for the user is Full Control; however, the NTFS cumulative permission is Modify. The most restrictive of the two is applied, which is Modify.

   B. **Correct:** When a user is a member of multiple groups, the cumulative Share and NTFS permissions are calculated and the most restrictive is applied. So Share (Full Control) and NTFS (Modify) equate to an effective permission of Modify.

   C. **Incorrect:** The Share permission applied to the folder for the user is Full Control; however, the NTFS cumulative permission is Modify. The most restrictive of the two is applied, which is Modify. Full Control would be the least restrictive.

   D. **Incorrect:** B is the correct answer.

3. **Correct answer:** D

   A. **Incorrect:** *Cipher.exe /c* displays information about an encrypted file.

   B. **Incorrect:** *Cipher.exe /x* backs up your encryption keys.

   C. **Incorrect:** *Cipher.exe /r* creates a new data recovery agent.

   D. **Correct:** *Cipher.exe /u /n* finds all encrypted files on a local drive.

4. **Correct answer:** C

   A. **Incorrect:** CD And DVD: Deny Read/Write/Execute Access applies only to CDs and DVDs, not all classes.

   B. **Incorrect:** Prevent Installation Of Devices That Match Any Of These Device IDs is an additional Group Policy setting you can configure but doesn't fit the scenario here.

   C. **Correct:** Set All Removable Storage Classes: Deny is the proper policy.

   D. **Incorrect:** Prevent Installation Of Devices Using Drivers That Match These Device Setup Classes is a valid policy but isn't the correct answer here.

5. **Correct answer:** E

   A. **Incorrect:** You can use BitLocker to protect 32-bit and 64-bit computers running Windows 8.1 Pro, Windows 8.1 Enterprise, and Windows Server 2012. However, the other answers are also correct.

   B. **Incorrect:** On computers that have a TPM version 1.2 or 2.0, BitLocker can also ensure that data is accessible only if the computer's startup features and settings haven't been compromised and if the disk is still installed in the original computer. However, the other answers are also correct.

   C. **Incorrect:** You can enable BitLocker before you deploy the operating system. When you do, you can opt to encrypt used disk space only or encrypt the entire drive. However, the other answers are also correct.

   D. **Incorrect:** You can automate deployment of BitLocker in an enterprise with the command-line tool Manage-bde.exe. However, the other answers are also correct.

   E. **Correct:** All of the above is correct.

6. **Correct answers:** A, B, C, E

   A. **Correct:** The encryption key is stored on the TPM chip, but an administrator must type a PIN and insert the startup key (available on a USB drive).

   B. **Correct:** The encryption key is stored on the TPM chip, and an administrator must insert a USB flash drive that contains a startup key.

   C. **Correct:** The encryption key is stored on the TPM chip, and an administrator must enter a PIN.

   D. **Incorrect:** An administrator must insert a USB flash drive with the startup key on it. The computer doesn't have to have a TPM chip, but this one does and you want to use it.

   E. **Correct:** The encryption key is stored on the TPM chip, and no administrator log on is required.

   F. **Incorrect:** D doesn't fit the suggested scenario.

7. **Correct answer:** A

   A. **Correct:** You can recover a remote computer at a command prompt by entering the following command:

      ```
      manage-bde. -ComputerName <ComputerName> -forcerecovery <Volume>
      ```

   B. **Incorrect:** To perform this task, you need to be at the client's computer. (This answer mentions nothing about remotely accessing the computer.)

   C. **Incorrect:** You can tell the user to access the MBAM Self-Service Center if you have that set up in your enterprise.

   D. **Incorrect:** The following Windows PowerShell cmdlet is valid:

      ```
      Manage-bde -protectors-delete C: -type RecoveryPassword
      ```

      However, the cmdlet shown with this answer isn't correct and can't be used to access a computer remotely.

CHAPTER 3

Support Windows clients and devices

This final chapter involves supporting the enterprise you have set up or been integrated into. Here you'll learn how to support and manage operating systems, hardware, mobile devices, and so on to ensure compliance with the policies and security settings you've configured. This chapter focuses quite a bit on Windows Intune for management tasks, including managing remote computers and devices from virtually anywhere you can access the Internet securely.

Objectives in this chapter:

- Objective 3.1: Support operating system and hardware
- Objective 3.2: Support mobile devices
- Objective 3.3: Support client compliance
- Objective 3.4: Manage clients by using Windows Intune

Objective 3.1: Support operating system and hardware

Part of your job as a network administrator involves supporting installed operating systems and hardware. This includes resolving problems when they arise and optimizing performance wherever you can. In this objective you'll learn about the support and optimization tools that are listed as exam goals; however, you won't see many other ways to support your clients.

> **This objective covers how to:**
>
> - Resolve hardware and device issues, including STOP errors and use Reliability Monitor
> - Optimize performance by using the Windows Performance Toolkit (WPT), including Xperf.exe, Xbootmgr.exe, XperfView.exe, and Windows Performance Recorder (WPR)
> - Monitor performance by using Data Collector Sets, Task Manager, and Resource Monitor
> - Monitor and manage printers, including NFC Tap-to-Pair and printer sharing
> - Remediate startup issues by using the Diagnostics and Recovery Toolkit (DaRT)

Resolving hardware and device driver issues

Problems with external or internal hardware or connected devices such as scanners and printers are generally related to the device drivers associated with them. You can often resolve the problems by reinstalling, updating, obtaining, and rolling back installed drivers. Device drivers also can cause problems for internal hardware, such as installed graphics cards. You can also use Reliability Monitor to uncover and troubleshoot unknown problems, if you aren't sure what device, application, Windows Update, or other issue is causing the problem.

Resolving hardware and device driver issues

Device drivers and computer hardware go hand in hand. Each requires the other to function properly. A long time ago, most devices came with their own device driver disks for installing the appropriate driver, but now, driver installation is generally automatic. In most instances, the necessary device driver is available in the Windows 8.1 Driver Store (on the computer itself) or from Windows Update (on the Internet), and the driver obtained there works fine. Occasionally, though, problems arise. This happens when a compatible, Windows 8.1 device driver isn't available, when the installed driver doesn't function properly, or when the driver isn't approved by Microsoft's Windows Hardware Certification Program (and is unsigned as a result).

TROUBLESHOOTING AND UPDATING A DRIVER WITH DEVICE MANAGER

You use Device Manager to view, install, uninstall, disable and otherwise manage hardware devices. You can access Device Manager a number of ways, including by right-clicking the Start button and clicking Device Manager from the resulting list. You can also find Device Manager in the Computer Management Console, under the System Tools node. By default, the list is organized by the various types of devices, but other viewing and sorting options are available.

When you use Device Manager to resolve a device driver issue, most often you'll opt to update the driver. To get started, locate the problematic device in Device Manager and double-click it. Click Update Driver on the Driver tab, or click Update Driver from the General tab as shown in Figure 3-1. In the Update Driver Software dialog box, choose how to locate the driver. If it's one you've downloaded and saved to your computer, click Browse My Computer For Driver Software. Otherwise, click Search Automatically For Updated Driver Software, which automatically looks for a driver in all the usual places. The latter is a good option if you think a driver is available from Windows Update, or if you've inserted a driver disk into the CD/DVD drive.

If this option doesn't resolve your hardware issue, you can try others. You'll have to try other options if the device doesn't appear in Device Manager, for instance. One way to resolve an issue is to open Action Center and see whether a solution is waiting for you. Although this is an end-user's solution to a driver problem and not necessarily a network administrator's, it's still an option that can be quite useful. Action Center can identify problems, search for solutions automatically, and, when a solution is found, offer it up.

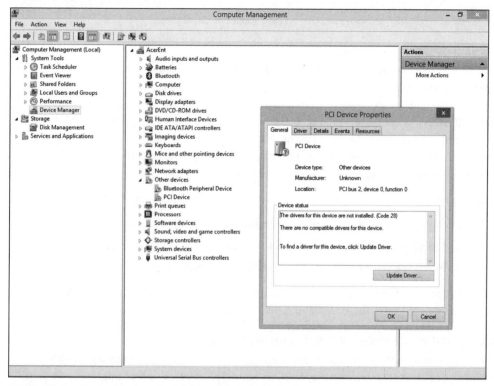

FIGURE 3-1 Use Device Manager to troubleshoot device drivers.

Another option for installing a device driver is to download it from the manufacturer's website, and then double-click an executable file that contains it. You have to do this manually; no automated task can do it for you.

You can perform additional tasks with Device Manager. You use similar methods to disable and troubleshoot drivers as you do to update them. Disable is an option from the Driver tab of the device's Properties dialog box. When you disable a device, you turn it off. This is different from uninstalling a device. When the device is turned off, Windows can't use it and won't try to reactivate it. In contrast, if you uninstall a device such as a graphics or audio driver, Windows reinstalls it on restart in most instances (if not before, when you scan for hardware changes in Device Manager). You might want to disable a specific device to determine whether it is causing a system conflict or problem. You also can disable devices that don't work properly or that you don't need in order to free up system resources. One example is a docking station with Ethernet versus a laptop with Wi-Fi. You could disable other unwanted hardware, such as modems.

Sometimes, installing a new driver over an older driver causes more problems than it resolves. In such a situation, you can roll back the driver. Roll Back Driver is available only after you install a second driver; otherwise, the option is grayed out. You can find this option from Device Manager from a Properties dialog box, from the Driver tab.

MANAGING LEGACY HARDWARE

Occasionally you'll need to manage legacy hardware. In many organizations, legacy hardware still plays a very important role in getting the job done. It might be a printer that connects to a parallel port, an infrared device, or even a modem. This hardware might not be detected automatically on a computer running Windows 8.1 (it won't be if it's a parallel-port printer, for example). An option in Device Manager can help you install these kinds of devices (Action menu, Add Legacy Hardware). To use this option, insert any installation media you have for the device (if you have it), and then follow these steps:

1. Open Device Manager. From the Action menu, click Add Legacy Hardware.

2. Click Next to start the wizard and then select either of these options:
   - Search For And Install The Hardware Automatically (Recommended)
   - Install The Hardware That I Manually Select From A List

3. Follow the resulting prompts. This might involve selecting a port for a printer, selecting the device from a list, or making other choices.

USING SIGVERIF.EXE TO CHECK FOR UNSIGNED DRIVERS

Device drivers have the potential to damage a computer when they are laced with hidden malware by dishonest programmers. Thus, technology is in place to test, approve, and then sign drivers to verify that they are safe to install and haven't been altered since the testing and approval process completed. When approved, the drivers are digitally signed by an approved authority (often a trusted organization or publisher). This signature is created using a cryptographic algorithm and is appended to the device driver. This verifies that the driver is authentic and secure when you get it, because the algorithm is verified before installation.

When installed, unsigned drivers can cause various computer problems, especially those that are difficult to diagnose, even if those drivers have no integral malware. You can check to see whether any unsigned drivers are installed on any computer by using the command-line tool Sigverif.exe. To perform this check, follow these steps:

1. Right-click the Start button and click Command Prompt (Admin).

2. At the command prompt, type **sigverif.exe** and press Enter.

3. Start the File Signature Verification, and then view the results.

4. Click Close.

USING PNPUTIL.EXE TO MANAGE DEVICE DRIVERS

You can use the command-line tool Pnputil.exe to manage device drivers manually at an elevated command prompt. You can also use the command to manage the driver store by adding, deleting, and listing driver packages. A driver package consists of all the data needed to install the driver, including but not limited to

- **Driver files**   Generally, this is a dynamic link library (DLL) with the .sys file extension.
- **Installation files**   These files have the file extension .inf and contain the installation files.
- **Driver Catalog file**   Included with the installation files, this .cat file contains the information related to the driver's digital signature.
- **Additional files**   These can be icons, device property pages, and even items related to an installation wizard.

The syntax for the Pnputil.exe command is

```
pnputil.exe –a <path to the driver> /<drivername>.inf
```

Here are some parameters to consider:

- *-a* specifies the path to the driver's .inf file.
- *-d* deletes a specific .inf file.
- *-f* forces the deletion of a specific .inf file.

To see the DriverStore folder, navigate to C:\Windows\System32\DriverStore\FileRepository.

Resolving STOP Errors

A STOP error is one that's so severe, the computer stops working and then generally offers up a long error code to try to shed some light on the problem. These problems are often hard to diagnose, unless you can write down the error code and look it up online. If you can find a resolution, you can generally work through the fix to bring the computer back up. Sometimes this involves installing an update from Microsoft. You can also try the Microsoft Fix It website at *http://support.microsoft.com/fixit/default.aspx*.

Some STOP errors don't have anything to do with a part of the operating system or a device connected to it though. For example, a STOP error might occur if a problem has occurred with Random Access Memory (RAM). If you suspect this is the problem, you can run a memory diagnostic test using the Windows Memory Diagnostic Tool. To access this tool, from the Start screen type **diagnose**, and then click Diagnose Your Computer's Memory Problems in the results. You can also run it from an elevated command prompt by typing **mdsched**. Either way, you have to restart the computer so that the test can run.

If you think the STOP error is related to problems on your hard disk, you can opt for a different tool. ChkDsk (pronounced Check Disk) scans your disk for errors and tries to resolve them. Like other options, you can search for ChkDsk from the Start screen or run it from an elevated command prompt with the *chkdsk* command. Figure 3-2 shows an example of ChkDsk in action.

You can also get STOP errors if a device driver tries to write to an incorrect memory address. If you get an error related to an interrupt request (IRQ), this might be the problem, and you might have to use Device Manager for help resolving it.

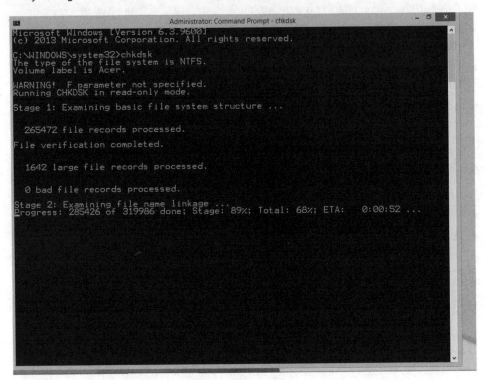

FIGURE 3-2 Use ChkDsk to check for errors on the hard drive.

Really, the possibilities for these kinds of errors are endless because of the sheer number of computer manufacturers, drivers, and devices. Here are a few STOP errors that have been reported and resolved by using Windows updates and hotfixes:

- The memory manager code was changed in order to remove a potential lock contention. This problem was first addressed in Windows Server 2012 R2 and Windows 8.1. A hotfix is now available for Windows Server 2012 and Windows 8. This STOP error is 0x9E and the Knowledge Base (KB) article that addresses it is 2916993.

- You have a Windows 8 or Windows Server 2012-based computer that has high performance disks, and low performance processors or a single core CPU. You put the computer into hibernate (S4). You try to resume the computer from hibernate but problems ensue. There is a cumulative update that resolves this issue. This STOP error is 0x000000A0 (parameter1, parameter2, parameter3, parameter4) and the KB article that addresses it is 2823506.

- You use the right mouse button as the primary mouse button, and you have enabled the Use numeric keypad to move mouse around the screen option. When you press some keys on a Windows 8.1 or Windows Server 2012 R2-based touch device, you receive a STOP error. There is an update for this. This STOP error is 0x0000003B and describes a SYSTEM_SERVICE_EXCEPTION issue. The KB article that addresses it is 2927067.

Using Reliability Monitor

The Reliability Monitor tool lets you explore a system's stability. It also can help you locate and resolve problems. To open the tool, type **Reliability** at the Start screen and click View Reliability History.

Figure 3-3 shows a sample report on a recently reinstalled computer. Clicking any of the blue icons on the report causes the list below the graph to populate. You can see that on this day (for this recently reinstalled machine) several successful Windows updates and driver installations occurred. If, for example, you were having intermittent problems with a monitor flickering on and off, and you discovered here that the graphics card driver installation was unsuccessful, you would certainly have a starting point for your troubleshooting.

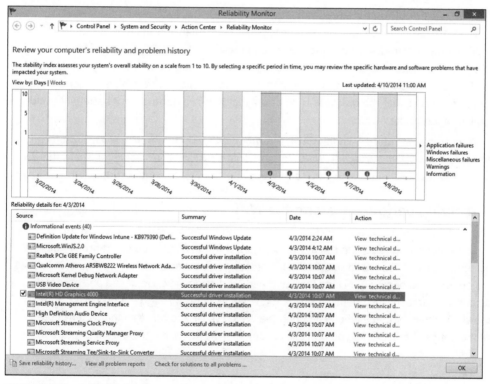

FIGURE 3-3 Use Reliability Monitor to discover problems.

You can also view the technical details of any entry. The technical details might offer a driver name and manufacturer; information about updates for Windows Defender, Windows Intune, or Windows Update; and so on. What you see depends on several factors, such as the type of entry you've requested more information about. Notice also that an option to check for solutions to all problems appears at the bottom of the Reliability Monitor window.

> **NOTE** **RELIABILITY MONITOR DETAILS**
>
> Reliability Monitor gathers information using the Reliability Access Component Agent (RACAgent). The Stability Index Score is based on the data collected over time and ranges from 1 to 10.

Optimizing performance

The Windows Performance Toolkit (WPT) is available from the Windows Assessment and Deployment Kit (Windows ADK). The WPT consists of two independent tools: Windows Performance Recorder (WPR) and Windows Performance Analyzer (WPA). The WPT enables you to monitor performance and create performance profiles of both operating system and installed applications.

The WPT can help you analyze various types of performance problems, including application start times, startup issues, deferred procedure calls (DPCs) and interrupt activity (ISRs), system responsiveness issues, application resource usage, and interrupt storms. You'll use this tool when you are told by a client that a system is slow, that it takes longer than usual for apps to open, that the disk light is on often, that they are getting poor battery life, and similar, vague, related issues.

You can download the Windows ADK for Windows 8.1 Update from *www.microsoft.com/ en-us/download/details.aspx?id=39982*. In this update, support is available for Xperf, the previous command-line tool related to this, but XperfView is no longer supported.

Optimizing performance with the WPT

The WPT contains two tools. It includes the WPR and the WPA. You use the WPR for troubleshooting; you use it to run a trace analysis. Using the WPR you could profile the CPU's performance, disk input and output (I/O), memory performance, and so on. Figure 3-4 shows the options. You begin by clicking Start and end by clicking Save. Go ahead and accept the default save area in Documents as prompted when working through the process. Figure 3-4 shows the screen you see when you open the WPR. I've clicked More so that you can see all the options here. Even if you don't select any specific items, a trace will still capture the relevant data. While the trace runs, make note of any dropped events, because this can signal a report that's not completely valid.

After the analysis is complete, you can use the WPA to review the information acquired. In the Analyzer window, click File, click Open, browse to the file location, and then follow the instructions offered to add a graph to Graph Explorer. Make sure that you can see the Diagnostic Console (see Figure 3-5) as well as the graph itself. You can add multiple graphs and interact with them with your mouse. Be sure to explore this before continuing. You or a technician can use the information to uncover the problems, which can include an overused disk, problems with storage and read/write times, problems that occur from too little memory, and so on. By resolving these problems, you improve system performance.

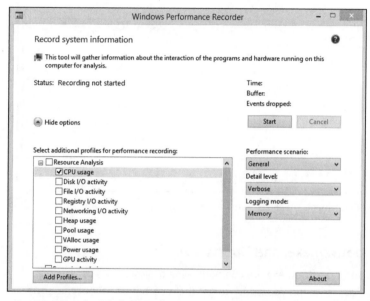

FIGURE 3-4 Use the Windows Performance Recorder to perform a trace analysis.

MORE INFO   **LEARN MORE ABOUT THE WPT**

The video at *http://channel9.msdn.com/events/BUILD/BUILD2011/HW-59T* shows how to change the view from Graph to other options, how to change the layout, how to review the data, and more.

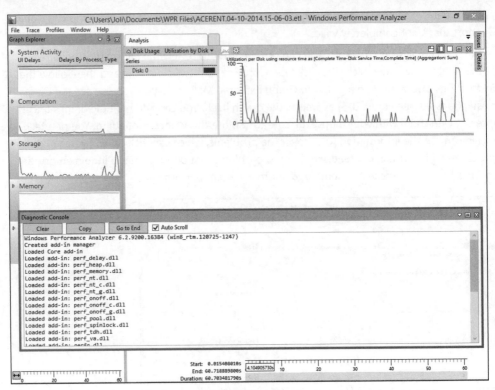

FIGURE 3-5 Use the Windows Performance Analyzer to review the trace logs you've acquired.

Using Xperf.exe, Xbootmgr.exe, and XperfView.exe

Xperf.exe, Xbootmgr.exe, and XperfView.exe are command-line tools you can use to create and manage trace recordings, assuming you prefer to get the recordings without the luxury of the GUI available from the WPT. However, the use of these tools appears to be fading. The WPT tools do still support Xperf.exe and Xbootmgr.exe, but with Windows 8.1 XperfView.exe is no longer supported. This means that you still can use the WPA to open recordings you've created by using Xperf, Xbootmgr, or the WPR, or recordings that are created from the Assessment Platform, if that's how you prefer to handle it. Although this objective might soon disappear from this exam, you should still review the command-line references available for Xperf and Xbootmgr. Review the following before continuing:

- At an elevated command prompt, type **xbootmgr.exe -help** to review the options associated with this tool.
- At an elevated command prompt, type **xperf.exe -help** to review the options available with this tool.

- To learn more, including how to use the options and parameters, read the article "Xperf Command-Line Reference" at *http://msdn.microsoft.com/en-us/library/windows/hardware/hh162920.aspx*.

Monitoring performance

You can monitor how well your systems perform in several ways. For example, you can use Performance Monitor to create Data Collector Sets and then review the logs to see where improvements can be made. You can use Task Manager to see what's using most of your computer's resources. You can also use Resource Monitor to view long-term performance data, including reviewing past problems that still need to be resolved.

Creating Data Collector Sets

You use Performance Monitor to view performance data in real time or to collect data in log files that you can review later. To do the latter, you need to configure a Data Collector Set, which gathers data related to the performance counters you select, as well as event trace sessions. Event trace data is collected from trace providers, which are features of the operating system or of individual applications that report actions or events. You can combine output from multiple trace providers into a trace session. You can also gather system configuration information (registry key values).

You can create a Data Collector Set from a template that's already configured to monitor specific data types, from an existing set of Data Collectors you've created, or by configuring your own Data Collector Set by selecting each individual item yourself. To open Performance Monitor, either search for it from the Start screen or type **perfmon** in a Run dialog box and click OK or press Enter.

The easiest way to collect a set of data is to create a Data Collector Set from a template, as follows:

1. In the Performance Monitor navigation pane, expand the Data Collector Sets node and right-click User Defined.
2. Click New, Data Collector Set.
3. Enter a name for your Data Collector Set.
4. Click Create From A Template and click Next.
5. Click the template you want to use (see Figure 3-6).
6. Click Finish. (You also can click Browse to define where to save the file.)

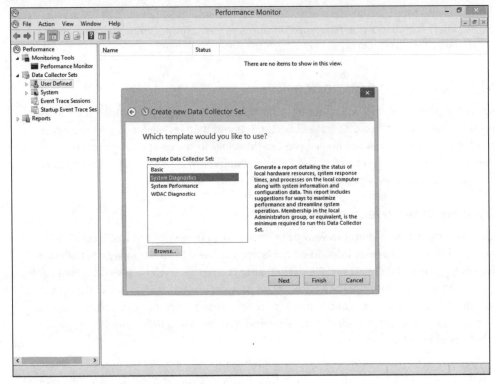

FIGURE 3-6 Creating a Data Collector Set from a template.

When you run the Data Collector Set, the collected data is saved on your root drive (unless you click Browse and choose a different folder) in a subfolder of a folder named PerfLogs. You can see the path and other relevant information by right-clicking the Data Collector Set that appears in the Navigation pane and clicking Properties. You also can see the options to view the results in the Navigation Pane of Performance Monitor under Reports.

To run the Data Collector Set, right-click it in the Navigation pane and then click Start. Click Stop when ready. You can right-click to see other options, including Save Template, Latest Report, and Data Manager. You can review the latest data collected in the Data Collector Set by right-clicking again and clicking Latest Report. Look closely at the report in Figure 3-7 and notice that the Hardware Device And Driver Checks has Failed beside it. This indicates a problem that you should address.

You can create Data Collector Sets in more ways than this. In the Navigation pane, notice several options in the Data Collector Sets option in addition to User Defined:

- **System** This consists of System Diagnostics and System Performance. You can run these predefined Data Collector Sets by right-clicking and clicking Start and then Stop.

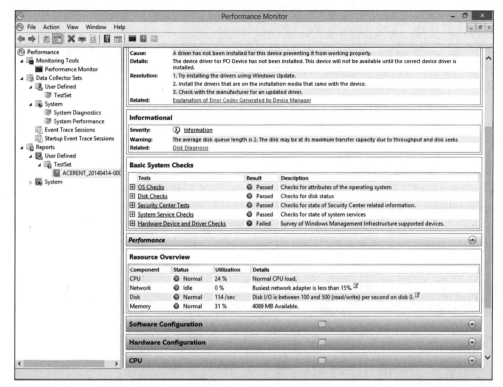

FIGURE 3-7 Reviewing Data Collector Set data.

- **Event Trace Sessions and Startup Event Trace Sessions** You can create a new Data Collector Set in both these locations in a manner similar to what's outlined in the prior steps, but you choose the event trace providers manually.

Continue to explore Performance Monitor as time allows. Continue on through this chapter when you are ready.

Using Task Manager

Task Manager is one of the most useful tools available in Windows 8.1 (and in earlier versions of Windows as well). Task Manager enables you to manage processes (discrete tasks) that use system resources and to see how those active processes affect those resources. Its simplicity enables end users to end problematic processes, disable apps that don't need to run at Startup, view logged-on users, and more. However, because Task Manager is such a powerful and feature-rich tool, the savviest network administrator can use it to monitor, diagnose, and improve computer performance quickly.

Because running processes are so important to system performance, Task Manager has been redesigned so you can see the *process tree*, which groups related processes together. The entire interface also is much more user-friendly. Task Manager has seven tabs. You need to know how you can use each tab to improve performance, and you need to know what each offers before you take the exam.

You can open Task Manager in several ways, but the simplest is to press Ctrl+Shift+Esc. Open Task Manager on your own computer now and explore the tabs as you read the rest of this section.

USING THE PROCESSES TAB

This tab shows all running processes grouped together as process trees. Processes with trees have a right-facing arrow beside them. Click that arrow to see the related processes. You can click a single process or a process tree name and then click End Task when you want to close one that is problematic. You can sort the processes based on resource usage. Figure 3-8 shows this tab.

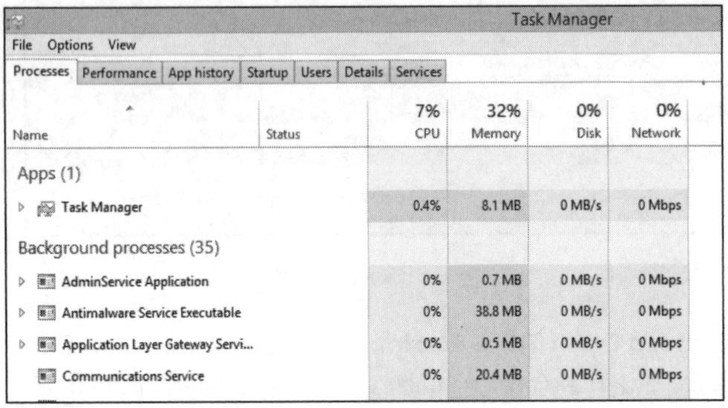

Task Manager
File Options View
Processes Performance App history Startup Users Details Services
Name Status 7% CPU 32% Memory 0% Disk 0% Network
Apps (1)
Task Manager 0.4% 8.1 MB 0 MB/s 0 Mbps
Background processes (35)
AdminService Application 0% 0.7 MB 0 MB/s 0 Mbps
Antimalware Service Executable 0% 38.8 MB 0 MB/s 0 Mbps
Application Layer Gateway Servi... 0% 0.5 MB 0 MB/s 0 Mbps
Communications Service 0% 20.4 MB 0 MB/s 0 Mbps

FIGURE 3-8 Use the Processes tab to select and end problematic processes.

USING THE PERFORMANCE TAB

This tab shows real-time statistics for CPU, Memory, Disk, Ethernet, Bluetooth, and Wi-Fi Usage. Under the graph you can see the adapter name, SSID, DNS name, connection type, IPv4 and IPv6 addresses, and signal strength. Right-click any entry on the left and click Summary View to minimize the window and to show only the left pane. Doing so lets you keep an eye on the usage without using up much of your desktop area.

USING THE APP HISTORY TAB

This tab shows usage associated with apps (not desktop apps). All apps are represented here, even if they aren't currently in use. You can use this tab to determine the load placed on the system from these apps. Columns here include CPU Time, Network, Metered Network, and Tile Updates. Like the Processes tab, you might see related trees. For instance, the Mail, Calendar, And People app has a right-facing arrow beside it. You can double-click any entry here to open the app or switch to it.

USING THE STARTUP TAB

This tab shows what applications start when the computer starts. You can select and disable any application listed here to keep it from starting when Windows does. When it's disabled, you can return here to re-enable it. You can also view the startup impact caused by the application, which can be marked None, Low, Medium, or High; its status (Enabled or Disabled); and more. You can also right-click any entry to open the file location for it.

EXAM TIP

In earlier operating system editions, you could type msconfig.exe in the Run dialog box to open the System Configuration window (and you still can), and from there you could click the Startup tab to configure what applications started when Windows did. If you do that now, under the Startup tab of the System Configuration window, you'll see only one option: Open Task Manager. I imagine that if a relevant question arises on the exam regarding configuring startup applications, the System Configuration window will be listed and will be (although technically a valid way to access the startup options) counted incorrect. You'll need to choose Task Manager.

USING THE USERS TAB

This tab shows all users logged on to the computer, including those logged on remotely. You can expand the tree associated with any user (click the right-facing arrow) to view the processes open for that user. You can select any of these processes and end them by clicking End Task at the bottom of the window, and you can disconnect a user by clicking the user name and clicking Disconnect in the same way. The active user will be prompted regarding the disconnect command when you use it.

USING THE DETAILS TAB

This tab shows what the old Processes tab showed in earlier versions of Task Manager. You can right-click any process to end the task, end the process tree, set a priority, set affinity, create a dump file, and more. Like other tabs, you can click any category name to sort the lists appropriately.

USING THE SERVICES TAB

This tab displays all enabled services. Like other tabs, you can right-click a service to perform a task. The options include Start, Stop, Restart, Open Services, Search Online, and Go To Details.

EXAM TIP

Explore the bottom of each tab of Task Manager. For the exam, you should know that the Performance tab has an option to open Resource Monitor and the Services tab has an option to open Services.

Using Resource Monitor

Resource Monitor is a powerful tool that you can use to see even more statistics regarding real-time resources. You can open Resource Monitor from the Performance tab of Task Manager, or you can use myriad other ways, including searching for it from the Start screen. You can also launch it directly by typing **Resmon.exe** in a Run dialog box. When you have it open, you need to spend some time reviewing each tab.

Figure 3-9 shows Resource Monitor, the Overview tab, the graphs available (which are available from any tab), and two suspended processes. Suspended processes can cause problems, so if you see them, take note. Understand that I did not manually suspend these processes myself; these processes were marked as suspended when I accessed this tab from Resource Monitor.

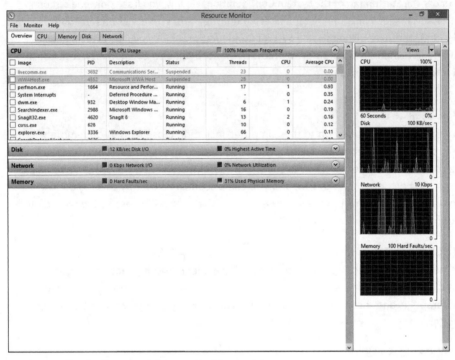

FIGURE 3-9 Use the Overview tab to see the bigger picture.

For the most part, you use Resource Monitor to troubleshoot problems that you couldn't uncover and resolve by using Task Manager and other tools. For instance, from the Memory tab, you can sort processes by how much memory is committed to them. You might find that a single process uses a lot of memory and is problematic. You might not even need to run the application. From there, you can right-click to end the process, and then return to Task Manager's Startup tab to stop the process from starting when Windows restarts to keep the problem from occurring in the future. This also reduces the memory load, which will, in the end, improve computer performance.

MORE INFO **RESOURCE MONITOR AND RELATED TERMS**

As you explore each tab, you'll see many terms that you'll need to know regarding Resource Monitor, including PID (the Process ID of the application) and Commit (the amount of memory committed by an application). Not enough space is available here to discuss all these terms, so you'll have to study them yourself. You can learn about Resource Monitor from this TechNet article: *http://technet.microsoft.com/en-us/library/dd883276(WS.10).aspx.*

Monitoring and managing printers

Although many companies are trying to get to a place where they can run a "paperless" office, printers generally are still a very large part of any enterprise. You might be assigned to manage those printers, including monitoring and sharing them, and you'll also need to understand how near field communication (NFC) Tap-to-Pair works and how to set it up.

Monitoring and managing printers as an end user or administrator

Devices And Printers, available from Control Panel or by searching for it from the Start screen, offers a place to view connected devices such as printers, mice, media devices, and fax machines. You can immediately discern whether a device has a known problem because of the exclamation point on top of it. You can right-click any device listed to configure device preferences, create a shortcut, troubleshoot the device, and view the device's properties.

Depending on what you click from the contextual menu, you see options that enable you to configure settings and preferences for the selected device (see Figure 3-10). For instance, if you click Printer Properties, you can access more than just options to print on both sides of the page or print a test page. You can also configure the following:

- **Sharing** This enables you to choose whether to share the printer and render print jobs on client computers. You can also opt to provide additional drivers to other workstations that need it.
- **Ports** This enables you to add, delete, and configure the port the printer is connected to. You can also enable printer pooling and bidirectional support.
- **Security** This enables you to choose the groups or users to allow or deny access to the printer.

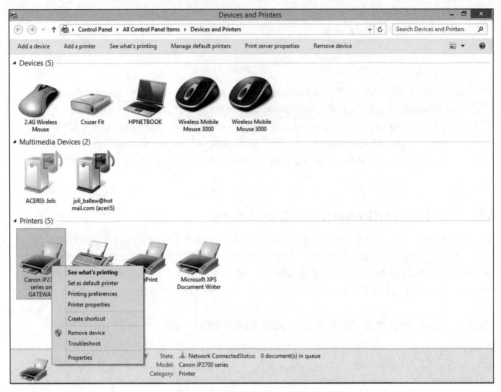

FIGURE 3-10 Devices And Printers offers a place to view connected devices .

You also can monitor a printer by right-clicking and selecting See What's Printing. When you are in the printer window, you can view the jobs waiting to print, pause print jobs, cancel all documents that are waiting to print, and delete a single entry from the print queue (right-click the entry). You also can access the printer's properties to perform tasks on the printer such as changing the print cartridges and performing other management tasks, and even manage the printer's color profiles.

The management and monitoring options for printers that have been discussed so far are really end-user management tools. Windows 8.1 Pro and Windows 8.1 Enterprise both include the Print Management console for administrators. You can use this console to manage your printers and gain access to more tools than are available to end users. For example, you can right-click any printer to delete or rename it, or to access options such as Open Printer Queue and Deploy With Group Policy (see Figure 3-11). Notice also the dimmed option: Enable Branch Office Direct Printing.

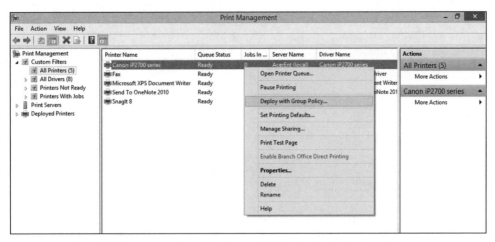

FIGURE 3-11 The Print Management console offers administrator-level printer options.

If you choose to deploy with a Group Policy Object, a new window opens that enables you to set the GPO name, as well as deploy the printer to the users or computers that this GPO applies to. Note that it doesn't open the Group Policy Management Console.

As you explore the window, be sure to expand each option, select each option, and right-click each option. Because too much is available to go over here, you'll have to cover that part on your own. However, I do want to point out the sharing options in the next section.

Sharing printers

To configure sharing options for any printer through the Print Management console, right-click the printer to share and click Manage Sharing. The printer Properties dialog box appears, with the Sharing tab displayed (see Figure 3-12). From here you can share the printer and add any drivers you have available for the computers that will access the printer.

Before continuing, you should explore every option in the Print Management console, including Printers With Jobs, Print Servers, and Deployed Printers. In the Print Servers section, what you see when you are in a domain and logged on as an administrator is quite extensive. For instance, you will also see the other computers in that domain and, for each computer listed, information about the driver versions used, form size (such as Legal or Ledger), ports used, and printers installed. On a local workgroup, you'll see your own computer there.

Finally, to add a network printer to a Windows 8.1 machine, open the Devices And Printers window, click Add Printer, and if the printer appears in the list of available printers, select it and work through the rest of the wizard. If you don't see the network printer there, click The Printer That I Want Isn't Listed, and type the path to the printer (see Figure 3-13). Then, work through the rest of the wizard.

FIGURE 3-12 Share a printer from its Properties dialog box.

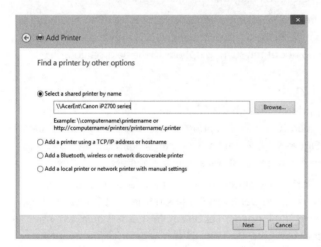

FIGURE 3-13 Locate the printer on the client to add it.

EXAM TIP

You might be asked how to troubleshoot a printer remotely by using Windows PowerShell. Make sure that you are familiar with the commands *Get-Printer*, *Get-PrintJob*, *Remove-PrintJob*, and others that you see at *http://technet.microsoft.com/en-us/library/ hh918357.aspx*.

Understanding NFC

NFC allows users to "tap" a device (such as a tablet) onto a physical device (such as a printer) and connect to it, in this case, to print. Users must be 4 cm or closer. NFC isn't Bluetooth, and there is no manual pairing; NFC uses short-range radio waves for discovery and for transmitting data. NFC requires users to employ some sort of NFC hardware, such as tags, stickers, key fobs, or cards, but the technology might be built right in to their laptops or tablets. Note that both devices must be NFC capable and enabled for this to work.

Here are a few more things to know about NFC in an enterprise:

- Administrators must be able to configure an NFC tag for their printer(s) or have printers with NFC built in.
- These connection types are acceptable for the printer: Universal Naming Convention (UNC), Web Services on Devices (WSD), and Wi-Fi Direct.
- Administrators can use the Windows PowerShell cmdlet *Write-PrinterNfcTag* to provision an NFC tag with information about a printer.

Remediating startup issues

The Diagnostics and Recovery Toolkit (DaRT) 8.1 supports Windows 8.1 and is part of the Microsoft Desktop Optimization Pack (MDOP) for Software Assurance. You can use DaRT to quickly repair unbootable or locked-out systems. You can also use it to diagnose what happened, restore missing files, and detect and remove malware.

Before you can use DaRT you must meet a few requirements:

- You must be a Microsoft Software Assurance customer.
- You must have the Windows Assessment and Development Kit 8.1 installed.
- You must have Microsoft .Net Framework 4.5.1.
- You must have the Windows 8.1 Debugging Tools to access the Crash Analyzer.

Because very little information about DaRT 8.1 is publically available, what you see in this section has been mined from the information available for DaRT 8.0. The steps involved in using DaRT likely haven't changed much, and this should be sufficient, at least until information about DaRT 8.1 becomes available.

To use DaRT, you must create a recovery image and copy it to a DVD, CD, or USB drive. You can also use a Windows Server Update Services (WSUS) server. A wizard will guide you through the process. You must select the image to use (it must match the platform of the computer you want to recover), clear any recovery tools you don't want your local user to access (you can still access them as an administrator), and include the latest Windows 8.1 Debugging Tools and Windows Defender malware definitions. With all that done, you can create your bootable recovery disk, which you'll use to start up to the DaRT recovery options. For the most part, you'll use DaRT to recover systems that can't start up to Windows, although you can also use it to reset passwords and recover lost files.

Recovering computers

You recover a computer by starting to the applicable DaRT recovery disk. Then, you navigate through the usual recovery screens to troubleshoot. You select the tool to use based on the type of problem you believe you're having.

- **Computer Management**   Use this tool to view system information and event logs, work with disks, manage services, manage drivers, and so on.
- **Crash Analyzer**   Use this tool to examine the dump file associated with the computer failure. The report might offer a name for the device driver that might have caused it. You can use the Computer Management tool, and the Services and Drivers node to disable the problematic driver.
- **Defender**   Use this tool to scan for and remove malware and viruses. This includes rootkit malware.
- **Disk Commander**   Use this tool to recover and repair disk partitions or volumes by restoring the master boot record (MBR), restoring partition tables, and saving those tables for backup. You should back up the partition tables before directing Disk Commander to repair it. DaRT can't recover dynamic disks.
- **Disk Wipe**   Use this tool to completely wipe a disk of all its data, using technology that meets current U.S. Department of Defense standards.
- **Explorer**   Use this tool to browse the files on the local system as well as network shares and to copy that data before you try to repair or reimage the computer.

- **File Restore**   Use this tool to restore deleted files that were too big for the Recycle Bin.

- **File Search**   Use this tool to search for files by type, path, date range, or size for the purpose of backing them up before attempting to recover the computer.

- **Hotfix Uninstall**   Use this tool to remove hotfixes or service packs installed on the computer, if you believe they caused the problem.

- **Locksmith**   Use this tool to set or change the password for the computer you are repairing.

- **Registry Editor**   Use this tool to add, remove, or edit registry keys and values.

- **SFC Scan**   This tool runs the System File Repair Wizard to repair/replace any system files that prevent Windows from starting.

- **Solution Wizard**   Use this tool to work through a series of questions when you don't know where to start with DaRT, and then review any solutions offered that might suit your needs.

- **TCP/IP Config**   When DHCP isn't available, you can use this tool to manually configure TCP/IP settings.

EXAM TIP

You might see a question on the exam that asks why DaRT can't be used to resolve a problem, or DaRT might be listed as an answer when it can't be used. For example, DaRT doesn't support dynamic disks but does support computers with Unified Extensible Firmware Interface (UEFI) and BIOS interfaces, GUID Partition Table (GPT) and MBR partition schemes, and 32-bit and 64-bit versions of Windows 8 and Windows Server 2012. When you see DaRT as an answer, make sure the requirements listed in the scenario meet the DaRT prerequisites.

Diagnosing system failures

You can use DaRT to diagnose system failures, using the available Crash Analyzer tool. The Crash Analyzer uses the Microsoft Debugging Tools for Windows (which you must install) to inspect a memory dump file to discover what caused the computer to fail (often a device driver). You generally run the Crash Analyzer on the problematic, local, end-user's computer. However, if you cannot access the Microsoft Debugging Tools for Windows or the symbol files on the end-user's computer, you can copy the dump file from it and analyze the information on a different computer. That secondary computer must have the stand-alone version of the Crash Analyzer installed on it. It must also have DaRT 8.0 installed.

To debug applications that have stopped responding, you also need access to the symbol files. Symbol files are automatically downloaded when you run the Crash Analyzer, but you must have Internet access to get them. Some ways to ensure that you'll have access to symbol files while debugging a computer are detailed at *http://technet.microsoft.com/en-us/library/jj713361.aspx.*

To run the Crash Analyzer on a local, end-user's computer, follow these steps:

1. In the Diagnostics and Recovery Toolset window on the problematic computer, click Crash Analyzer.

2. Provide the required information for the Microsoft Debugging Tools for Windows, the symbol files, and the memory dump file. You can find the location of the memory dump file by using these steps:

    A. In a Run dialog box, type **sysdm.cpl** and press Enter.

    B. Click the Advanced tab.

    C. In the Startup and Recovery area, click Settings.

    D. Note the location listed for the dump file before continuing.

3. Use the information to decide how you will attempt to resolve the problem. You might have to disable or update a device driver by using the Services and Drivers node of the Computer Management tool in DaRT 8.1.

Thought experiment

Repairing/restoring an unbootable computer

In this thought experiment, apply what you've learned about this objective. You can find answers to these questions in the "Answers" section at the end of this chapter.

You need to recover a computer that won't start. You think it might suffer from malware or a virus. You prefer not to reimage the machine if possible. You work for a large enterprise that has a Software Assurance agreement with Microsoft.

1. What tool is available to help you resolve this startup issue with the least amount of effort?

2. What will you use in this toolset to start the problematic computer?

3. What tool should you use first to try to salvage the data files on the machine?

4. What tool will you select to try to remove the malware?

Objective summary

- Device Manager is often your first choice when you need to view, install, uninstall, update, roll back, disable, and otherwise manage hardware devices, including legacy hardware.
- Use Sigverif.exe to view unsigned drivers and Pnputil.exe to manage drivers and the driver store from an elevated command prompt.

- When you see STOP errors, you might have to search online for a solution based on the error number, use the Windows Memory Diagnostic Tool, use ChkDsk, and/or review inconsistencies in Device Manager.

- Use Reliability Monitor to gauge the stability of a system and to search for errors involving Windows updates, driver installations, application failures, Windows failures, and more.

- The WPT consists of two independent tools: WPR and WPA. The WPR lets you monitor performance and create performance profiles; WPA lets you review the results.

- Use Performance Monitor to create Data Collector Sets and review the logs to see where you can make performance improvements.

- Use Task Manager to see what's using most of your computer's resources, to end processes, to stop applications from starting when Windows does, and more.

- Use Resource Monitor to view long-term performance data, such as past problems that still need to be resolved.

- You can share and manage printers in multiple ways, including by using the Devices And Printers window and the Print Management console.

- You can configure NFC printers to be used by other NFC-enabled devices to tap and connect.

- DaRT can help you recover from myriad startup problems and can be used when Windows is offline.

Objective review

Answer the following questions to test your knowledge of the information in this objective. You can find the answers to these questions and explanations of why each answer choice is correct or incorrect in the "Answers" section at the end of this chapter.

1. You have connected a legacy scanner by using a parallel part. You can't access the scanner, and Windows doesn't recognize the device. What should you do?

    A. In the Devices And Printers window, click Add A Device and work through the wizard.

    B. In Device Manager, from the Action tab, click Add Legacy Device.

    C. Windows doesn't recognize the device because the device driver isn't signed. Installing the device isn't possible.

    D. At an elevated command prompt, type **pnputil.exe –f** *<path to the driver>* **/***<drivername>***.inf** and press Enter.

2. You receive a STOP error on a client's computer. The Event ID suggests it is associated with the loss of the ability to write data to the hard disk. What command should you run to find out whether this is the problem?

   A. *Sigverif.exe*

   B. *Mdsched*

   C. *ChkDsk*

   D. *Perfmon*

3. What tool should you use when a client tells you that a computer is "running slowly," is often "unresponsive," and that the hard disk light is on a lot?

   A. Performance Monitor

   B. Reliability Monitor

   C. Sigverif.exe

   D. Windows Performance Toolkit (WPT)

4. You are using Task Manager to find out what exactly is using the most computer resources, specifically CPU resources. Which tab of Task Manager is the best to use to review this information?

   A. The Processes tab.

   B. The App History tab.

   C. The Services tab.

   D. You shouldn't use Task Manager; you should type **msconfig.exe** in a Run dialog box to access the System Configuration window.

5. Which of the following ways can enable you to share a printer on a Windows 8.1 Pro computer?

   A. In the Devices And Printers window, right-click the printer, click Printer Properties, and click the Sharing tab.

   B. In the Devices And Printers window, right-click the printer and click Sharing.

   C. In the Print Management console, right-click the printer and click Manage Sharing.

   D. In the Print Management console, right-click the printer and click Sharing.

6. You are attempting to resolve a startup problem by using DaRT. You believe that the problem involves a recently installed device driver, and you know the driver name. Which DaRT option should you try first to resolve the problem?

   A. Solution Wizard

   B. Explorer

   C. Disk Commander

   D. Computer Management

Objective 3.2: Support mobile devices

When mobile devices first became widely available, companies generally purchased them outright and then provisioned them to employees to use. This has fallen out of favor in many enterprises; instead, management allows users to bring their own devices to work (known as Bring Your Own Device or BYOD). This objective focuses on understanding the tools you'll need to incorporate to support this strategy. The devices considered here include Windows RT, Windows 8.1, and various mobile phones (those running Windows 8.1, Android, and iOS) that your users already own and want to use at work. Specifically, this objective looks at how to secure those devices, how to allow them to connect and sync, and how to manage them for the long term.

This objective covers how to:

- Support mobile device policies, including security policies, remote access, and remote wipe

- Support mobile access and data synchronization, including Work Folders and Sync Center

- Support broadband connectivity, including broadband tethering and metered networks

- Support mobile device management via Windows Intune, including Windows RT, Windows Phone 8, iOS, and Android

---

Supporting mobile device policies

Because users own devices such as tablets and phones, and because they want to use those devices on your enterprise network to do work, at some point you'll likely need to configure Bring Your Own Device (BYOD) policies and create an infrastructure that supports those devices. When the policies are in place, you can register and enroll those clients to authenticate them on your network. You'll do all of this before you let your users access any data on corporate servers, including their own data, apps you make available in the company portal (perhaps), and data that's available to all your users, perhaps from an intranet site.

Configuring mobile device policies

Before you can configure mobile device policies, you must be very sure that you know exactly how you want your mobile clients to function. Should the devices be encrypted? What apps and data will you allow users to access from those devices? What will you do when a device goes missing? What types of passwords will you allow your employees to use? As you might guess, you have a lot more questions to answer before you can start configuring policies.

After you decide what policies to apply, you need to create an infrastructure to support those policies.

You can choose from several options when planning a mobile device policy strategy, putting the applicable infrastructure in place, and so on. Some of the more popular options include Windows Intune and Microsoft System Center 2012. Other possibilities are available, but because this exam likely will focus on Windows Intune over others, this section puts its focus there. You learned a little about Windows Intune in Chapter 1, "Support operating system and application installation."

A popular mobile device management solution, Windows Intune—with or without System Center Configuration Manager—lets you deploy mobile devices, create security policies, upload and publish software packages, and manage inventory without any type of onsite infrastructure. Windows Intune offers various levels of security that you can configure and apply to your users and mobile devices, although not all options apply to every type of device that you might want to register and enroll. Although you can review the entire list of compliance options at *http://technet.microsoft.com/en-us/library/dn600287.aspx*, this section lists a few just to give you an understanding of what's available. You can apply the items in this list to every supported device type, including Windows 8.1, Windows RT 8.1, Windows Phone 8 and Windows Phone 8.1, iOS 6 or later, and Android 4.0 and later:

- Minimum password length
- Number of repeated sign-in failures to allow before the device is wiped of corporate data
- Minutes of activity before the screen turns off
- Password expiration
- Password history
- Links to the Windows Store, Windows Phone Store, App Store, and Google Play Store
- Featured apps

You can apply many other compliance (security) policies to some but not all mobile devices, either because they are unique to the device or not supported on all devices. For example, you can enable Smart Screen on Windows RT 8.1 or Windows 8.1 but not on anything else, because Smart Screen is unique to Windows. You can allow backup to iCloud on iOS devices and no others, because iCloud is unique to iOS. You can allow a pop-up blocker on Windows RT 8.1, Windows 8.1, and iOS, but not on Android or Windows Phone 8.

To explore Windows Intune as you read along, you need to sign up for and set up a free Windows Intune trial account. With that done, sign in, navigate to the administrator console, and click Policy in the left pane (see Figure 3-14).

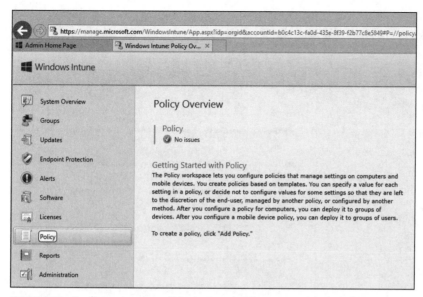

FIGURE 3-14 Configure security policies in the administrator console, in Policy.

You can use a predefined template to create your first security policy, but if you opt for a custom policy, you can better see all your options:

1. In the left pane, click Policy. This opens the Policy workspace.

2. Click Add Policy under Tasks.

3. In the Create a New Policy Wizard, leave Mobile Device Security Policy selected, and then click Create And Deploy A Custom Policy.

4. Click Create Policy.

5. From the Overview tab, name the policy, type a description, scroll down, and then carefully read and configure each option as desired (see Figure 3-15).

6. Click the Security tab, the Cloud tab, and the other tabs to review the options.

7. When you're ready, click Save Policy.

After you save the policy, you can choose to deploy it. If you do, you can continue working in the console to choose the users and groups to apply the policy to, as well as configure other options.

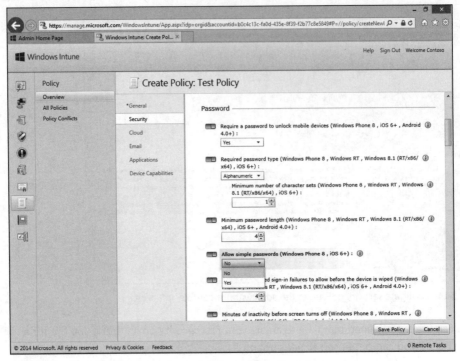

FIGURE 3-15 Use Windows Intune to create a custom security policy.

Exploring access policies

The preceding section focused on creating security policies. Other policies available include those that relate to Windows Firewall Settings. As with the security policy option, the Windows Firewall Settings policy option also includes a template you can use, but if you opt to create a custom policy instead, you can review all the available settings. To see these options, follow the steps in the preceding section to open the Create a New Policy Wizard, and this time choose Windows Firewall Settings. Again, opt for Create And Deploy A Custom Policy. The options you see in Figure 3-16 let you control incoming and outgoing network traffic on devices to which the policy is deployed. The policies are grouped by profile: Domain, Private, and Public.

Some options you can enable or disable for any profile includes whether or not to:

- Block all incoming connections.
- Configure exceptions for things such as BranchCache, Connect to a Network Projector, File and Printer Sharing, and Core Networking.
- Notify users when Windows Firewall blocks a program.
- Allow or deny Remote Assistance, Remote Desktop, and/or Remote Administration.

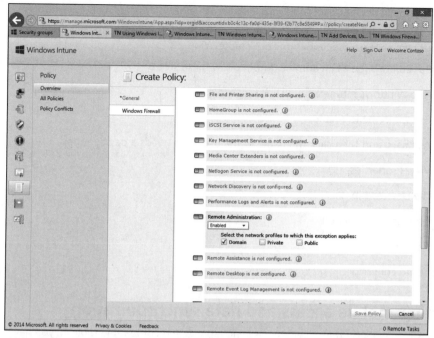

FIGURE 3-16 Use Windows Intune to create a custom firewall policy.

You can configure these policies and apply them to users and groups to maintain control over what kinds of data can enter or leave your network. As you can see in Figure 3-16, you can enable Remote Administration for any profile, and here, Domain is selected. Below this you might be able to see Remote Assistance and Remote Desktop, which enable you to control what kinds of access your users have to the resources on the enterprise network.

Exploring Remote Wipe

Windows Intune provides tools you can use to perform a remote wipe of a device. Remote Wipe is an important option because mobile devices often hold sensitive data that's unique to your enterprise, and those devices also offer access to your company's resources. If a user loses a device or if a device is stolen, that data can be compromised. Thus, knowing how to perform a remote wipe quickly is important. Users can also initiate a remote wipe from the company portal; this might be something you also would want to inform your users about. Finally, you'll want to wipe a device when you are ready to retire it.

Two types of wipe are available: Full and Selective. The article at *http://technet.microsoft. com/en-us/library/jj676679.aspx#bkmk_pass* provides lots of information about the differences between a full wipe and a selective wipe, including under what circumstance a wipe can occur. For example, what can be wiped selectively depends on the platform you are working with. Although you can wipe email from Windows 8.1 and Windows RT 8.1 devices that are enrolled as mobile devices, you can't wipe email from other platforms such as Windows RT, Windows Phone 8 and 8.1, iOS, or Android. You really need to read the aforementioned article on your own to learn the limitations of Remote Wipe.

To initiate a remote wipe as an administrator, follow these steps:

1. Open the Windows Intune administrator console.

2. Click Groups in the left pane.

3. Click All Users, and then click the name of the user who needs a device wiped.

4. Click View Properties.

5. Click the Devices tab.

6. Select the device to wipe.

7. Click Retire/Wipe.

8. Click Yes to confirm.

Supporting mobile access and data synchronization

If your users will do work on their devices (meaning laptops and compatible tablets), you have to provide them some way to sync data between those devices and your network servers. Two types of data access and synchronization to discuss are Work Folders and Sync Center.

You can use Work Folders with Windows RT 8.1 and Windows 8.1 laptops and tablets only. You can use Sync Center for older Windows clients that don't support Work Folders, such as Windows Vista and Windows 7, or when you don't want to put a Work Folders infrastructure in place. Sync Center has been around a long time, since Windows XP, and is still available in Windows 8.1.

Both options enable users to keep cached copies of important files on their devices so that they can access the data when they can't access the network. Group Policy settings are available to configure to manage these relationships.

Implementing mobile device synchronization of Work Folders

A new feature in Windows 8.1, Work Folders allows users to sync data from their user folders, located in their company's domain or data center, to their devices and back again. This is done automatically and is part of the file system. Before this feature was introduced, users had to be joined to the domain or at least required to input domain credentials before syncing could occur. Now, users can retain local copies of their work files on their devices, with automatic synchronization back to the company file servers occurring behind the scenes.

End users can find the Work Folders option in the Windows 8.1 Control Panel. They can select the Set Up Work Folders option, if you have set it up and configured it on the company network. The Work Folders window appears with Set Up Work Folders available for configuring (see Figure 3-17).

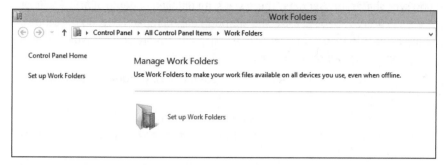

FIGURE 3-17 Users can set up their own Work Folders after the infrastructure is in place.

When users opt to set up Work Folders, they must work through a few setup tasks:

1. They must input a company email address.

2. They must wait while the wizard searches the network for their Work Folders.

3. After the folders are found, the users must accept (or change if applicable and available) where the files will be saved on their computers.

4. The users must read the security policy and then accept those polices.

5. Users can now access the documents under the Work Folders location from any compatible device, and the documents are kept in sync by Work Folders automatically. (Work Folders appears as a folder in File Explorer when This PC is selected in the navigation pane.)

> **NOTE ENSURING FULL FUNCTIONALITY OF WORK FOLDERS**
>
> The client and server must be running the same milestone release for Work Folders to function properly. For example, if the server is running this milestone release of Windows Server 2012 R2, the client must be running the same milestone release of Windows 8.1 if the client wants full functionality.

> **MORE INFO WORK FOLDERS**
>
> To learn more about Work Folders, refer to this TechNet article: *http://technet.microsoft.com/en-us/library/dn265974.aspx*.

Designing a Work Folders implementation in a domain involves several steps, including installing Work Folders on a domain-joined file server, creating security groups for Work Folders, and creating sync shares for user data. These steps are detailed in depth at *http://technet. microsoft.com/en-us/library/dn528861.aspx*, and although this material is beyond the scope of this book, you might want to read it anyway. Group Policy settings are also available for Work Folders that you as an administrator should be aware of, including these two:

- From User Configuration, Policies, Administrative Templates, Windows Components, WorkFolders you can specify Work Folders settings.

- From Computer Configuration, Policies, Administrative Templates, Windows Components, WorkFolders you can force automatic setup of Work Folders for all users.

Supporting mobile device synchronization with Sync Center

Sync Center enables your users to sync files between a compatible device (such as a laptop running Windows 7 Enterprise) and applicable network servers in a domain or workgroup. Sync Center is available in Windows 8.1 as well as earlier operating systems. You use Sync Center when your users need to be able to keep a copy of their data on their own devices so that they can access that data when they aren't connected to your network.

> **SEE ALSO   GROUP POLICY FOR OFFLINE FILES**
>
> In the next section, "Supporting broadband connectivity," read the subsection "Exploring Group Policy" to learn more about controlling the behavior of offline files.

To get started, you must first create a sync partnership on the client computer. To do this, navigate to a share on a different computer (not on the client) or file server, right-click that share, and click Always Available Offline. Then, on the client computer, open Sync Center (type **Sync Center** at the Start screen on a Windows 8.1 client). You should see what's shown in Figure 3-18. Make a note of the options on the left side before moving forward here; you can use these options as soon as syncing is configured to manage syncing tasks. You'll want to return here and click each option to see what's offered there. One option, Manage Offline Files, lets you view the Offline Files dialog box, where you can disable offline files, view offline files, check disk usage, encrypt your files, and more.

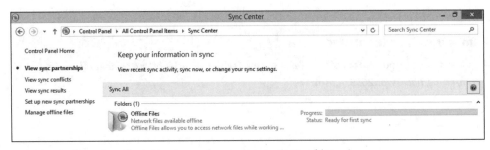

FIGURE 3-18 Open Sync Center to view and manage sync partnerships.

In Sync Center, as soon as a sync partnership is available, you can opt to sync everything (Figure 3-18 shows Sync All) or you can select the Offline Files folder, click Schedule (not shown), and work through the wizard provided to configure sync settings. Two options are available:

- **At a scheduled time**   For example, every Monday at 11 A.M. or every day at 2 A.M.
- **When an event occurs**   For example, every time you log on to your computer

Depending on your choice, you set more scheduling options, such as only syncing when the computer has been idle for a specific amount of time or if the computer is running on external power (and not on its battery). You can also opt to trigger synchronization to coincide with a specific event, such as when the client logs on, when the computer is idle for a specific amount of time, when the client locks Windows, and when the client unlocks Windows.

Note that two types of syncing options are available. A one-way sync is used when only data on the computer is transferred to the device, but nothing from the device is synced back. More common in an enterprise is a two-way sync, in which data can be transferred in both directions.

> **NOTE   FORCING A SYNC**
>
> Users can force a sync from Windows Mobility Center by clicking Sync in the Sync Center box anytime they like.

> **NOTE   SYNC CONFLICTS**
>
> When multiple versions of a file exist and those versions are synced, a sync conflict occurs. When this happens, the user is prompted regarding what to do. Users might want to keep both versions, or they can choose one over the other.

Supporting broadband connectivity

Some users have mobile devices that let them connect to the Internet when traditional options are unavailable. Traditional options include free and personal Mi-Fi networks, VPNs, workgroup and domain networks, broadband connections from ISPs, and Ethernet connections to networks. When these options are unavailable, users can opt for a built-in or personal cellular or metered broadband connection option, or another person's shared Internet connection.

Windows 8.1 comes with built-in support for these newer connectivity models. For instance, any Windows 8.1 user can connect to a broadband connection from their personal device (if the device is so enabled) from the Networks pane using familiar connection options. Users can also connect through a shared personal hotspot, assuming they have the required credentials.

Connecting to a shared personal hotspot

Users can connect to shared, metered connections configured as personal hotspots by others through the traditional Networks pane they use to connect to all other networks. They also can use that pane to disconnect. Figure 3-19 shows the Networks pane in which a shared hotspot is available. The user has connected to this network in the usual way, by clicking it and typing the applicable network information and password.

FIGURE 3-19 Users can connect to shared hotspots.

Connecting with a personal broadband connection

Some mobile devices, including those enabled for Long-Term Evolution (LTE), come with mobile broadband technology built in. Users connect in the same manner as always, by locating the network connection in the Networks pane and entering the desired credentials. These connections can also start automatically when no other network is available.

Windows 8.1 enables users to share their personal connections with others. Briefly, users connect to the Internet using the connection available on their own devices, and then opt to share the connection. This is done in PC Settings, Network, Connections and by clicking the connection to share. After the connection is shared, users can also change the service set identifier (SSID)—the password for the Wi-Fi network—and see how many people are sharing the connection. The person sharing the connection has to have purchased a data plan that supports tethering for this to work.

> **MORE INFO** **WINDOWS 8.1 FEATURES FOR BROADBAND**
>
> Refer to this article for more information about the new features for broadband in Windows 8.1: *http://msdn.microsoft.com/en-us/library/windows/hardware/dn247045.aspx*.

Managing metered connections

If the user's connection is metered, you should configure the Networks pane to show the estimated usage so that your users can more easily manage that connection. Marking that connection as metered is also important. You can find these options under PC Settings, Network, Connections. Figure 3-20 shows the options to show the estimated usage and configure the network as metered.

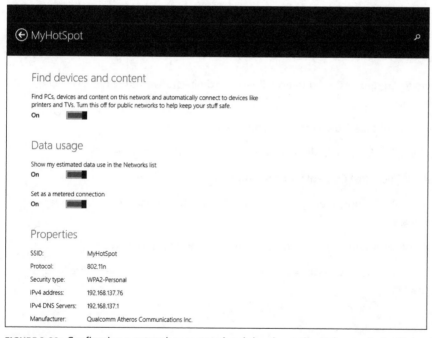

FIGURE 3-20 Configuring a network as metered and showing estimated usage in the Networks pane.

Exploring Group Policy

You should explore Group Policy settings that enable you to better maintain control over what happens when users are connected to a metered network. Specifically, here you look at how offline files are handled when users are on metered networks.

To enable background file synchronization of offline files on metered networks (which isn't enabled by default), follow these steps:

1. Open Group Policy Management.

2. Right-click the applicable GPO and click Edit. The Group Policy Management Editor appears.

3. Navigate to Computer Configuration, Policies, Administrative Templates, Network, Offline Files.

4. Right-click Enable File Synchronization On Costed Networks, and then click Edit.

5. Click Enabled, and then click OK.

You can enable Always Offline mode so that users can have faster access to cached files and redirected folders. Always Offline also lessens the amount of bandwidth used because users are always working offline, even when they are connected through a high-speed network connection. To enable Always Offline mode, follow these steps:

1. Open Group Policy Management.

2. Right-click the applicable GPO and click Edit. The Group Policy Management Editor appears.

3. Navigate to Computer Configuration, Policies, Administrative Templates, Network, Offline Files.

4. Right-click Configure Slow-Link Mode, and then click Edit.

5. In the Configure Slow-Link Mode window, click Enabled. See Figure 3-21.

6. Click Show. The Show Contents window appears.

7. In the Value Name box, specify the file share for which you want to enable Always Offline mode.

8. To enable Always Offline mode on all file shares, type * (asterisk).

9. In the Value box, type **Latency=1** to set the latency threshold to one millisecond, and then click OK.

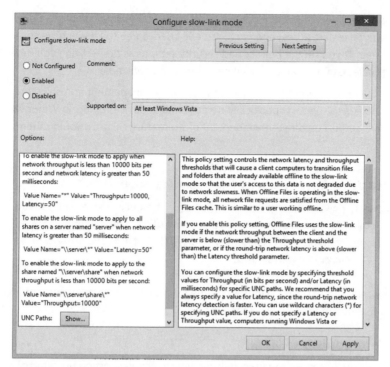

FIGURE 3-21 Configuring applicable Group Policy settings.

EXAM TIP

Before taking the exam, you must review all Group Policy settings located in the Computer Configuration, Administrative Templates, Network, Offline Files area so that you are aware of other policies that you can enable (or disable). A few include Enable Transparent Caching, At Logoff, Delete Local Copy Of User's Offline Files, and Encrypt The Offline Files Cache.

Supporting mobile device management

Windows Intune offers enterprises, small to medium companies, and network administrators complete mobile device management options for their clients who use Windows RT, Windows Phone 8 or 8.1, iOS, and Android devices both on the local network and off. Windows Intune enables you to secure corporate data; manage mobile inventory; offer access to applications you create and access to applications created elsewhere; and wipe data from devices when they are lost, stolen, or ready to be retired or reassigned (as you learned earlier in this chapter). Users can control, manage. and personalize their own devices while you maintain control of device enrollment and enterprise data access and management. Users agree to let you have corporate control when they enroll; you set the policies and security settings as desired, and you have the right to wipe corporate data off their devices if necessary and at any time.

You have a lot to consider when creating a mobile device management infrastructure, but the objective here is to support specifically named mobile devices by using Windows Intune, which means setting up direct management of those devices, provisioning them, and enrolling them.

> **MORE INFO** **WINDOWS INTUNE MOBILE DEVICE MANAGEMENT**
>
> Only a few pages can be used here to devote to the topic of mobile device management with Windows Intune, but you can find pages upon pages of documentation regarding this topic at *http://technet.microsoft.com/en-us/library/jj733654.aspx* and *http://technet. microsoft.com/en-us/library/dn408185.aspx.*

Many steps are required to set up Windows Intune for mobile device management and to enroll devices, as outlined in the following sections.

Meeting the prerequisites

To get started, you must first meet the prerequisites, which includes setting up external dependencies for the devices you want to enroll. These dependencies vary for each type of device:

- **For Windows Phone 8**   Deploy the applicable company portal app to the phone along with the required security certificates.
- **For iOS**   Obtain an Apple Push Notification service certificate. This enables Windows Intune to communicate securely with the Apple Push Notification service.
- **For Android**   Download the Windows Intune Company Portal app from the Google Play Store.
- **For app management of Windows 8, Windows 8.1, or Windows RT**   Obtain side-loading keys and sign all apps.

Setting up the Windows Intune administrator console

Next, you must choose how to manage your devices: the Windows Intune administrator console (see earlier) or the Configuration Manager console. To use the Windows Intune administrator console, follow these steps:

1. Click the Admin Console.

2. Click Mobile Device Management.

3. Click Set Mobile Device Management Authority.

4. Click Yes to continue the setup process.

Setting up direct management for the devices to support

You can set up direct management for the device types you want to support. The process varies for each device type. To set up direct management for Windows devices, follow these steps:

1. In the Windows Intune administrator console, click the Administration icon.

2. Under Mobile Device Management, click Windows (see Figure 3-22).

3. Under Step 1: Enrollment Server Address, type the name of the verified domain, and then click Test Auto-Detection.

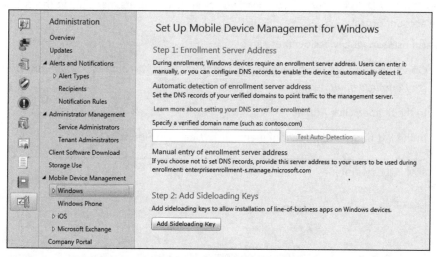

FIGURE 3-22 Setting up mobile device management for Windows.

NOTE SIDELOADED APPS

Sideloaded apps don't have to be certified by (or installed from) the Windows Store. However, they can be installed only on devices capable of sideloading, and you must have and add the applicable sideloading product activation keys.

To add sideloading keys, follow these steps:

1. Under Step 2: Add Sideloading Keys, click Add Sideloading Key.

2. Enter a key name, the product activation key, the number of activations, and an optional description.

3. Click OK.

To set up direct management for iOS devices, follow these steps:

1. In the Windows Intune administrator console, click Administration, click Mobile Device Management, and then click iOS.

2. Click Upload An APNs Certificate.

3. Click Browse to locate and then select the Apple Push Notification service (APNs) certificate you obtained in the prerequisite setup process.

Provisioning users for device enrollment

Now you must add the members you want to enroll into the Windows Intune user group. You have two options. If you have Active Directory Domain Services (AD DS) in your environment, you can configure Active Directory synchronization. When you do, local users and security groups are synchronized and can appear in the Windows Intune administrator console. If you don't have AD DS in your environment, you need to add users manually to the Windows Intune account portal.

To add users manually, follow these steps:

1. Open the Windows Intune account portal from *https://account.managem.microsoft. com/admin/default.aspx.*

2. In the header, click Admin.

3. In the left pane, under Management, click Users (see Figure 3-23).

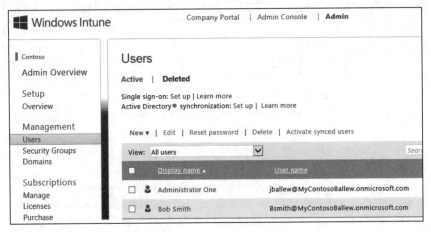

FIGURE 3-23 Adding users manually.

4. Click New, and in the drop-down list that appears, click User.

5. Input the user information. Click Next.

6. Click Yes to assign the user an administrator role, if desired. Otherwise, select a role from the available drop-down list.

7. Select the user's work location, and then click Next.

8. Accept Windows Intune as the user group and click Next.

9. Leave Send Email selected to send an email to yourself and add the recipients of your choice by typing their email addresses. Click Create.

10. Click Finish.

Enrolling the devices

Finally, you must enroll the devices. Users generally do this, but you can do it yourself if you have access to the device.

1. **For Windows Phone 8**   Open system settings and select company apps. Select Install company app or Hub.

2. **For Windows RT**   Select Start, type **System Configuration**, and open Company Apps. Enter credentials to authenticate.

3. **For Windows RT 8.1**   From the Settings Charm, click Change PC Settings. Click Network, Workplace. Enter the user ID, click Turn On, and agree to allow apps and services when prompted. Click Turn On.

4. **For iOS 6 or later**   Get the Windows Intune Company Portal app from the app store. Open the app to work through the enrollment process. Users also can enroll online at *m.manage.microsoft.com*.

5. **For Android 4.0 or later**   Users download the Windows Intune Company Portal app from the Google Play Store. Open the app to work through the enrollment process.

Monitoring the devices

Now you can monitor the devices. You've already explored some of the management options, including wiping data from a device. To access all management options, follow these steps:

1. In the left pane of the Windows Intune administrator console, click Groups.

2. Expand All Mobile Devices, and then click All Direct Managed Devices.

From the General tab you can see the status of various items, including Alert Status, Update Status, Endpoint Protection Status, Policy, Software Status, and Device Health Status. If any problems exist, click the information offered to see what's wrong and how to resolve it. You also can manage devices individually from the Devices tab, shown in Figure 3-24.

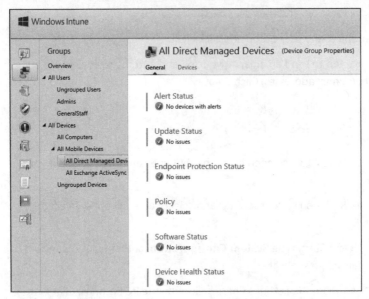

FIGURE 3-24 Managing devices from the Windows Intune administrator console.

Thought experiment

Setting up offline files

In this thought experiment, apply what you've learned about this objective. You can find answers to these questions in the "Answers" section at the end of this chapter.

You want to give your users the option to keep cached copies of important files on their devices so that they can access the data when they can't access the network. You support many different types of clients. You do have an AD DS domain and have set up the required infrastructure for setting up this option for users.

1. What offline files option would you choose for your Windows 8.1 laptop and tablet users so that they can sync data from their user folders, located in their company's domain or datacenter, to their devices and back again, automatically?

2. Where would those Windows 8.1 users go to set up this option?

3. What offline files option would you use for your Windows 7 clients?

4. What are some of the available options regarding when to sync those Windows 7 clients beyond syncing when the client logs on?

5. Which is the most common scenario for syncing data in an enterprise: one-way or two-way?

Objective summary

- Windows Intune is a popular mobile device management solution. Windows Intune (with or without Configuration Manager) lets you deploy mobile devices, create security policies, upload and publish software packages, remotely wipe devices, and manage inventory without any type of onsite infrastructure.

- You can configure security policies from scratch or by using a template to create rules for password history, password expiration, and so on. You create access policies in the same way to create rules unique to accessing data over a specific network type: Domain, Private, or Public.

- Work Folders and Sync Center enable users to keep cached copies of important files on their devices so that they can access the data when they can't access the network. Group Policy settings are available to configure to manage these relationships.

- Windows 8.1 users can connect to a broadband connection from their personal devices from the Networks pane using familiar connection options. Users can also connect through a shared personal hotspot, assuming they have the required credentials.

- To manage mobile devices, you can set up Windows Intune, provision and enroll the devices, and then learn where and how to manage them for the long term.

Objective review

Answer the following questions to test your knowledge of the information in this objective. You can find the answers to these questions and explanations of why each answer choice is correct or incorrect in the "Answers" section at the end of this chapter.

1. Which of the following Windows Intune security policies are available to apply to all your mobile clients (Windows 8.1, Windows RT 8.1, Windows Phone 8, iOS, Android 4.0 and later)? (Choose all that apply.)

   A. Password expiration

   B. Allow a pop-up blocker

   C. Password history

   D. Maximum password length

2. From the Windows Intune administrator console, where do you perform a remote wipe of a device?

   A. In the Software pane, from the Manage Deployment option

   B. In the Groups pane, from All Users, and from the user's Properties page

   C. In the Administrator pane, from Mobile Device Management, from the applicable device type section

   D. In the Policy pane, from All Polices

3. Some of your users access your network and the data on it from metered cellular or broadband connections. You want to reduce how much bandwidth they use and offer faster access to cached files. Which of the following Group Policy settings should you enable and how should you configure them? Choose two.

   A. Enable file synchronization on costed networks.

   B. In the Value box, type **Latency=0** to set the latency threshold to one millisecond.

   C. In the Value box, type **Latency=1** to set the latency threshold to one millisecond.

   D. Configure slow-link mode.

4. How and where do you, as an administrator, provision mobile users for device enrollment if you don't have AD DS in your environment?

   A. In the Windows Intune administrator console, from the Administrator pane in Mobile Device Management

   B. In the Windows Intune administrator console, from the Groups pane, in All Mobile Devices

   C. In the Windows Intune account portal, under Admin, from the Users tab

   D. In the Windows Intune account portal, under Admin Console, from the Users tab

   E. In the Windows Intune Company Portal

Objective 3.3: Support client compliance

You can use several strategies to keep your client computers healthy. You could simply list all the things your clients need do to keep their machines safe (scan with Windows Defender, install Windows updates, and so forth) and tell them to do those things, but chances are this wouldn't work for the long term. Another option is to manage the security of these machines yourself by using tools such as Windows Intune, Group Policy, and Microsoft System Center 2012 Endpoint Protection. This objective discusses these things and more, including Internet Explorer 11 security and new and improved Group Policy features.

> **This objective covers how to:**
> - Manage updates by using Windows Update and Windows Intune, including non-Microsoft updates
> - Manage client security by using Windows Defender, Windows Intune Endpoint Protection, or Microsoft System Center 2012 Endpoint Protection
> - Manage Internet Explorer 11 security
> - Support Group Policy application, including Resultant Set of Policy (RSoP), policy processing, and Group Policy caching

Managing updates by using Windows Update and Windows Intune

Microsoft has provided Windows updates as part of its ongoing attempt to keep its operating systems safe and secure week after week, year after year, for decades. These updates often offer new features or functionality, but for the most part they are pushed out to fix security issues, address new security threats, and provide new device drivers. This is a necessary part of any company's maintenance plan, because someone always will try to hack into systems, unleash viruses, hide malware, and so on. You need to be protected. Thus, you have to install these updates, and creating a policy for doing so is the best way to go.

In small organizations that don't use an Active Directory infrastructure but instead are small peer-to-peer networks, most client computers are simply configured to install updates automatically. Often, such companies have no policy and no one to oversee the process. In larger organizations, even those configured as workgroups (and not Active Directory domains), administrators often prefer to set policies for updates via Local Group Policy. Companies with Active Directory domains commonly have isolated labs where updates are tested before they are rolled out, and sometimes even have specialized servers that cache those updates first, to lessen the required bandwidth if each client gets their updates directly from Microsoft. With this approach, updates also can be tested before releasing them to clients. Of course, administrators can use Group Policy settings for Windows updates to manage them as well.

If you prefer not having to manage the updates in any of these ways, or none of these fit your infrastructure properly (perhaps because of specific mobile clients and network type), you can use Windows Intune instead. The Windows Intune administrator console includes an Updates tab (to access the Updates workspace) that enables you to fully manage the process. Updates can be Microsoft or non-Microsoft updates, and you can view pending updates, approve or decline updates, configure automatic approval settings, and set a deadline for update installation by configuring an automatic approval rule.

EXAM TIP

You might see questions that ask you to propose a solution for configuring approval and automatic updates, given a specific scenario. If that scenario includes Windows RT devices, remember that Windows RT can't join a domain, so any domain-based solution won't work. In these cases, consider Windows Intune as an answer if given.

Using Windows Update

Windows Update is the client side of the equation. For stand-alone computers and computers in small workgroups, Windows Update might be ideal, assuming that you configure the settings appropriately. The settings you need to access are available in the Windows Update window, from Control Panel, System And Security, Windows Update. You'll find the options Check For Updates, Change Settings, View Update History, Restore Hidden Updates, Installed Updates, and Add Features To Windows 8.1. You'll also see any available scheduled updates to install, optional updates, and information about when you receive any updates. Figure 3-25 shows this window.

FIGURE 3-25 Clients can manage their own updates from Windows Update in Control Panel.

NOTE **USING WINDOWS UPDATE**

You can use PC Settings, Update And Recovery to quickly see whether a client machine is configured to receive updates. You can also view the update history and choose how updates are installed. However, most network administrators still prefer the Windows Update window, available from Control Panel, because all options are available there, not just the ones that end users would likely access.

To configure update settings from Control Panel, follow these steps:

1. Click System And Security, and then click Windows Update.

2. From the Windows Update window shown in Figure 3-25, click Change Settings.

3. Make your preferred choices, using the options available in the drop-down list under Important Updates:

   - Install Update Automatically (Recommended)

   - Download Updates But Let Me Choose Whether To Install Them

   - Check For Updates But Let Me Choose Whether To Download Or Install Them

   - Never Check For Updates (Not Recommended)

4. Click the scheduling option shown. The default entry is Updates Will Be Automatically Installed During The Maintenance Window.

5. If desired, use the drop-down list next to Run Maintenance Tasks Daily At to choose a different time. The default is 3 a.m.

6. If desired, select Allow Scheduled Maintenance To Wake Up My Computer At The Scheduled Time.

7. Click OK twice.

> *NOTE* **MANAGING UPDATES**
>
> - When a new device is connected to a computer, Windows 8.1 searches for a driver on the computer, and if it doesn't find one, it looks to Windows Update.
> - Standard users can install drivers that have been downloaded from Windows Update without a User Access Control (UAC) prompt.
> - Optional updates might be available in the Windows Update window that weren't installed automatically, so occasionally check to see whether any are available.

When you need more control over how Windows updates are applied to client machines, you can enable local and domain Group Policy settings. You'll find the settings in the applicable Group Policy Editor from Computer Configuration, Policies, Administrative Templates, Windows Components, Windows Update. Be sure to review these before continuing here. Remember, too, that when you enable a specific Group Policy setting, you are configuring the policy to do exactly what it says it will do. So if the policy setting starts with the words "Do not display...", when you enable the setting, whatever it is will not be displayed. A policy starting with the words "Turn on..." means that when you enable that policy, the thing is turned on. Alternatively, and unless otherwise stated, when you disable a policy, the result is the same as not configuring it at all.

Applying updates with Windows Intune

Applying updates with Windows Intune is only one part of the much larger concept of managing device security. Part of managing security is to manage the updates. Managing updates with Windows Intune includes:

- Selecting the product categories to include. This includes many Microsoft products by default (Office, Windows, Windows elements such as language packs and dictionary updates, Windows Live, and Works), but you can select more (Active Directory, Bing, Exchange, and so on).
- Creating Automatic Update Approval rules. This enables you to automatically approve desired updates.
- Approving or declining specific updates.

- Creating a non-Microsoft Update Software Package for distributing non-Microsoft updates.

You'll go through these tasks next, but you can learn more about Windows Intune and the larger security management tasks at *http://technet.microsoft.com/en-us/library/jj676558.aspx*.

To select product categories for updates you'd like to receive, follow these steps:

1. Open the Windows Intune administrator console.

2. Click Administration in the left pane to open the Administrator workspace.

3. Click Updates (see Figure 3-26).

4. In the Product Category area, select the specific products or categories that represent the items you want to manage.

5. In the Update Classification area, select the classifications to include.

6. Click Save.

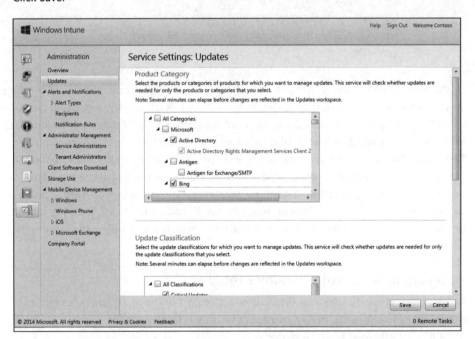

FIGURE 3-26 Use the Windows Intune administrator console to select product categories for updates you'd like to receive.

To create an Automatic Update Approval rule and run the rule now, follow these steps:

1. Open the Windows Intune administrator console.

2. Click Administration in the left pane and then click Updates.

3. Scroll down to the Automatic Approval Rules area, and then click New.

4. Type the name of the new automatic approval rule (and optionally a description), and then click Next.

5. Specify the products for which you want to have updates approved automatically by selecting the check boxes, and then click Next.

6. Specify the update classifications that you want to have approved automatically, and then click Next.

7. Click the desired groups or devices to apply the rule to and click Add.

8. If desired, select the Enforce An Installation Deadline For These Updates check box, and then select an installation deadline interval after the rule is approved.

9. Click Next and then click Finish.

10. Note the new rule in the Automatic Approval Rules area, as shown in Figure 3-27. Also note the option to edit the rule or to run it now.

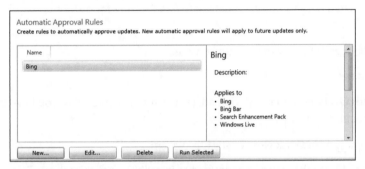

FIGURE 3-27 New rules appear in the Automatic Approval Rules section.

To approve an update, follow these steps:

1. Open the Windows Intune administrator console.

2. In the left pane, click Updates.

3. On the Updates Overview page, in the Update Status area, click New Updates To Approve. (You won't see this unless new updates are available.)

4. Select an update and click Approve on the taskbar. (You can Ctrl+click to select multiple updates.)

5. Click the desired groups or devices to apply the rule to and click Add.

6. For each group on the approval list, choose either Required Install, Do Not Install, or Uninstall.

7. From the Deadline list, select one of the following:

   ▪ **None** No deadline is enforced, and users can decline the update.

- **As Soon As Possible**
- **Custom**   Specify the date and time when approved updates are installed.

8. Click Finish.

To decline an update, follow these steps:

1. Open the Windows Intune administrator console.

2. Click Updates.

3. On the Updates Overview page, in the Update Status area, click New Updates To Approve. (You won't see this unless new updates are available.)

4. Select an update to decline and click Decline in the taskbar.

5. Click Decline again to verify.

6. In the Decline dialog box, click Decline to decline this update, or click Cancel.

To create and upload a non-Microsoft Update Software Package for distributing updates, follow these steps:

1. Open the Windows Intune administrator console.

2. Click the Updates tab.

3. In the Uploads Overview pane, click Upload. (The first time you do this, you have to install the required software.)

4. Sign in if prompted, and click Next to start the wizard.

5. Click Browse to locate the setup files required to install the update package. This can be a Windows Installer (.msi) file, Windows Installer patch (.msp) file, or .exe program file.

6. If additional files or folders are required to successfully install the update, select the Include Additional Files And Subfolders From The Same Folder check box.

7. Click Next.

8. Type a name for the publisher and make other changes to the prepopulated areas as desired. Click Next.

9. Select the desired architecture (Any, 32-bit, or 64-bit) and operating system for the target computers. Click Next.

10. The Detection Rules page lets you specify how Windows Intune determines whether the update already exists on targeted client computers. Specify a way to detect whether the update is installed. You can choose to use the default detection rules, or create your own rule as shown in Figure 3-28. You can add multiple rules. If you create your own rule, select it, click Add, and work through the rest of the creation process.

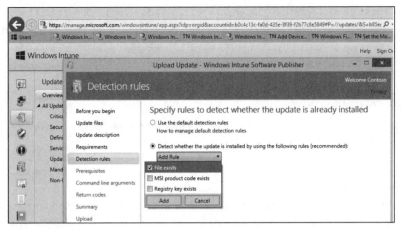

FIGURE 3-28 Choose how to detect whether the update is already installed.

11. Click Next.

12. If applicable, specify the software on which the update depends and click Next. Otherwise, click None and then click Next.

13. If applicable, specify any command-line arguments. Otherwise, click No and click Next.

14. Specify whether you want return codes interpreted (these are considered failures).

15. Review the summary and click Upload.

16. The Upload page displays the status of the update as it uploads to Windows Intune.

17. After the upload successfully completes, click Close.

Managing client security

You need to protect your computer and the ones you are responsible for from viruses, spyware, and malware in general. You need real-time protection that's available 24/7. You have many choices for this, but this section focuses on three of them: Windows Defender, Windows Intune Endpoint Protection, and Microsoft System Center 2012 Endpoint Protection.

Exploring Windows Defender

Windows 8.1 provides malware protection through Windows Defender. For the most part, Windows Defender is an end-user solution, although you can rely on it for protecting stand-alone computers in homes and in business workgroups. If you see an exam question about Windows Defender, it will likely ask on which tab you find a particular feature. With that said, you should open Windows Defender and explore those tabs thoroughly.

Although this book could dedicate several pages to Windows Defender alone, I believe that you can review this information on your own and the pages can be used to talk about other technologies you might not yet be familiar with. However, the following sections briefly discuss what you'll find on each Windows Defender tab.

> **NOTE** **WINDOWS DEFENDER**
>
> The Windows Defender window looks just like the Windows Intune Endpoint Protection window, detailed next. The same tabs and features are available.

USING THE HOME TAB

On the Home tab you can see the status of your real-time protection, including whether it's turned on and whether the virus and spyware definitions are up to date. It also shows when the last scan was run. You can also run a manual scan for malware (Quick, Full, or Custom) if you believe the computer was put at risk since the last scan. This is also where you can access the option to change the scan schedule, which simply takes you to the Settings tab.

USING THE UPDATE TAB

Windows Defender updates virus and spyware definitions automatically, and you can review information regarding this update from here. You can see the date on which the last definitions were created, when the definitions were last updated, the virus definition version, and the spyware definition version. You can also click Update here to update the definitions manually.

USING THE HISTORY TAB

Here you can review past problems that were detected. For example, you can view items that were prevented from running but not removed from your PC; and these are Quarantined Items. You can view items you were warned about but opted to run anyway: Allowed Items. Finally, you can see all the detected items under All Detected Items. With administrative privileges you can also remove or restore items listed here.

USING THE SETTINGS TAB

The Settings tab offers many options for configuring how Windows Defender should run (see Figure 3-29). Here are a few of the things you can do here:

- Run a scheduled scan or change when scans run.
- Choose what happens when a potential threat is found.
- Configure real-time protection.
- Set excluded files, locations, processes, and file types.
- Configure advanced settings, such as when to remove quarantined files; whether to scan removable drives; whether to create a system restore point before removing, running, or quarantining detected items; and so on.

- Join MAPS, the Microsoft Active Protection Service. This automatically reports malware and other unwanted software to Microsoft so that the company can improve its services.

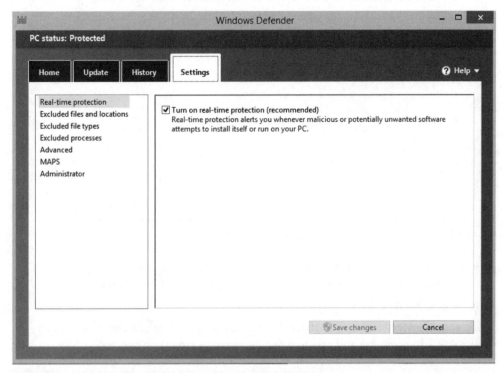

FIGURE 3-29 Windows Defender lets you configure various settings.

Exploring Windows Intune Endpoint Protection

Windows Intune Endpoint Protection is another way to incorporate real-time protection for your clients. It does the same thing Windows Defender does—updates virus definitions, scans for malware, and so on—but you, not Windows or your employees, are in charge of how it's used. As with other Windows Intune tasks, you use the Windows Intune administrator console—specifically, the Endpoint Protection workspace—to perform tasks. As you can see in Figure 3-30, Endpoint Protection has two tabs: Overview (shown) and All Malware.

In this workspace you can see the status of your computers quickly, and if problems exist you can take control of the situation immediately. You can also configure notifications be sent via email to yourself or others when problems are detected.

You can perform a multitude of tasks with Windows Intune regarding endpoint protection, and I'm not sure about which you'll be tested on. The following list includes most of these tasks, and you can review how to perform them at *http://technet.microsoft.com/en-us/library/jj676558.aspx*.

- Create a Windows Intune policy (such as a firewall policy).
- Configure Windows Intune updates.
- Monitor computers, report issues, and configure alerts when issues arise.

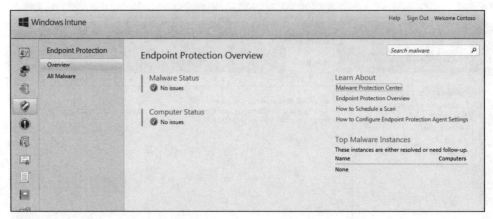

FIGURE 3-30 Windows Intune offers an Endpoint Protection workspace.

- Run remote tasks such as forcing an Endpoint Protection update, running a scan, remotely wiping a computer, restarting a computer, and refreshing policies.
- Troubleshoot device security.

You should understand how to do two things regarding Windows Intune: how to run a remote scan of a computer and how to schedule a scan by creating a new policy.

> **NOTE   RUNNING AND SCHEDULING SCANS**
>
> A quick scan checks locations, memory processes, and registry files on the hard disk in which malware generally appears. A full system scan checks all files on the hard disk and all currently running programs. Quick scans are less taxing on the computer than full scans, and full scans can cause the computer to run slowly. The best time to schedule these scans is when the user isn't at the computer.

To run an on-demand remote scan, follow these steps:

1. Open the Windows Intune administrator console.
2. Click Groups, and then do one of the following:
   - Click Overview. In the Search pane type the name of the computer to scan.
   - Click Expand All Devices, click the group name, and then click the Devices tab. Select the computer or Ctrl+click to select multiple computers.

3. On the Remote Tasks list on the taskbar, click one of the following:

- Run A Full Malware Scan
- Run A Quick Malware Scan

4. Review the summary message, and then click Close.

5. To view the task status, click the Remote Tasks link in the lower-right corner of the Windows Intune administrator console. If necessary, take any required action to complete the scan process.

To schedule a scan by using a policy, follow these steps:

1. Open the Windows Intune administrator console.

2. Click Policy.

3. Click Add Policy under Tasks.

4. In the Create A New Policy dialog box, shown in Figure 3-31, do the following:

   A. Under Template Name, click Windows Intune Agent Settings.

   B. Under How Would You Like To Use The Selected Template, do one of the following:

   - Select Create And Deploy A Policy With The Recommended Settings, click Create Policy, and then skip to step 11.
   - Select Create And Deploy A Custom Policy and continue here.

   C. Click Create Policy.

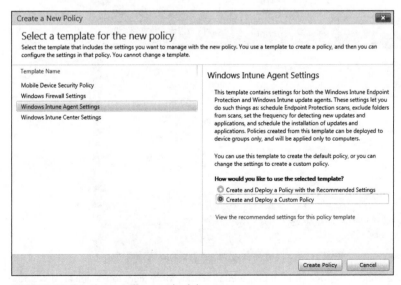

FIGURE 3-31 Creating a policy to schedule a scan.

5. Type a name and description for your new policy.

6. Scroll down to the Scan Schedule area, and then

   A. Specify whether to schedule a daily quick scan and when the scan is to run.

   B. Specify whether to schedule a full scan and when the scan is to run.

   C. Configure additional options as necessary.

7. Scroll down and configure settings for the Excluded Files And Folders, Excluded Processes, and Excluded File Types, as needed.

8. Click Save Policy.

9. Click Yes to deploy the policy immediately, or No to deploy the policy later.

10. If you clicked Yes in step 9, select the device groups to which you want to deploy this policy and then click Add.

11. Click OK.

As soon as you configure Windows Intune to run on a client computer, Windows Defender is no longer available. If you want to see how Windows Intune Endpoint Protection is configured on a client, type **Endpoint Protection** on the Start screen and then click it in the results. Figure 3-32 shows the window available on the client, which offers a place to manage the client somewhat at the computer itself. The tabs here are the same as those in Windows Defender, so if you didn't read that information earlier, do so now.

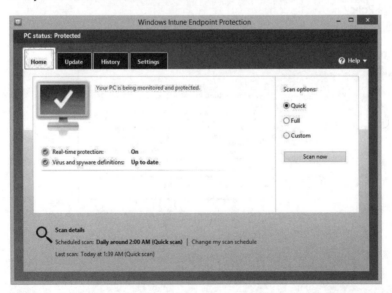

FIGURE 3-32 The Windows Intune Endpoint Protection window on a client looks similar to Windows Defender.

Understanding Microsoft System Center 2012 Endpoint Protection

You can extend your device management capabilities by integrating System Center 2012 SP1 or System Center 2012 R2 Configuration Manager into your existing infrastructure. When partnered with the Windows Intune connector site system role available through the Configuration Manager console, you can manage onsite Windows PCs, Macs, and UNIX/Linux servers, as well as mobile devices that run Windows, Windows Phone, Apple iOS, and Android. (An excellent article at *http://technet.microsoft.com/en-us/library/jj884158.aspx* details how to manage mobile devices using these technologies.) This enables you to manage your infrastructure more completely through a single, unified administrator console. This is important for big companies that need the flexibility of both System Center and Windows Intune. You can also incorporate these Endpoint Protection tools and features:

- Deploy and configure the Endpoint Protection client from a single, central location.
- Configure your own antimalware policies and apply them to computer groups.
- Create and deploy your own Windows Firewall settings to computer groups.
- Automatically download the latest antimalware definition files to keep client computers up to date.
- Incorporate the Endpoint Protection Manager Security role to allow others to manage the antimalware policies and Windows Firewall settings.
- Configure Endpoint Protection so that you and others will get email notifications when computers you manage report that malware has been detected.
- View detailed information from the Configuration Manager console.

> *MORE INFO*   **ENDPOINT PROTECTION WITH MICROSOFT SYSTEM CENTER 2012**
>
> You can find more information about Endpoint Protection at *http://technet.microsoft.com/ en-us/library/hh508836.aspx* and *http://technet.microsoft.com/en-us/library/gg682041. aspx.*

The steps involved in the process of setting up System Center 2012 so that you can install a client and enroll, manage, and protect them—at least in relation to mobile clients—includes several steps. The required steps follow, but you need to consider other optional steps. For more information on each of these steps, refer to the TechNet article at *http://technet. microsoft.com/en-us/library/gg712327.aspx*.

The required steps are as follows:

1. Deploy a web server certificate to site system servers.
2. Deploy a client authentication certificate to site system servers.
3. Create and issue a certificate template for mobile device enrollment.

4. Configure the management point and distribution point.

5. Configure the enrollment proxy point and the enrollment point.

6. Configure client settings for mobile device enrollment.

7. Enroll mobile devices.

To enroll devices, you deploy the System Center 2012 Endpoint Protection (SCEP) client, available with System Center 2012, to the devices you want to manage. Enrolling a device installs the Configuration Manager client on the device, requests and installs the required certificate, and then points the client to the enrollment site. You can opt to provide the client with the applicable link in an email, among other options.

You can deploy the client in several ways:

- Push the software to the client.
- Use the Configuration Manager software update feature.
- Use Group Policy.
- Use logon scripts.
- Manually install the client.
- Automatically upgrade the client.
- Use client imaging.

After a client device is set up, the client interface looks like Windows Defender or Windows Intune Endpoint Protection and contains the same tabs: Home, Update, History, and Settings. Also, the interface you'll use is similar to the Windows Intune interface you're already familiar with, but with many more features. This interface includes the Configuration Manager, where you can create policies, monitor devices, remediate problems, and force compliance, among other things.

Managing Internet Explorer 11 security

Just like you have to lock down and manage devices, the data users can access, and how they can connect, you must also keep Internet Explorer 11 safe, too. Internet Explorer 11 offers various security and privacy options that you can explore and apply. To start, click the Tools button and click Internet Options. Two tabs deal with security: Security and Privacy. These two tabs offer options related to security settings for the four zones (Internet, Local Intranet, Trusted Sites, and Restricted Sites) and how you want to protect your privacy (such as never allowing websites to require your physical location, using the Pop-Up Blocker, and so on).

The other tabs also offer a few security and privacy options. For example, the General tab offers the ability to delete your browsing history each time you exit Internet Explorer 11. The Content tab lets you manage AutoComplete settings and how you'd like to use certificates for encrypted connections and identifications. You should explore each of these tabs to see what's available and to ensure that you know how to make changes when needed. Under-stand that the changes you make here also affect the Internet Explorer app on the Start screen. You might use these options for managing stand-alone computers and those in small workgroups; however, for the most part, you'll control Internet Explorer through Group Policy.

You need to be familiar with many Internet Explorer 11 Group Policy settings. Make sure that you understand what happens when you enable, disable, or don't configure various policies. Figure 3-33 shows some of the options available in Group Policy to configure in the Local Group Policy Editor. Note all the options under Internet Explorer, including but not limited to Corporate Settings, Delete Browsing History, Privacy, and what's shown in Figure 3-33, Security Features with Restricted Protocols Per Security Zone. You can double-click any entry in the right pane to enter restricted protocols for a specific zone to further secure Internet Explorer for any group of users.

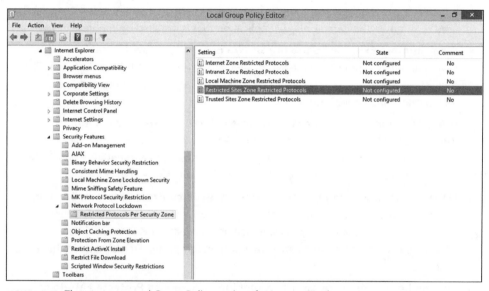

FIGURE 3-33 There are a several Group Policy settings for Internet Explorer.

You can explore other areas of Group Policy beyond the Security Features options. For example, if you click Internet Explorer in the left pane, in the right you'll see options that include Security Zones: Do Not Allow Users To Change Policies and Disable Automatic Install Of Internet Explorer items.

EXAM TIP

No one knows how heavily you'll be tested on the Group Policy settings for Internet Explorer 11, so you should go through them all at least one time. In doing so, you can see what features are available in Internet Explorer to both users and administrators. This can help you become more proficient with Internet Explorer 11.

You should also familiarize yourself with the newly added entries to Group Policy for Internet Explorer. Some of these directly relate to security and privacy settings. This list contains what's new for Internet Explorer 11:

- **Turn off loading websites and content in the background to optimize performance**   When this setting is enabled, Internet Explorer preemptively loads websites and content in the background. This helps speed up performance.

- **Allow Microsoft services to provide enhanced suggestions as the user types in the Address bar**   If this setting is enabled, Internet Explorer provides enhanced suggestions when the user types something to search for in the Address bar.

- **Turn off phone number detection**   This policy setting determines whether phone numbers are recognized and turned into hyperlinks. When enabled, this setting can be used to summon the default phone application that is installed on the device.

- **Allow Internet Explorer to use the SPDY/3 network protocol**   Enable this setting to have Internet Explorer use the SPDY/3 network protocol. SPDY/3 works with HTTP requests to improve how fast network requests are returned by using compression, multiplexing, and prioritization.

- **Don't run antimalware programs against ActiveX controls (Internet, Restricted Zones)**   Use this policy setting to determine whether Internet Explorer will run antimalware programs against ActiveX controls to check to see whether those ActiveX controls are safe to run on any particular webpage in the specified zone.

- **Don't run antimalware programs against ActiveX controls (Intranet, Trusted, Local Machine Zones)**   Use this policy setting to determine whether Internet Explorer will run antimalware programs against ActiveX controls to check to see whether those ActiveX controls are safe to run on any particular webpage in the specified zone.

- **Turn on 64-bit tab processes when running in Enhanced Protected Mode on 64-bit versions of Windows**   Enable this option to run all Content Processes at 64 bits (while in Protected Mode). When not enabled, Content Processes will run at 32 bits for compatibility with 32-bit ActiveX controls, toolbars, and so on.

- **Turn off sending UTF-8 query strings for URLs**   Use this setting to determine whether Internet Explorer uses 8-bit Unicode Transformation Format (UTF-8) to encode query strings in URLs before those strings are sent to servers or proxy servers.

- **Turn off sending URL path as UTF-8**   Use this setting to determine whether to let Internet Explorer send the path part of a URL using the 8-bit Unicode Transformation Format (UTF-8) standard. This standard defines characters so they can be read in any language. You can also exchange Internet addresses (URLs) with characters available in any language.

- **Turn off the flip ahead with page prediction feature**   This policy setting determines whether a user can swipe across a screen or click Forward to go to a website's next preloaded page. This feature is available only in the Internet Explorer app.

- **Prevent deleting ActiveX Filtering, Tracking Protection and Do Not Track data**
  - **In Internet Explorer 9 and 10**   If enabled, this setting prevents users from deleting ActiveX Filtering and Tracking Protection data. Users can also enable the Personalized Tracking Protection List, which blocks third-party items during any Internet Explorer session.
  - **With Internet Explorer 11**   If enabled, this setting prevents users from deleting ActiveX Filtering, Tracking Protection data, and Do Not Track exceptions that are stored for any website they've visited.
  - **Always send Do Not Track header**   This policy setting allows you to configure how Internet Explorer sends the Do Not Track (DNT) header.

EXAM TIP

You might be asked about InPrivate Browsing on the exam. InPrivate Browsing prevents Internet Explorer from collecting any data during the session including cookies, tracking, browsing history, passwords, and user names. Like other features, you can control InPrivate Browsing behavior through Group Policy.

Another desktop area of Internet Explorer 11 to explore is the Manage Add-ons dialog box, shown in Figure 3-34.

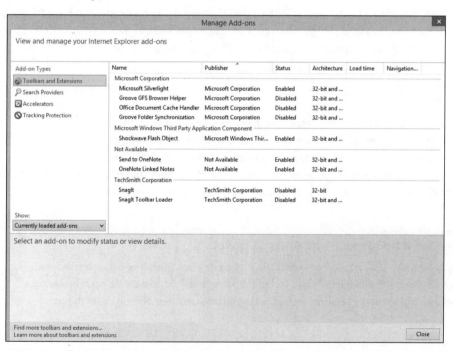

FIGURE 3-34 The Manage Add-ons dialog box lets you enable and disable features that the user has added.

From this dialog box, you can view information about the following and see how they are configured on the local computer:

- **Toolbars And Extensions**   You can see what toolbars have been added to Internet Explorer 11 and disable them, if desired. These are sometimes from Microsoft Corporation and sometimes from third parties. This is where some malware appears, too. Click any entry to see options to enable or disable it.

- **Search Providers**   You can see what search providers are in use on the local computer. You'll see Bing, but you might also see additional providers such as eBay, Ask.com, Amazon Search Suggestions, and so on. You can select any item in the list and remove it, set it as the default, or disable suggestions from it. You can also change the order of the list. Select and then right-click any entry to see additional options that don't appear in the dialog box itself.

- **Accelerators**   You can view what accelerators are configured for the local machine. You'll probably see Map with Bing, Translate with Bing, and perhaps others. These help users perform tasks in a single click (such getting directions to a place with Bing Maps). Click any entry to remove, disable, or set it as the default.

- **Tracking Protection**   You can get a Tracking Protection List online and use it to help enhance your privacy by preventing websites from automatically sending data they collect about your visit to other websites and content providers. Those providers use the information to tailor advertisements based on what you do online. You have to click Your Personalized List and then click Enable to get started. When you select a list, you can configure settings for it, such as blocking all content or choosing the content to block or allow.

EXAM TIP

Explore each tab of the Internet Properties dialog box available from the Tools menu. Know that the Content tab offers a way to access the installed certificates, that the Connections tab lets you add a VPN or view Local Area Network (LAN) settings, that the Programs tab lets you set one Internet Explorer app as the default, and that the Advanced tab offers all kinds of options for accessibility, browsing, HTTP settings, and so on.

NOTE **USING THE ALT KEY IN INTERNET EXPLORER**

When in Internet Explorer, you can press the Alt key to show the Menu bar, and from the Tools menu perform all kinds of tasks including but not limited to deleting your browsing history, managing media licenses, and reporting unsafe websites, among other things.

Supporting Group Policy application

You know about Group Policy, how to apply policies to groups, and what applying those policies means to your users. What you might not know are the effects of a policy or groups of policies on a single computer or for a specific user, domain, or organizational unit. You might need new ways to process those policies, too, or more effectively update those policies without taxing your network. You can use three new tools that can help you support Group Policy application in Windows Server 2012 and Windows 8 (and Windows 8.1): Resultant Set of Policy (RSoP), policy processing, and Group Policy caching.

Using RSoP

Resultant Set of Policy (RSoP) is a report of all your Group Policy settings. The report can show how those settings affect your network, users, computers, and devices. You can use the RSoP snap-in to create these reports.

RSoP has two modes: logging and planning. Logging mode displays policy settings that are applied to computers or logged-on users. Planning mode simulates policy settings that you plan to apply to a computer or user. Planning mode also lets you review policy settings for a computer that's currently unavailable or a user who's not currently logged on.

You need to set up RSoP before you can use it, though. To add the snap-in to a Microsoft Management Console (MMC), follow these steps:

1. In a Run window, type **mmc** and press Enter.

2. In the empty MMC that appears, click File, and then click Add/Remove Snap-In.

3. In the left pane, click Resultant Set Of Policy, and then click Add.

4. Click OK.

> **NOTE OPENING RSOP AS AN MMC SNAP-IN**
>
> To open RSoP as an MMC snap-in and display RSoP logging mode for the currently logged on user and computer, type **rsop.msc** in a Run dialog box and click OK.

You can run an RSoP query on a computer account, a user account, a domain, an organizational unit, a site, and a local computer. Because the focus is on Windows 8.1 here, this section introduces the latter. To run an RSoP query in logging mode on a local computer (you can't run planning mode on a local computer) follow these steps:

1. In the MMC you created in the preceding steps, right-click Resultant Set Of Policy, and then click Generate RSoP Data.

2. In the Resultant Set of Policy Wizard (see Figure 3-35), click Next.

3. Click Logging Mode, and then click Next.

4. Click This Computer and click Next.

5. Leave Current User selected and click Next.

6. Review the information and click Next.

7. Click Finish.

Now, you can expand any node in the left pane and dive into any item to review. When you do, you'll see the results of your Group Policy settings. Figure 3-36 shows sample results for the Sleep settings configured for a computer: Require A Password When A Computer Wakes (Plugged In) is listed as Enabled.

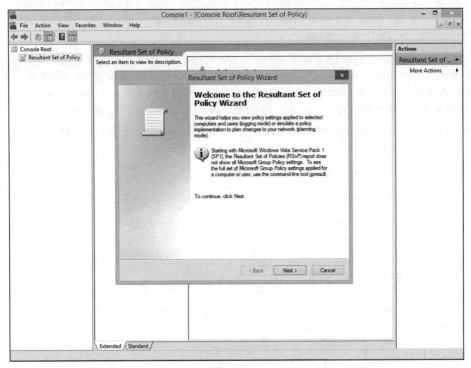

FIGURE 3-35   Use the Resultant Set of Policy Wizard to simulate a policy implementation.

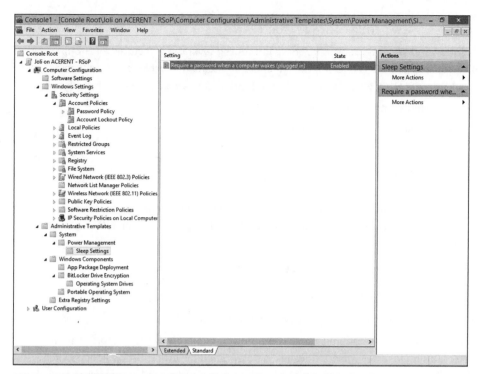

FIGURE 3-36 Use RSoP to review all Group Policy settings for a local computer.

Understanding policy processing

If you've used RSoP but aren't getting the results you want from a local or remote computer, you can force a Group Policy update by using Gpupdate.exe. This command-line tool lets you verify that the computer has indeed received and processed the latest Group Policy settings. With Windows Server 2012 and Windows 8, you can refresh these settings remotely for all computers in an organizational unit (OU) from the Group Policy Management Console (GPMC) on the applicable server. You can optionally use the Windows PowerShell cmdlet *Invoke-GPUpdate* to refresh Group Policy on any group of computers, including those not included in the OU structure.

Before moving on, you should learn about a few new features, such as Local Group Policy support for Windows RT. Although this is turned off by default, you can enable it as a local administrator:

1. From the Start screen, type **Services.msc**.

2. Double-click Group Policy Client.

3. Set the Startup type to Automatic, and then click Start.

You also can use sign-in optimizations when slow links are used. These improvements allow users to sign in faster when a slow link is determined by letting Group Policy switch automatically to asynchronous processing. See the following Note to learn more about asynchronous processing if you aren't familiar with it. (Note that if speed can't be determined, Group Policy defaults to slow-link mode.)

A new policy setting also enables administrators to configure all 3G connections as slow links. To disable 3G slow-link connections, enable the Configure Group Policy Slow Link Detection policy setting and then select the Always Treat WWAN Connections As Slow Link check box. You'll find this in the Group Policy Management Editor here: Computer Configuration, Policies, Administrative Templates, System, Group Policy.

NOTE **ASYNCHRONOUS PROCESSING AND SYNCHRONOUS PROCESSING**

Asynchronous processing refers to processes that don't require other processes to complete before they can run. Thus, the processes can run simultaneously, which means that the client computer is ready faster, and the user can sign in more quickly. In contrast, synchronous processing refers to processes that depend on other process outcomes, which must complete before other processes can run.

The Fast Startup feature reduces the amount of time required to shut down and start a computer. This allows the computer to go into hibernation rather than completely shut down. However, Group Policy settings and scripts that are configured to be applied during the start-up or shutdown process might not be applied, which can be a source of trouble if Fast Startup is enabled for your clients. You can read more about the effects of allowing Fast Startup and how it affects Group Policy at *http://technet.microsoft.com/en-us/library/jj573586*.

One more additional change is that you can configure the Group Policy Client service to sleep when it is idle for more than ten minutes. This way, the clients can perform better by letting Group Policy refresh as a scheduled task, not as a service refresh. By default, refreshes occur about every 90 minutes.

EXAM TIP

Be sure to review the links offered in this section before taking the exam so that you are familiar with the other new and changed functionality in Group Policy.

Configuring Group Policy caching

Cached data can be accessed faster than when it must be retrieved from a remote source. Thus, Group Policy caching (theoretically) improves performance when configured to do so. A new policy, Configure Group Policy Caching, is available for this purpose. When Configure Group Policy Caching is enabled, the local computer first gets the latest version of a policy from the domain controller, and then writes that policy to its local store. The next time the computer starts up in synchronous mode, it retrieves the Group Policy settings from its own local store rather than download it anew. You might consider enabling this feature for computers you know are on slow connections to help improve performance.

To configure Group Policy Caching in Windows 8.1, follow these steps:

1. In a Run dialog box, type **gpedit.msc** and press Enter.

2. Navigate to Computer Configuration, Administrative Templates, System, Group Policy.

3. Double-click Configure Group Policy Caching (see Figure 3-37).

4. Click Enabled.

5. Click OK.

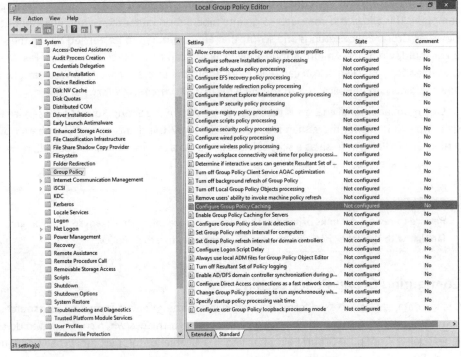

FIGURE 3-37 Review Group Policy settings in the Local Group Policy Editor.

Before continuing, review every Group Policy setting shown in Figure 3-37 (by double-clicking it and reading the information offered). Specifically, note the following:

- Turn Off Background Refresh Of Group Policy
- Turn Off Local Group Policy Objects Processing
- Configure Group Policy Slow Link Detection
- Set Group Policy Refresh Interval For Computers
- Configure Logon Script Delay
- Turn Off Resultant Set Of Policy Logging
- Change Group Policy Processing To Run Asynchronously When A Slow Network Connection Is Detected
- Specify Startup Policy Processing Wait Time
- Configure User Group Policy Loopback Processing Mode

Thought experiment
Providing a malware solution

In this thought experiment, apply what you've learned about this objective. You can find answers to these questions in the "Answers" section at the end of this chapter.

You need to protect your clients from malware and viruses. You want the solution to meet the following criteria: provide real-time protection for workstations and mobile clients, get alerts when a computer in your organization is at risk, and run remote tasks such as wiping a compromised computer. You don't need to manage servers or Linux/UNIX machines, and you don't want to spend any more money than you have to.

1. From the options introduced in this section, which protection option would you choose?

2. Using the technology you selected in question 1, how do you run a scan of a remote computer you believe has been affected by malware?

3. How can you manage this technology while sitting in front of the client machine?

Objective summary

- Windows updates often offer new features or functionality, but for the most part they are pushed out to fix security issues, address new security threats, and provide new device drivers.

- You can manage, control, approve, and decline Windows updates in your organization with Windows Intune. You can also upload and manage non-Microsoft updates here.

- Windows Defender, Windows Intune Endpoint Protection, and Microsoft System Center 2012 Endpoint Protection can all be used to provide real-time protection from viruses, malware, and other threats.

- Internet Explorer 11 offers its own set of built-in protection tools, including but not limited to security zones, ways to manage add-ins and toolbars, and options to manage privacy.

- Resultant Set of Policy (RSoP) offers a report of all your Group Policy settings. The report can show how those settings affect your network, users, computers, and devices. You can use the RSoP snap-in to create these reports. RSoP uses two modes: logging and planning.

- You can configure clients in various ways to process Group Policy, including but not limited to letting the Group Policy refresh on its own synchronously or asynchronously at intervals you configure by using Windows PowerShell, the command line, and more.
- You can enable Group Policy Caching to let clients cache Group Policy settings for fast startup.

Objective review

Answer the following questions to test your knowledge of the information in this objective. You can find the answers to these questions and explanations of why each answer choice is correct or incorrect in the "Answers" section at the end of this chapter.

1. Where in the Group Policy Management Editor can you find settings for Windows Update?

   A. Computer Configuration, Windows Settings, Windows Components, Windows Update

   B. Computer Configuration, Administrative Templates, Windows Components, Windows Update

   C. User Configuration, Administrative Templates, Windows Components, Windows Update

   D. User Configuration, Windows Settings, Windows Components, Windows Update

2. You are trying to approve Microsoft updates by using the Windows Intune administrator console. You've navigated to the Updates tab, the Updates Status area, and clicked New Updates. But you don't see any updates there. Why?

   A. You need to be in the Admin Console, not the administrator console.

   B. You need to click the Administration tab in the left pane, not the Updates tab.

   C. You have to upload the updates that you want to approve first.

   D. No new updates are available to approve.

3. In Windows Defender, what tab do you use to configure when scheduled scans are run?

   A. Home

   B. Update

   C. History

   D. Settings

4. When performing scans with Windows Intune Endpoint Protection, which of the following is true?

   A. A quick scan checks the locations, processes in the memory, and registry files on the hard disk where malware generally appears.

   B. A full system scan checks all files on the hard disk and all currently running programs.

   C. The best time to schedule these scans is when the user isn't at the computer.

   D. All of the above.

5. You want to set up System Center 2012 Endpoint Protection in your enterprise. What is the first thing you need to do?

   A. Deploy a web server certificate to site system servers.

   B. Deploy a client authentication certificate to site system servers.

   C. Create and issue a certificate template for mobile device enrollment.

   D. Configure the management point and distribution point.

   E. Configure the enrollment proxy point and the enrollment point.

   F. Configure client settings for mobile device enrollment.

   G. Enroll mobile devices.

6. You have enabled the Group Policy setting Turn Off The Flip Ahead With Page Prediction Feature for Internet Explorer 11. Some clients complain they can't use the feature, even though it's enabled. Why?

   A. You must also enable the setting Allow Internet Explorer To Use The SPDY/3 Network Protocol.

   B. You have disabled the setting Turn Off Loading Websites And Content In The Background To Optimize Performance.

   C. This feature is available only in the Internet Explorer app, but the problematic users are using the Internet Explorer 11 desktop app.

   D. This feature is available only in Windows RT 8.1, and the problematic users are using another version of Windows 8.

7. You've applied Group Policy but notice that a few clients aren't compliant. What could be the problem and how can you resolve it?

   A. The client needs to refresh; you can refresh the client in various ways, including by using GPupdate.exe.

   B. The Group Policy might be in conflict with other policies and groups; run the RSoP and review the results.

   C. The Group Policy isn't being applied at startup. You need to enable Fast Startup.

   D. The policies aren't being cached. You need to enable Group Policy Caching through Computer Configuration, Policies, Administrative Templates, System, Group Policy.

Objective 3.4: Manage clients by using Windows Intune

You've already learned quite a bit about Windows Intune in this book. This last objective looks at it one more time. Here, you'll learn how to create and manage user and computer groups, how to configure monitoring and set an alert when something goes awry, how to manage policies, and how to manage computers remotely.

> **This objective covers how to:**
> - Manage user and computer groups; configure monitoring and alerts; and manage policies
> - Manage remote computers

Managing user and computer groups

With Windows Intune configured and with users and devices added and enrolled, you can now manage them. Management tasks include creating user and computer groups as well as monitoring them, creating alerts, and configuring policies, among other things.

Managing groups with Windows Intune

If you've ever managed users or devices in any setting—whether it's a local workgroup or an enterprise domain—you likely know something about groups. In enterprises using AD DS, administrators generally create user accounts, create groups to house those accounts (users), and then apply the desired permissions to these groups for the purpose of managing multiple users at once. With groups, administrators can easily remove and add users, as well as manage hundreds or thousands of users more easily. Deciding how groups will be created in this scenario involves quite a bit of planning, and taking your time to do so is important.

Like with AD DS, you can create a group structure using Windows Intune. Also like with AD DS, you can establish a group plan for your organization in many ways. For example, you can group users by geographic location if you want to manage users and computers based on where they are located. You can also group members by department (such as Accounting or Sales) or by other characteristics. When dealing with computers, for instance, you can group devices by what kind of hardware they run on, what type of device they are, or what operating system they use. A device or a user can belong to more than one group, although users and devices never appear in the same group.

Windows Intune has four built-in, ready-to-use groups that can't be removed: All Users, Ungrouped Users, All Devices, and Ungrouped Devices. You can tell by their names that these groups are very general. However, they offer access to everything you've enrolled, all the computers you manage, and all the users you've added. You build down from there, creating your own structure as desired.

Here are a few caveats to creating groups:

- Groups contain either users or devices. They never contain both.
- Groups can be empty.
- You can name the groups you create and edit the names (descriptions and so on) when needed.
- You don't need AD DS to create groups in Windows Intune. If AD DS isn't used, though, you do need to add users and groups manually in the Windows Intune account portal.
- Groups can be dynamic, and you can query them to sort what's included when necessary. You can create your own dynamic groups. You also can create static groups, such as Accountants, that include only specific members.
- If you want to include mobile devices in a group, the devices must be discovered and added to the Windows Intune inventory.

You create a group in the Groups workspace in the Windows Intune administrator console. You saw this tab earlier if you've worked through this chapter. Figure 3-38 shows this, with All Users selected.

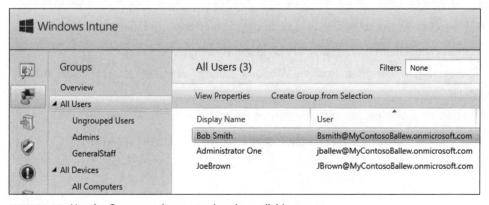

FIGURE 3-38 Use the Groups workspace to view the available groups.

The following steps show how to create a new computer group from the Windows Intune administrator console and then how to create a new user group. Later you'll see how to create a security group from the Windows Intune account portal.

To create a new computer group from the Windows Intune administrator console, follow these steps:

1. Click Groups in the left pane, click Overview, and click Create Group under Tasks.

2. Type a group name and description, select All Devices (see Figure 3-39), and then click Next (not shown).

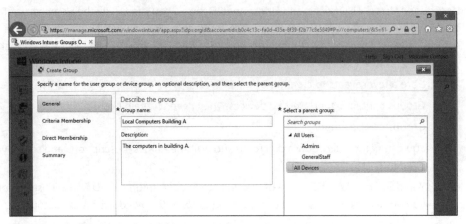

FIGURE 3-39 Creating a new computer group.

3. Select the applicable Device Type. There are three options: All Devices (Computers And Mobile Devices); Computer; Mobile. (Note that this group is dynamic because membership can and will change.)

4. If applicable, choose how to start the group. There are two choices: All Computers In The Parent Group; Empty Group.

5. Choose to include or exclude members from OUs or domains, as desired. Click Next.

6. If applicable, opt to include or exclude specific members from the group. Click Next.

7. Review the items on the Summary page and click Finish.

To create a new user group from the Windows Intune administrator console, follow these steps:

1. Click Groups in the left pane, click Overview, and click Create Group under Tasks.

2. Type a group name and description, select All Users, and then click Next.

3. Click All Users and click Next.

4. Choose how to start the group. There are two choices: Empty Group; All Users In The Parent Group.

5. Opt to include or exclude members from security groups, as desired.

6. Open to include or exclude members with these managers, as desired, and click Next.

7. If applicable, opt to include or exclude specific members from the group. Click Next.

8. Review the items on the Summary page and click Finish.

You can now locate both of these new groups in the Groups list. The new computer group is listed under All Devices; the new user group is listed under All Users. Click either and note the options available. Under Tasks, for example, you can edit the group, create a group, or delete the group. You can view the total users or devices, review the membership criteria, and see the date the group was created. You can also check for any software deployment issues or policy issues. When you see problems here, you can use this workspace to try to resolve them.

EXAM TIP

You might be asked on the exam to explain why Windows Intune can't be used in a particular situate, or, you might be given a scenario with Windows Intune as an option for resolving a problem. You'll need to know these things to answer those types of questions: Windows Intune can't be used to manage 64-bit Windows XP Professional or 32-bit Windows 8 operating systems. Windows Intune Client software needs to be installed on compatible desktop operating systems such as Windows 8 Enterprise and Pro, Windows 7 Enterprise, Ultimate, or Professional, Windows Vista Enterprise, Ultimate, or Business, and Windows XP Professional SP3. Client software isn't installed on devices that run Windows RT, Windows Phone, iOS, or Android.

You might also want to create a security group, which you can use to assign permissions to shared resources. If you use AD DS in your environment, you can specify synchronized security groups as membership conditions. To manually add security groups, you use the Windows Intune account portal (*http://account.manage.microsoft.com*):

1. At the top of the Windows Intune account portal, click Admin.

2. In the left pane, under Management, click Security Groups.

3. Click New.

4. Type a display name and description for the group, and then click Save.

5. In the List Type list, select Users or Groups (for this example, click Users).

6. Select the members to include (see Figure 3-40) and then click Add.

7. Click Save and Close.

FIGURE 3-40 Creating a new security group.

MORE INFO **CREATING GROUPS**

For more information about users and groups in Windows Intune, refer to the TechNet article at *http://technet.microsoft.com/en-us/library/dn646967.aspx#Step3*. Specifically, refer to Step 2: Add Windows Intune Users and Step 3: Create Groups To Organize Users And Devices.

Configuring monitoring and setting alerts with Windows Intune

The next logical step after setting up Windows Intune, adding users, creating groups, and so on is to monitor inventory and configure alerts when something is amiss.

MONITORING STATUS

You can monitor the status of almost anything regarding your Windows Intune infrastructure from the applicable tab (workspace) in the Windows Intune administrator console. In this instance, the word *monitor* simply means to look at the entries to see the current status of a specific thing. You can try to resolve any issues from the same area. Another type of monitoring deals with creating alerts, and you configure those alerts by selecting severity levels, using filters to determine when an alert is necessary, configuring threshold settings, and so on. This section focuses on the former; the next section focuses on the latter.

For this example, you'll monitor the mobile devices on your network. You can use the same technique to access and monitor other items, including users (although you won't see nearly as much data for users as you do computers).

To get started, open the Windows Intune administrator console and follow these steps:

1. In the left pane, click Groups.

2. Click All Mobile Devices, All Computers, Ungrouped Devices or any other applicable subgroup.

3. Review the information offered.

The information you'll find in step 3 includes the following, which you can monitor as often as you like (under the General tab). Remember, if a problem exists, you can click the available link to learn more or resolve the issue.

- **Alert Status**   This shows you whether any alerts specific to the inventory selected have occurred.

- **Update Status**   This shows you whether any problems related to updates are occurring.

- **Endpoint Protection Status**   You can see whether any problems with endpoint protection have developed.

- **Policy**   You can see whether issues have occurred with policies you've created and configured.

- **Software Status**   This lists the status of installed software.

- **Device Health Status**   This shows the health of devices.

- **Membership Criteria**   You can review the criteria for membership.

- **Computer Summary**   You can review information regarding inventory, including but not limited to the top five manufacturers and top five operating systems used in your inventory list.

MORE INFO   **MONITORING MOBILE DEVICES**

To learn more about monitoring mobile devices, refer to the following TechNet article: *http://technet.microsoft.com/en-us/library/jj733634.aspx*.

You can use Windows Intune to monitor in other ways. For example, in the Windows Intune administrator console, from the System Overview tab, you can view and monitor alerts (see Figure 3-41). You also can change how you view the alerts; View By Date is the default, but you can switch to View By Category or View By Severity. You can also opt to view more information about the alerts. You can see any service announcements here, too, in an area named Notice Board. You can export these if desired.

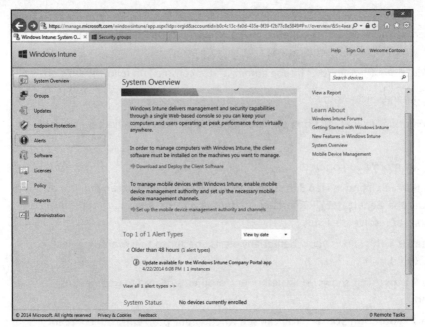

FIGURE 3-41 Viewing and managing alerts from the System Overview workspace.

As with the Windows Intune System Overview tab (which offers information about alerts), you can access the Windows Intune Updates tab (which offers information about updates, update status, and cloud storage status). You explored this tab when you configured automatic approval settings earlier in the chapter.

Explore the other tabs now, too: Endpoint Protection Overview (status of malware and computers), which you explored when you opted to schedule a scan of a remote computer; Software (software status and cloud storage status), which you explored when you needed to add non-Microsoft software to Windows Intune for deployment; Licenses (licenses status); and Policy (the status of policies you've created), which you'll explore shortly.

> *NOTE* **CREATING A REPORT**
>
> You can create a report in the Windows Intune administrator console. Click the Reports tab, and then click the type of report to create (Update, Detected Software, Computer Inventory, Mobile Device Inventory, License Purchase, or License Installation). Work through any tasks required. Then, save or view the report as applicable. If you don't get any output, disable the pop-up blocker in your web browser.

CONFIGURING ALERTS

Things will go wrong, and you might not always be in front of the Windows Intune administrator console when they do. Thus, it's best to configure Windows Intune so that when problems arise, you are notified. You can also configure it so other people are notified.

Alerts all have similar properties. For example, they all offer the time the alert was created; the number of times the alert happened; the source of the alert; whether the alert is still active, modified, or has been resolved; and any applicable path related to the issue.

When configuring alerts, you have lots of options. You can decide how severe the problem must be before you receive a notification about it. You can display a threshold to determine how often a single alert must occur before it's considered important enough to garner a notification. You can enable and disable alerts as desired. And you can configure settings that are unique only to a single type of alert. Alerts are categorized as follows:

- **Endpoint Protection** These alerts deal with malware warnings and unprotected devices.

- **Monitoring** These alerts are created when a service is stopped, when a disk is highly fragmented, and when disk space is running low.

- **Notices** These alerts deal with service announcements.

- **Policy** These alerts are created when a device has an issue with a policy setting and can't apply or comply.

- **Remote Assistance** These alerts are created when a managed computer requests remote assistance.

- **System** These occur when a client deployment has failed. You can also be alerted if a mobile device has a connectivity issue.

- **Updates** These alerts are specific to updates waiting for approval, including Security and Critical updates.

Alerts can be assigned to one of three severity levels:

- **Critical** A serious problem that needs immediate attention

- **Warning** A potentially serious problem you should look into

- **Informational** A smaller issue that still requires attention

To configure an alert, follow these steps:

1. Open the Windows Intune administrator console and click the Administration tab.

2. Click Alerts And Notifications and then Alert Types (see Figure 3-42).

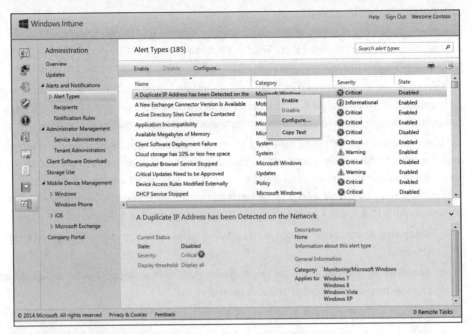

FIGURE 3-42 Configuring an alert.

3. Right-click any alert type, and then click Configure.

4. Change the state from Disable to Enable.

5. If desired, change the Severity.

6. If desired, change the Display Threshold.

7. Click OK.

Now you can create a notification based on this alert. To do this in the Windows Intune administrator console, follow these steps:

1. Click the Alerts tab, and then click Configure Notification Rules.

2. Click Create New Rule.

3. Type the name for the rule.

4. Select the category to apply the rule to. (These match the alert categories listed earlier.)

5. Select the severity.

6. Click Next.

7. Select Device Groups and click Next.

8. Specify the email addresses that will be notified.

As you continue to work with alerts, right-click as you explore. You'll find options to close an alert in some instances, view an alert's properties, and so on.

Managing policies with Windows Intune

The Policy workspace in the Windows Intune administrator console lets you create policies that help you control the computers and mobile devices you manage. You can force these policies or not configure them at all. For settings you don't care to manage, you can leave the decision to your end users. You create policies based on available templates, which you can change or accept the defaults for. The defaults for these templates match up with Microsoft Best Practices.

> **NOTE CREATING AND DEPLOYING POLICIES**
>
> You create policies for computers and deploy them to device groups. You create policies for mobile devices and deploy them to user groups.

How much the exam objective "Manage Policies" covers can't be predicted, but this section covers what I think you'll see. This includes creating and deploying a policy, but I'll also include how to view existing policies, edit and delete those policies, and review and address policy conflicts. You can learn more about Windows Intune policies from this set of TechNet articles at *http://technet.microsoft.com/en-us/library/jj662710.aspx*.

You can create four types of policies:

- **Mobile Device Security Policy**   This policy helps you configure things such as password length, whether to allow simple passwords, whether to require encryption, and so on.

- **Windows Firewall Settings**   This policy helps you configure things such as turning on the firewall, creating exceptions for specific network profiles, and so on.

- **Windows Intune Agent Settings**   This policy lets you configure other policies that include things such as installing endpoint protection, creating a system restore point before you try to remediate malware, enabling real-time protection, and so on.

- **Windows Intune Center Settings**   This policy lets you configure what users see when they open the Windows Intune Center, which is installed on all the computers you manage. This can contain support contact information such as a name, phone number, email address, website name, and so on.

CREATING AND DEPLOYING A POLICY WITH RECOMMENDED SETTINGS

As noted earlier, when you create a policy with recommended settings, you let Microsoft do all the work by applying the settings that are in the best interests of most enterprises. To create and deploy a policy with the recommended settings, follow these steps:

1. In the Windows Intune administrator console, click the Policy tab.

2. From the Policy Overview page, click Add Policy.

3. Select a template that matches the type of policy to configure:

- Mobile Device Security Policy
- Windows Firewall Settings
- Windows Intune Agent Settings (selected in Figure 3-43)
- Windows Intune Center Settings

4. Click Create And Deploy A Policy With The Recommended Settings, and then click Create Policy.

5. Select the groups to which you want to deploy the policy, click Add, and then click OK.

6. If you are prompted to deploy the policy, click Yes to deploy now, or No to deploy later.

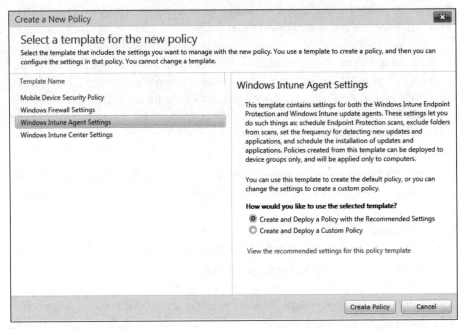

FIGURE 3-43 Creating a policy.

> **MORE INFO   DEPLOYING A POLICY**
>
> If you didn't deploy the policy when you created the policy or if you want to deploy the policy to more groups, refer to this article on TechNet: *http://technet.microsoft.com/en-us/ library/jj662643.aspx*.

To create and deploy a custom policy, follow these steps:

1. In the Windows Intune administrator console, click the Policy tab.

2. From the Policy Overview page, click Add Policy.

3. Select a template that matches the type of policy to configure:

   - Mobile Device Security Policy
   - Windows Firewall Settings
   - Windows Intune Agent Settings
   - Windows Intune Center Settings

4. Click Create And Deploy A Custom Policy, and then click Create Policy.

5. Type the name and description of the policy.

6. Configure the applicable policy settings.

7. Select the groups to which you want to deploy the policy, click Add, and then click OK.

8. Click Save Policy.

9. Click Yes to deploy the policy now or No to deploy the policy later.

REVIEWING A POLICY LIST AND MANAGING LISTED POLICIES

You can review a list of configured policies from the Windows Intune administrator console, in Policy, from the All Policies tab. From there you can also add, edit, delete, and manage the deployment of policies. When you opt to edit a policy, the Create a New Policy Wizard opens and you can simply reconfigure the parts of the policy as desired.

HANDLING CONFLICTS

Sometimes multiple policies conflict with one another. When this happens, one of the policies must be the "winner," and the winning policy is applied automatically. The winning policy setting is determined as follows:

- If a computer is a member of two groups and the policies applied to those groups vary, the policy associated with the deepest group in the group tree structure wins.
- If two policies are deployed to the same group, or if two groups are at the same depth in the group structure, the setting with the most recent Last Modified Time entry wins.

Sometimes multiple policies are applied to users, too. The winning policy setting is determined as follows:

- If a user is a member of two groups and the policies applied to those groups vary, the policy associated with the deepest group in the group tree structure wins.
- If two policies are deployed to the same group, or if both groups are at the same depth in the group structure, the older policy setting wins.
- When a conflict occurs and the older policy setting is applied, a Policy Conflict alert is raised. You'll see these in the Policy Conflicts area of the Policy workspace.
- If a user's device is managed by Windows Intune direct management and Exchange ActiveSync, the policies are compared. The most secure policy wins.

Review the Policy Conflicts tab in the Policy workspace. This is where you review and manage conflicts when they arise.

Finally, take a minute to look at the Exchange Access For Mobile tab in the Policy workspace. If you incorporate Exchange in your network infrastructure, you can create rules here. Note the three options:

- Allow All Mobile Devices To Access Exchange, Unless A Custom Rule States Otherwise
- Block All Mobile Devices From Accessing Exchange, Unless A Custom Rule States Otherwise
- Quarantine All Mobile Devices So I Can Decide Later For Each Individual Mobile Device, Unless A Custom Rule States Otherwise

Notice that you can also view quarantined devices, set user notifications, and set administrator notifications here.

> **MORE INFO** **EXCHANGE ACCESS FOR MOBILE**
>
> The Windows Intune administrator console also offers a place where you can manage mobile devices through Exchange ActiveSync. To learn about this, review the article "Windows Intune Capabilities for Directly Managed and Exchange ActiveSync-Managed Mobile Devices" at *http://technet.microsoft.com/en-us/library/jj662631.aspx*.

Managing remote computers with Windows Intune

You can use Windows Intune to perform remote tasks on computers (and mobile devices) you manage. Several tasks are available:

- You can force an Endpoint Protection Definition Update in Windows Intune.
- You can run a Windows Intune Endpoint Protection scan.
- You can protect data with Remote Wipe, Remote Lock, or Passcode Reset by using Windows Intune.
- You can restart a computer by using Windows Intune.
- You can refresh Windows Intune policies.
- You can refresh inventory in Windows Intune.

This chapter already covered the first two (about Endpoint Protection). You also saw how to perform a remote wipe and how to refresh policies. This section looks at a few other tasks: performing a remote lock, resetting a password, restarting a computer, and refreshing inventory.

SETTING A REMOTE LOCK

When a user loses a device, or perhaps leaves it in another office or at home, you can opt to lock the device to secure it. Remote Lock isn't supported on all platforms, but you can lock iOS and Android devices easily. You can also lock Windows RT and Windows RT 8.1 devices if the device's current user is the same person who enrolled it. This is also true for Windows 8.1

computers. You can't remotely lock a Windows Phone 8 yet—at least, not at the time this book was written.

To lock a mobile device, open the Windows Intune administrator console, and then follow these steps:

1. Click Groups, expand All Devices, and expand All Mobile Devices (or the applicable group).

2. Click any applicable subgroup.

3. From the Devices tab, click the device (or devices) you want to lock, and then click Remote Tasks (you might have to first click a double-facing arrow).

4. Click Remote Lock.

RESETTING A PASSWORD

Another common task you'll perform remotely is resetting a password. You do this when a user forgets his or her password (passcode). By resetting a password, you force a new, temporary password, which the user must type in, and then the user can regain access.

You can reset a password on iOS and Android devices. For now, you can't reset a password for Windows Phone 8, Windows RT, Windows RT 8.1, or Windows 8.1.

To reset a password, open the Windows Intune administrator console, and then follow these steps:

1. Click Groups, All Devices, All Mobile Devices.

2. Click any applicable subgroup.

3. From the Devices tab, click the device or devices that you want to reset the password for, click Remote Tasks, and then click Passcode Reset.

RESTARTING REMOTELY

You can restart a managed computer remotely. When you do, you can also watch the status of the restart from the Windows Intune administrator console. To restart a device, open the Windows Intune administrator console, and then follow these steps:

1. Click Groups.

2. Click All Devices or the appropriate group.

3. Select a computer or device. You can select more than one.

4. Click Remote Tasks, and then click Restart Computer.

5. On the Summary page, click Close.

You can encounter any of four status messages during the restart process:

- **Queued**   The request has been sent but not yet delivered to the device.
- **Running**   The task was received by the remote device and is running now.

- **Completed** The task has completed.
- **Failed** The task failed.

REFRESHING INVENTORY

You can refresh data involving inventory in your enterprise. Follow these steps:

1. Open the Windows Intune administrator console.

2. Click Groups, and then click All Devices (or the appropriate group).

3. Select a computer or a group of computers, click Remote Tasks, and then click Refresh Inventory.

4. Click Close.

Thought experiment
Protecting your computers

In this thought experiment, apply what you've learned about this objective. You can find answers to these questions in the "Answers" section at the end of this chapter.

You manage a combination of 100 computers, mobile devices, and laptops. One of your responsibilities is to ensure that those computers are protected from malware. You use Windows Intune Endpoint Protection and want to configure alerts so that you are notified quickly when a problem is found.

1. Of the available alert categories, which category will you choose to configure alerts that have to do with malware?

2. You want to catch any problems as quickly as possible and remediate them. What severity level would you choose when creating the alerts?

3. In the Windows Intune administrator console, what workspace do you use to create alerts?

Objective summary

- Windows Intune has four built-in, ready-to-use groups that can't be removed: All Users, Ungrouped Users, All Devices, and Ungrouped Devices.

- You can create Windows Intune groups to give you options for managing everything you've enrolled and all the users you've added.

- You can configure alerts so that you are notified when problems occur. Alerts offer the time the alert was created; the number of times the alert happened; the source of the alert; whether the alert is still active, modified, or has been resolved; and any applicable path related to the issue. Several alert categories are used.

- The Policy workspace in the Windows Intune administrator console lets you create policies that help you control the computers and mobile devices you manage. You can force these policies or not configure them at all.

- You can remotely manage computers with Windows Intune and remotely lock or wipe enrolled devices, reset passwords, and restart computers, among other things.

Objective review

Answer the following questions to test your knowledge of the information in this objective. You can find the answers to these questions and explanations of why each answer choice is correct or incorrect in the "Answers" section at the end of this chapter.

1. Which of the following is true regarding Windows Intune groups that you create?

   A. As soon as you create a group, you can't change its name.

   B. A single group can contain both computers and users.

   C. You must have AD DS to create groups in Windows Intune.

   D. Groups can be empty.

2. What's the main difference between a Windows Intune user group and a Windows Intune security group? Choose two.

   A. You create the user group in the Windows Intune administrator console and a security group in the Windows Intune account portal.

   B. User groups contain users, but security groups assign permissions to shared resources.

   C. You can delete a user group you've created, but you can't delete a security group you've created.

   D. You can delete a security group you've created, but you can't delete a user group you've created.

3. You need to create an alert that informs you if any device you manage can't or didn't install a required update. What kind of alert would you create?

   A. Policy

   B. Software Status

   C. Update Status

   D. Computer Summary

4. What types of policies can you create in Windows Intune? (Choose all that apply.)

   A. Mobile Device Security Policy

   B. Windows Firewall Settings

   C. Windows Intune Agent Settings

   D. Windows Intune Center Settings

   E. All of the above

5. When policies conflict because two policies are deployed to the same group, which policy is applied?

   A. The policy with the most recent Last Modified Time entry.

   B. The policy that is deepest in the tree structure.

   C. The most stringent policy wins.

   D. The least stringent policy wins.

6. On what types of devices can you reset a passcode with Windows Intune? (Choose all that apply.)

   A. Windows 8.1 computers

   B. Windows 8.1 mobile computers

   C. iOS

   D. Android

   E. Windows 8 phones

   F. Windows RT and Windows RT 8.1 devices

Answers

This section contains the solutions to the thought experiments and answers to the lesson review questions in this chapter.

Objective 3.1: Thought experiment

1. DaRT is the best tool for this problem if you are a Software Assurance customer. Otherwise you'll have to come up with a different solution, perhaps reimaging, scanning with Windows Defender, or using a third-party tool.

2. You need to create and use a recovery image that you create with DaRT.

3. Explorer lets you copy data files before trying to repair the computer.

4. Defender can help you resolve issues with malware and viruses.

Objective 3.1: Review

1. **Correct answer:** B

   A. **Incorrect:** If you click Add A Device in the Devices And Printers window, Windows looks for a wireless or network device.

   B. **Correct:** This is the applicable option.

   C. **Incorrect:** You should be able to install the device if you can find an applicable device driver.

   D. **Incorrect:** Although Pnputil.exe can be used to manage device drivers, the −*f* parameter is used to force the deletion of a driver and thus isn't applicable here.

2. **Correct answer:** C

   A. **Incorrect:** Sigverif.exe is used to scan the computer for unsigned drivers, not check for bad disk sectors.

   B. **Incorrect:** Mdsched is used to schedule a scan using the Windows Memory Diagnostic tool to check for memory errors.

   C. **Correct:** ChkDsk scans the hard disk for bad sectors.

   D. **Incorrect:** PerfMon opens the Performance Monitor.

3. **Correct answer:** D

   A. **Incorrect:** You generally use Performance Monitor to create Data Collector Sets to see where performance improvements can be made.

   B. **Incorrect:** You can use Reliability Monitor to review events, installations, and other information about a computer's performance, but the WPT is better suited to the problem detailed here.

   C. **Incorrect:** You use Sigverif.exe to locate unsigned drivers. This would be a good tool to use if you thought a driver was causing the issue, but because the hard disk light is on and additional vague problems are occurring, trying the WPT first would be best.

   D. **Correct:** The Windows Performance Toolkit (WPT) is the best tool to use in this situation.

4. **Correct answer:** A

   A. **Correct:** This tab shows all running processes, grouped together as process trees, and offers columns that show the resources allotted and their usage.

   B. **Incorrect:** The App History tab shows usage associated with apps (but not desktop apps). Although you can review the load apps place on the computer, App History isn't the best place to review processes for the entire computer.

   C. **Incorrect:** This tab displays all the enabled services and enables you to manage them.

   D. **Incorrect:** Msconfig.exe opens the System Configuration window and only offers access to the Task Manager and no way to monitor discrete processes.

5. **Correct answers:** A, C

   A. **Correct:** In the Devices And Printers window, right-click the printer, click Printer Properties, and click the Sharing tab.

   B. **Incorrect:** Sharing isn't an option in the Devices And Printers window when you right-click the printer.

   C. **Correct:** In the Print Management console, right-click the printer and click Manage Sharing.

   D. **Incorrect:** Sharing isn't an option in the Print Management console when you right-click the printer.

6. **Correct answer:** D

A. **Incorrect:** The Solution Wizard lets you work through a series of questions when you don't know where to start with DaRT, and then review solutions offered that might suit your needs. Because you believe the problem to be a device driver, this likely isn't the best option.

B. **Incorrect:** Explorer lets you browse the files on the local system as well as network shares, and copy that data before you try to repair or reimage the computer. Although this might be a good first step, it won't help you resolve the driver issue.

C. **Incorrect:** Disk Commander lets you recover and repair disk partitions or volumes by restoring the master boot record (MBR), restoring partition tables, and saving those tables for backup. This isn't the best solution here.

D. **Correct:** Computer Management enables you to view system information and event logs, work with disks, manage services, manage drivers, and so on. You can locate the driver here and uninstall it or disable it.

Objective 3.2: Thought experiment

1. Work Folders.

2. Control Panel, Work Folders.

3. Sync Center.

4. You can configure syncing to occur when the computer has been idle for a specific amount of time or if the computer is running on external power (and not on its battery). You can also opt to trigger synchronization to coincide with a specific event, such as when the computer is idle for a specific amount of time, when the client locks Windows, and when the client unlocks Windows.

5. Two-way is most common because syncing occurs from device to server and server to device.

Objective 3.2: Review

1. **Correct answers:** A, C

A. **Correct:** Password expiration is available to set for all named devices.

B. **Incorrect:** Allowing a pop-up blocker isn't available for Windows Phone 8 or Android devices.

C. **Correct:** Password history is available to all named devices.

D. **Incorrect:** Maximum password length isn't correct, although minimum password length is an available policy for all.

2. **Correct answer:** B

   A. **Incorrect:** You can't wipe a device from here. This is where you add software and agreements.

   B. **Correct:** This is where you opt to wipe a device.

   C. **Incorrect:** You can manage devices here, but it's used for enrollment and other mobile device management tasks.

   D. **Incorrect:** You set policies here. You don't wipe devices from here.

3. **Correct answers:** C, D

   A. **Incorrect:** Enabling file synchronization on costed networks requires more bandwidth because you enable the option to sync files over metered networks.

   B. **Incorrect:** Setting the Latency=0 isn't the correct option for the latency threshold; the correct value is 1.

   C. **Correct:** In the Value box for configuring slow-link mode, type **Latency=1** to set the latency threshold to one millisecond.

   D. **Correct:** You configure slow-link mode to achieve the desired results.

4. **Correct answer:** C

   A. **Incorrect:** The Windows Intune administrator console, from the Administrator pane in Mobile Device Management, is not the desired solution here.

   B. **Incorrect:** Although you can manage devices in the Windows Intune administrator console from the Groups pane in All Mobile Devices, you can't add users manually here.

   C. **Correct:** You add users manually from the Windows Intune account portal, under Admin, from the Users tab.

   D. **Incorrect:** No Users tab is available (which is what you need to locate) in the Windows Intune account portal, under Admin Console.

   E. **Incorrect:** You can't add users manually in the Windows Intune Company Portal.

Objective 3.3: Thought experiment

1. Windows Intune provides support for all these items. Windows Defender won't support all mobile clients, nor will it offer alerts. System Center 2012 Endpoint Protection is too much in this scenario because servers and Linux/UNIX machines aren't a part of what you need to manage.

2. Open the Windows administrator console. From the Groups tab, locate the device to manage, and then click Run A Full Malware Scan (or Run A Quick Malware Scan).

3. Open the Windows Intune Endpoint Protection window (which looks like the Windows Defender window) and choose the desired tab to make the appropriate changes.

Objective 3.3: Review

1. **Correct answer:** B

   A. **Incorrect:** Windows Update isn't available from Windows Settings.

   B. **Correct:** Computer Configuration, Administrative Templates, Windows Components, Windows Update is the proper area.

   C. **Incorrect:** Windows Update isn't available in User Configuration; it's a computer element.

   D. **Incorrect:** Windows Update isn't available in User Configuration; it's a computer element.

2. **Correct answer:** D

   A. **Incorrect:** The administrator console is the proper place to look for new updates to approve.

   B. **Incorrect:** The Updates tab in the left pane is the proper place to look for new updates to approve.

   C. **Incorrect:** You have to upload the non-Microsoft updates that you want to approve first, but not the Microsoft updates.

   D. **Correct:** No new updates are available to approve.

3. **Correct answer:** D

   A. **Incorrect:** Home is where you can see the status of your real-time protection, including whether it's turned on and whether the virus and spyware definitions are up to date.

   B. **Incorrect:** Update is where you can see the date on which the last definitions were created, when the definitions where last updated, the virus definition version, and the spyware definition version.

   C. **Incorrect:** History is where you review past problems.

   D. **Correct:** Settings is where you schedule scans.

4. **Correct answer:** D

   A. **Incorrect:** A quick scan does check the locations, memory processes, and registry files on the hard disk where malware generally appears, but the other answers are also correct.

   B. **Incorrect:** A full system scan does check all files on the hard disk and all currently running programs, but the other answers are also correct.

   C. **Incorrect:** Scheduling these scans when the user isn't at the computer is best, but the other answers are also correct.

   D. **Correct:** All the answers are correct.

5. **Correct answer:** A

   A. **Correct:** The first thing you must do is appropriate the proper certificates.

   B. **Incorrect:** This is the second thing you do.

   C. **Incorrect:** This is the third thing you do.

   D. **Incorrect:** This is the fourth thing you do.

   E. **Incorrect:** This is the fifth thing you do.

   F. **Incorrect:** This is the sixth thing you do.

   G. **Incorrect:** This is the very last thing you do.

6. **Correct answer:** C

   A. **Incorrect:** The setting Allow Internet Explorer To Use The SPDY/3 Network Protocol isn't required for Flip Ahead.

   B. **Incorrect:** The setting Turn Off Loading Websites And Content In The Background To Optimize Performance isn't required for Flip Ahead.

   C. **Correct:** This feature is available only in the Internet Explorer app and the problematic users are using the Internet Explorer 11 desktop app.

   D. **Incorrect:** This feature is available in all versions of Windows 8 for the Internet Explorer 11 app.

7. **Correct answers:** A, B

   A. **Correct:** The client might need to have new policies refreshed.

   B. **Correct:** You should use RSoP to see if any conflicts exist.

   C. **Incorrect:** Fast Startup reduces the amount of time required to shut down and restart a computer by allowing the computer to go into hibernation rather than completely shut down. However, Group Policy settings and scripts that are configured to be applied during the startup or shutdown process might not be applied, which can be a source of trouble if Fast Startup is enabled for your clients.

   D. **Incorrect:** You can enable Group Policy caching from here, but doing so won't resolve the problem.

Objective 3.4: Thought experiment

1. Endpoint Protection alerts

2. Critical

3. Administration

Objective 3.4: Review

1. **Correct answer:** D

   A. **Incorrect:** As soon as you create a group, you *can* change its name.

   B. **Incorrect:** A single group can't contain both computers and users.

   C. **Incorrect:** You don't need AD DS to create groups in Windows Intune.

   D. **Correct:** Groups can be empty.

2. **Correct answers:** A, B

   A. **Correct:** You create a user group in the Windows Intune administrator console and a security group in the Windows Intune account portal.

   B. **Correct:** User groups contain users, but security groups assign permissions to shared resources.

   C. **Incorrect:** You can delete any group you create.

   D. **Incorrect:** You can delete any group you create.

3. **Correct answer:** C

   A. **Incorrect:** Policy alerts deal with policies you've created and deployed.

   B. **Incorrect:** Software Status alerts deal with the status of installed software.

   C. **Correct:** Update Status is the applicable alert type.

   D. **Incorrect:** Computer Summary lets you review inventory information, including but not limited to the top five manufacturers and top five operating systems used in your inventory list.

4. **Correct answer:** E

   A. **Incorrect:** Mobile Device Security Policy is a valid policy type, but other answers are also correct, so the correct answer is E.

   B. **Incorrect:** Windows Firewall Settings is a valid policy type, but other answers are also correct, so the correct answer is E.

   C. **Incorrect:** Windows Intune Agent Settings is a valid policy type, but other answers are also correct, so the correct answer is E.

   D. **Incorrect:** Windows Intune Center Settings is a valid policy type, but other answers are also correct, so the correct answer is E.

   E. **Correct:** All of the above.

5. **Correct answer:** A

   A. **Correct:** In this case, the policy with the most recent Last Modified Time entry is applied.

   B. **Incorrect:** The question states that the groups are equal in the tree structure.

   C. **Incorrect:** The most stringent policy doesn't win in this case. However, if a user's device is managed by Windows Intune direct management and Exchange ActiveSync, the policies are compared and the most secure wins.

   D. **Incorrect:** The least stringent policy doesn't win.

6. **Correct answers:** C, D

   A. **Incorrect:** Windows 8.1 computers can't be reset in this manner.

   B. **Incorrect:** Windows 8.1 mobile computers can't be reset in this manner.

   C. **Correct:** iOS devices can be sent a passcode reset.

   D. **Correct:** Android devices can be sent a passcode reset.

   E. **Incorrect:** Windows 8 phones can't be reset in this manner.

   F. **Incorrect:** Windows RT and Windows RT 8.1 devices can't be reset in this manner.

Index

Symbols

6to4 transition technology, 99–100
802.1x wireless technology standard, 110
802.11ac wireless technology standard, 110
802.11a wireless technology standard, 109
802.11b wireless technology standard, 109
802.11g wireless technology standard, 110
802.11i wireless technology standard, 110
802.11n wireless technology standard, 110
/? parameter (Cipher.exe command), 188

A

Accelerators (Manage Add-Ons dialog box), 280
access control lists (ACLs), 181
accessing resources
    authentication and authorization, 150–165
        account policies, 160–161
        computer authentication vs user
            authentication, 159–160
        credential caching, 161–162
        Credential Manager, 162–164
        homegroups, workgroups, and
            domains, 156–159
        local accounts vs Microsoft accounts, 164–165
        multifactor authentication, 151–156
        Secure Channel, 160
        Workplace Join, 165
    data security, 180–200
        BitLocker Drive Encryption, 191–200
        EFS (Encrypting File System), 186–189
        permissions, 180–186
        removable devices, 190
    data storage, 169–177
        BranchCache, 173–175

DFS, 169–170
OneDrive, 175–177
Storage Spaces, 171–173
network connectivity, 93–123
    automatic IP address assignment, 96–97
    IPv4, 94–96
    IPv6, 97–99
    names resolution, 101–106
    security, 113–123
    transition technologies, 99–101
    wireless networks, 106–113
remote access, 127–147
    DirectAccess, 134–138
    NAP, 141–147
    RDP, 131–134
    remote administration, 138–141
    VPNs, 127–131
Access (Office 365), 59
access policies, mobile devices, 246–247
Account Lockout Duration policy, 161
Account Lockout Policies, 161
Account Lockout Threshold policy, 161
account policies, authentication and
        authorization, 160–161
Accounts: Block Microsoft Accounts setting, 165
ACLs (access control lists), 181
ACT (Application Compatibility Toolkit), 29–36
    fixing problems, 33–36
    inventory collector packages, 30–31
    reviewing report data, 33
    runtime-analysis packages, 31–33
    tools, 30
activating sideloading key, 69–72
Active Directory Certificate Services (AD CS), 151
Active Directory Users And Computers snap-in, 160
active partitions, 9
AD CS (Active Directory Certificate Services), 151

P

S

About the author

JOLI BALLEW is an award-winning, best-selling author of over 50 books, including *Windows 8.1 Step By Step* and *Windows 8.1 Plain and Simple*, both with Microsoft Press. Joli is a Microsoft MVP (10 years) and holds many Microsoft certifications, starting with the original MCSE for Windows Server 2000. Joli is a Microsoft Certified Trainer and a professor at Brookhaven Community College, where she also serves as the Microsoft Academy Coordinator. Joli teaches certification classes, including the class related to this exam, Supporting Windows 8.1 (70-688) and the one that precedes it, Configuring Windows 8.1 (70-687).

From technical overviews to drilldowns on special topics, get
free ebooks from Microsoft Press at:

www.microsoftvirtualacademy.com/ebooks

Download your free ebooks in PDF, EPUB, and/or Mobi for
Kindle formats.

Look for other great resources at Microsoft Virtual Academy,
where you can learn new skills and help advance your career
with free Microsoft training delivered by experts.

Microsoft Press

Now that you've read the book...

Tell us what you think!

Was it useful?
Did it teach you what you wanted to learn?
Was there room for improvement?

Let us know at http://aka.ms/tellpress

Your feedback goes directly to the staff at Microsoft Press,
and we read every one of your responses. Thanks in advance!

 Microsoft